Profile of
a Nation

Profile of a Nation

Canadian Themes and Styles

ALAN DAWE

Macmillan of Canada/Toronto/1969

Reprinted, 1970, 1971

PHOTOGRAPHS:

Page 62, Isachsen, Northwest Territories (photo by Herb
Taylor). Page 98, Frederick Varley self-portrait (National
Gallery of Canada). Page 140, "View of the Taking of Quebec
September 13th 1759" (from an engraving in the Public
Archives of Canada). Page 180, "Main Street, Winnipeg,
Manitoba, c. 1909" (Public Archives of Canada). Page 224,
an Eskimo school at Tuktoyaktuk (photo by Paul Almasy).
Page 256, Toronto skyline from the Toronto Dominion Centre
(photo by Ron Vickers Ltd.).

Printed in Canada

Acknowledgements

For permission to use copyrighted material grateful acknowledgement is made to the following authors and publishers:

Mrs. Ralph Allen for excerpt from *Land of Eternal Change* by Ralph Allen.

Pierre Berton for excerpt from *The New City, a Prejudiced View of Toronto*.

Art Buchwald for permission to reprint *Fold, Bend, Mutilate*.

Canadian Broadcasting Corporation for "Impasse in Race Relations" taken from the first of the 1967 Massey Lectures by Martin Luther King commissioned and broadcast by the CBC and published by them in paperback under the title *Conscience for Change*. Copyright © Martin Luther King Jr. 1967.

The Canadian Historical Association for excerpt from *Louis Riel, Patriot or Rebel?* by G. F. G. Stanley, published by The Canadian Historical Association.

Chatto and Windus Ltd. and Mrs. Laura Huxley for excerpt from *Brave New World Revisited* by Aldous Huxley.

Clarke, Irwin & Company Limited for excerpts from: "With Its Face To The West" by Roderick Haig-Brown in *The Face of Canada* by Bennet et al.; *Mostly in Clover* by Harry J. Boyle; *A Painter's Country: The Autobiography of A. Y. Jackson*; *A History of Canada, Volume I* by Gustave Lanctot; and *The Table Talk of Samuel Marchbanks* by Robertson Davies.

J. M. Dent & Sons (Canada) Limited for excerpt from *The North American Nations* by Edgar McInnis.

Peter Desbarats for excerpt from *Century 1867-1967, The Canadian Saga*, published by Southam Press Limited.

Doubleday & Company, Inc., for excerpt from *The Search for Identity* by Blair Fraser. Copyright © 1967 by Blair Fraser. Also for excerpt from *Toronto* by Bruce West. Used by permission of Doubleday & Company, Inc.

W. J. Gage Limited for excerpt from *Canadian English* by W. S. Avis in the Introduction to *Dictionary of Canadian English: The Senior Dictionary* by W. S. Avis and others © 1967 by W. J. Gage Limited.

Ray Gardner for excerpt from "Percy Williams at the Olympics" published in the November 24, 1956 issue of *Maclean's* Magazine.

Chief Dan George for "Lament for Confederation".

Alan Gowans and The Oxford University Press for excerpt from an essay entitled "Architecture in New France" in *The First Five Years*.

Harper & Row, Publishers, Incorporated, for excerpt from *Only Yesterday* by Frederick Lewis Allen. Copyright, 1931 by Frederick Lewis Allen; renewed 1959 by Agnes Rogers Allen. Also for excerpt from *Atoms and People* by Ralph E. Lapp. Copyright © 1956 by Ralph E. Lapp.

Harvard University Press for excerpt from *The United States and Canada* by Gerald M. Craig. Reprinted by permission of the publishers Cambridge, Mass.: Harvard University Press, Copyright, 1968, by the President and Fellows of Harvard College.

Reservation, Caughnawaga" by A. M. Klein from *The Rocking Chair and Other Poems*. Also excerpt from *Breaking Smith's Quarter Horse* by Paul St. Pierre.

F. R. Scott for "Laurentian Shield".

Simon & Schuster, Inc., for excerpt from *The Gilded Age of Sport*, copyright 1945, 1950, 1951, 1952, 1953 © 1954, 1955, 1956, 1958, 1959, 1960, 1961 by Herbert Warren Wind.

Time Magazine for excerpt from their story on Bobby Hull. Copyright Time Inc. 1968.

University of Toronto Press for excerpt by Nathan Keyfitz from *Urbanism and the Changing Canadian Society*, edited by S. D. Clark. Also for excerpt from *The Story of Canadian Roads* by Edwin C. Guillet.

The Viking Press, Inc., for excerpt from *Wolf Willow* by Wallace Stegner. Copyright © 1962 by Wallace Stegner.

Outline
of Contents

Detail
of Contents

PART TWO: Canadian Themes and Styles

List of selections arranged according to the rhetorical and literary principles they illustrate

Structure

Development

Sentence Structure

Diction

Rhetorical Devices

Beginning and Ending

Preface

Like most anthologists, I cannot refrain from hoping that my anthology will justify its existence by being different in some way from all others. Since this potential difference cannot lie in the fact that the focus of this collection of poems, essays, and narratives is both thematic and rhetorical (for this is a commonplace among anthologies now), it must be because the material contained in *Profile of a Nation* is mostly Canadian, largely contemporary, and extremely broad in the spectrum of writers it represents. Over eighty per cent of the selections are by Canadians; over half of them were first published after 1960; and poets, essayists, novelists, short-story writers, historians, sociologists, humorists, amateurs, and other occasional writers are represented here. Canada – or so everyone seems to enjoy saying – may not as yet have produced a *great* writer, but I am convinced that it has recently been turning out a plentiful supply of very *good* ones.

As with any anthologist who tries to cover an unconscionable amount of ground (I have unabashedly tried to cover Canada's 3,851,809 square miles), I have had to live with the threat that I am likely to cover the ground rather thinly. If I have not let this threat concern me too much, it is because I am convinced that the selections I looked for, liked, and brought together here cannot fail to serve as useful springboards for further discussion and reading both inside and outside the college classrooms where I expect my anthology will find its proper use. The organization of this text should make it clear that such discussion can profitably be concerned not only with issues related to several aspects of the general subject "Canada", but also with principles of exposition relevant to college students.

The main problem that must be faced by an anthologist who wants to ride off simultaneously in two different directions is deciding which of his two possible paths he will ultimately follow. My decision has been to take the thematic rather than the rhetorical path, although I have attempted to leave numerous rhetorical signposts along the way. These are found in the introductory essay that precedes the anthology, in the second table of contents where the selections have been arranged rhetorically, and in the second paragraph of the headnote that prefaces each selection. An instructor making use of *Profile of a Nation* has, then, at least three approaches open to him. He can follow the thematic path, or the rhetorical path, or – better still – both paths at once, for although this latter manoeuvre is an awkward one for the anthologist, it can be performed quite gracefully by the reader.

There is one pleasant problem that any anthologist must face. This is finding a way to tender thanks to the numerous people who knowingly or unknowingly provided assistance. May I do all that tradition allows and offer these simple words of gratitude to the following people. First of all, my thanks to those colleagues and students at Vancouver City College who either concurred with or corrected my taste during our trial runs with the material. Specifically, I would like to express my gratitude to Mr. Ted Langley, Mrs. Betty Stubbs, and Mrs. Nora Tolman, each of whom directed me to selections that would not have been included here had they not brought them to my attention. And I most sincerely thank Mrs. Kay Lewis who so cheerfully typed so many words about Canada. Nor can I, among many omissions, fail to acknowledge my indebtedness to several staff members at Vancouver City College for the suggestions and encouragement they offered during the early stages of this project, especially to my colleague Mr. John Parker, my department chairman Miss Mary Fallis, and my principal Mr. John Newberry. Finally I would like to acknowledge most sincerely the editorial advice I received from Mrs. Diane Mew of The Macmillan Company of Canada Limited. Despite the miles and mountains between Toronto and Vancouver, Mrs. Mew never failed to extend a gracious and steadying hand.

Alan Dawe
September 1, 1968

Profile of
a Nation

Introduction

This book is meant to serve the reader in two specific ways. First of all, it illustrates the fundamental principles of effective writing. Second, it offers a wide range of reading selections on several important Canadian and contemporary themes. Two basic assumptions have influenced the shaping of *Profile of a Nation*. The first is that the activities we call reading and writing are in reality but the two sides of the same coin; the second, that the ability to put words *on* to paper effectively is closely related to the ability to take words *off* the printed page. Like so many other human activities, writing is something that most people learn largely through imitation, although "imitation" in this sense does not mean merely *copying* what others have thought and said, but rather, *emulating* the quality of thought and the power of expression of those writers we most admire. However, such emulation is obviously not possible unless we have first understood exactly what an author has said, and have analysed clearly why his saying of it has been effective. It is hoped that this book, with its double focus on content and style, will help the students who use it to become readers who write well.

It must be understood, though, that the development of maturity as a reader and writer is not something that will take place suddenly. Learning to read and learning to write both take time; both skills can be developed only through sustained and intelligent practice. The average person can no more become expert in the relatively sophisticated activities of reading and writing without regularly working with words than he can, say, become a good swimmer without frequently getting wet. Fortunately, a number of things can be learned to help speed up the maturing process. Several of these basic strategies for improving reading and writing are discussed and illustrated in Part One. They are referred to again in the headnote that precedes each of the selections in Part Two, and they are illustrated in the selections themselves. And even though it *is* assumed that reading and writing are the two sides of the same coin, each side is, in the interests of clarity, discussed separately. Section I of Part One, sub-titled "The Reader's Responsibility to the Page", discusses a number of concepts related to reading; section II, "The Writer's Responsibility to the Reader", sets up a standard for prose composition; section III, "Some Technical Matters", defines and illustrates a number of terms and concepts with which the student of writing should be familiar.

One comment about the anthology section of this book needs to be made. The reader is expected to approach the selections *critically*. Reading is far from being a passive activity, and the reader should always be prepared to keep a critical eye on what a writer is saying and on how well he has expressed himself. Although Part Two, "Canadian Themes and Styles", does contain many thoughtful and well-written selections, it is not expected that the fifty-four pieces collected there will be approached as if they were sacrosanct literary masterpieces beyond intelligent discussion. It cannot be assumed that any selection represents the final word on its subject, nor that the many different styles found in the anthology will appeal to every reader. What is intended is that each of these essays, poems, and narrations will be, as Francis Bacon urged three centuries ago, weighed and considered, not only for what it says, but also for its manner of saying it. The reader should attempt to measure each selection against the truth and reality that he himself has experienced, remembering as he does so that a statement does not become true, and an idea does not become established, merely because it has found its way into print. And the reader should also remember that the person who admires nothing that he reads is just as blind as the uncritical person who admires everything.

PART ONE

Reading for Writing

I. The Reader's Responsibility to the Page

The reader's responsibility to the page is to take from it everything the writer has put on to it. A number of strategies useful in achieving this aim are discussed and illustrated in this section. The stress here will be on close, critical reading. Other approaches to the page – skim reading or speed reading – have their own uses and their own strategies, but they are not the special concern of the comments on reading that follow.

1. Know What You Are Reading

To be clear about what you are reading involves many things. In the first place, it involves knowing *who* the writer is and what his qualifications are. Does the author, the reader should ask, really know something about the subject he is dealing with? Is he a careful reporter who gets his facts correct, and has he earned the right to express opinions that can be taken seriously?

Secondly, it will be useful to know *when* something was written, since the passage of time will often date a comment and limit its value. For example, an essay on Canadian-American relations written in 1910 may be of historical interest, but it would be erroneous to consider it a dependable basis for evaluating these relations as they exist today. Obviously, there are numerous literary works in which the date of composition does not seriously affect their value. A comic essay (for example, one by Stephen Leacock) written in 1910 may be just as effective today as when it was first published. None the less, most expository prose should be read with the date of composition clearly in mind.

And thirdly, when considering a piece of writing, it is important to know whether the work is complete in itself or whether it is only a part of some longer work, as many of the selections in this anthology are. The fact that a particular piece of writing is only a fragment does not mean that it is not worth reading. Still, the reader should know when he is looking at only part of what a writer has said about a subject. In the brief notes that precede each of the selections in this anthology, much of the necessary background material concerning the author, the date of publication, and the source of the selection has been given.

The three things discussed briefly above are preliminary details that the reader should know. But there are other things that must be considered. The most important of these is to recognize the *type of material* that is being read. Writing can be classified in several different ways. One common classification is based on the selection's literary form. This usually involves distinguishing between poems, essays, plays, novels, and short stories. Some reference will be made to these forms throughout this anthology, but the fundamental classification that will be employed here is the twofold one based on whether the material being presented is a *narration* or an *exposition*. A narration is concerned with giving an account of some *event* or series of events, an exposition with the presentation of an *idea* or a series of ideas. It will be immediately clear to the reader into which category each of the following paragraphs can be placed.

PARAGRAPH 1

Although last Saturday was very wet, Sam attended to jump as per advertisement, and leaped from the masthead of the Niagara into the river, performing the feat with great ease and dexterity. At three o'clock a considerable number of persons had assembled on both sides of the river, and the jumping apparatus appeared in order for use in front of Goat Island. It consisted of a ladder, or ladders, elevated 118 feet perpendicular above the margin of the waters in the eddy between the British and American Falls, stayed by ropes, and accommodated with a platform at top. Sam came forth with great punctuality, descended the Biddle staircase, ascended the ladder, and stood for some time upon the platform surveying the spectators and the gulf of waters below. A boat crossed over in front of us, and took its station below the ladder. At last Sam sprang off the platform, eight or ten feet out; but the apparatus not being very firm, he swung a little round, and descended, holding out his arms, the one a little above the other below a horizontal direction; his feet, when he struck the water, were not close together, but one of them was drawn up, and, as it were, cramped a little. When he came to the water he made a great splash, and disappeared like a stone, but came up in less than half a minute farther up the river, and swam to the land on his back. He thought at first he had dislocated his thigh, but found, on coming to shore, that he had suffered no harm.

PARAGRAPH 2

Of the interest and importance of his [Simon Fraser's] explorations there can be no question. His was the third expedition to span the continent of North America. The first, led by Alexander Mackenzie in 1793, was essentially a reconnaissance trip, to spy out the land in the interests of the fur trade. The second, the famous Lewis and Clark expedition of 1805-6, was sent out by President Jefferson soon after the United States acquired the vast and somewhat indeterminate Louisiana territory from France; it, too, was a reconnaissance trip, although Lewis and Clark had the political future of the Pacific region in mind as well as its trading possibilities. Fraser, on the other hand, was not merely a bird of passage; he crossed the Rocky Mountains in 1805 and again in 1806 to take possession and to build trading posts. His great journey down the Fraser River in 1808, though the first exploration of one of the world's most difficult and dangerous rivers, was undertaken primarily to find supply routes for those posts. He was the pioneer of permanent settlement in what is now the mainland of British Columbia.

Although this type of classification is useful, the reader must also accept the fact that the two categories can, and often do, overlap. Paragraph 3 below (it is also about a man and a river) provides an example of prose that is a *blend* of narrative and expository material. The fact that this paragraph also contains elements that might be called descriptive need not force us to add "description" as a third category to our two-part system, for long descriptive prose passages existing in their own right are generally out of fashion now. Descriptive elements are usually at the service of the narration or exposition in which they are found.

PARAGRAPH 3

"When you reach Lytton," a British Columbian told me in Montreal, "be sure to stand on that little bridge where the Thompson enters. It's a wonderful sight. Thompson water is blue-green and Fraser water is yellow gumbo. You can see them both together – two separate streams in the same course." I thought I understood what he meant, for the year previous I had been on the Mackenzie and seen the phenomenon of the Liard's brown water flowing along the left bank while the clean Mackenzie water keeps to the right. The two streams are distinguishable side by side for nearly two hundred miles below Fort Simpson. It takes the Mackenzie, one of the most powerful streams in the land, all this distance to absorb its chief tributary. When I stood on the Lytton bridge the sight was indeed wonderful, but it bore no resemblance to anything I had expected. The Thompson is the Fraser's chief tributary, a major stream in its own right, a mountain stream also, and it does not so much enter the Fraser as smash its way into it like a liquid battering ram. From the bridge I saw its water plunging into the Fraser just as the man said, the blue-green into the Fraser's yellow froth. Then it completely disappeared. The Fraser swallows the Thompson in less than a hundred yards.

In the anthology, further examples of these three types of material will be found. For example, Selection No. 15 ("Bell, Book and Scandal" by

Alec Shaw) is primarily a narration; No. 27 ("Checks and Balances" by Pierre Elliott Trudeau) is an exposition; and No. 8 ("Saskatchewan" by Edward McCourt) is a blend of narration and exposition.

Reading a narration

Classifying reading into any kind of system is useful only if it increases our ability to ask the right questions about what we read. In dealing with a narration, for example, we will want to know what kind of event the writer is describing. Is it an account of some *first-hand* experience, as we can assume it is in No. 14 of the anthology ("The Birth of Rawhide" by Max Ferguson), or is it an account of something the writer has learned "second-hand", either by talking to someone or by reading? An example of this second type will be found in No. 25 ("Clifford Sifton's Medicine Show" by Ralph Allen). It must not be assumed, however, that these so-called second-hand experiences are necessarily less interesting or less reliable than first-hand accounts. There are good and bad writers, not good and bad types of experiences. But the two types of narration do differ, and the reader should be aware of what type he is dealing with before he attempts to evaluate it.

When we read narrative passages it is also important to distinguish between *real* and *fictitious* events. For example, in No. 13 in the anthology ("Landscape Painters" by A. Y. Jackson), we can assume that we are being told about things that actually took place, an assumption that we cannot make with No. 19 ("Bicultural Angela" by Hugh Hood), although it is *possible* that events "something like" those in Mr. Hood's short story might actually have happened. Once again the reader must not assume that anything approaching a judgment is involved in making this distinction between real and fictitious events. Accounts of real events are not necessarily more valuable than accounts of imaginary ones. Each type can record a valid aspect of human experience; each can inspire a narrative worth reading. And, certainly, each requires its own type of evaluation. The reader should expect that anything that purports to be a true account of an actual event will have been carefully observed and accurately reported. And he can hope that the writer of a fiction will have told of things that are psychologically and emotionally true. (A further note on reading fiction will be found on pages 22-3.)

Reading an exposition

In dealing with expository material, the reader must pay attention to somewhat different things. He must, first of all, ask whether what he is reading consists primarily of facts or of opinions, a distinction that is clearly illustrated by the following two paragraphs.

PARAGRAPH 4

It is probably sound to regard moves among provinces, like those of Canadians to the United States, as essentially a movement to the cities. Cityward migration has characterized our whole history. Thus a hundred years ago the population called urban was a very small part of the total; in 1956 it was 58 percent of the census definition (including all incorporated places however small). Incorporated places of over 1,000 population contained 50.9 percent of the total in 1941, 53.6 percent in 1951, and 54.9 percent in 1956. Cities are increasing their share of the population of the country by almost 3 percent per decade. If this pace continues until 1980, some two-thirds of the population will be urban.

PARAGRAPH 5

Vancouver is a port city. Port cities possess an enormous advantage over those built inland, for the combination of sea and land is inevitably more varied and interesting than either by itself; and for all men the sea holds the attraction of the mysterious and unknown. A port city acquires glamour merely through the presence of ships in its harbour, for a ship is of man-made things inherently the most romantic. All devices of transport, even the creaking Red River cart, are romantic because they are invested with some hint of the magic of distance. But the ship is one of the oldest of such devices; it is the most graceful and except for the airplane goes the farthest. The airplane offers no competition because it is a Johnny-come-lately without a history to match against that brought instantly to mind by mention of such names as the *Santa Maria*, the *Golden Hind*, the *Mayflower*, the *Erebus*, and the *Terror*, or of the unnamed curragh in which St. Brendan crossed the Atlantic – as all right-thinking Irishmen agree – and discovered America a thousand years before Columbus.

Once again there is no intention here to suggest that expositions that present facts are necessarily better than those that present opinions, for both factual statements and opinion statements are indispensable items in any balanced reading or thinking diet. But an opinion should not be mistaken for a fact, and the critical reader will automatically ask whether the facts presented are true, and whether the opinions have been formed on the basis of knowledge and experience. In the democratic world of reading and writing, everyone has the right to express an opinion on any subject. But the reader also has a democratic right to reject as dubious, or worthless, the opinions of authors who seem to know little or nothing about their subject.

2. Read for Ideas

One thing that we can assume about both narrative and expository writing is that the author had some purpose in writing what he did. It may be necessary here to distinguish between an author's *motive* (his desire to become famous, earn money, spread propaganda, or express his feelings) and his *purpose*, which in most writing involves the presentation of an idea, either *directly* as is usually the case with expositions, or *indirectly*, as is often the case with narrations.

Ideas in a narration

In a narration the events themselves usually get most of our attention, but we often find within the events an implied idea. So after we have read the "plot" (or even while we are reading it), we should make some effort to translate the events into some kind of meaning. We often do this automatically in everyday experience, as, for example, when we assume that the driver in the adjacent car at a stoplight is expressing impatience or annoyance when he drums his fingers on the steering-wheel while waiting for the light to change. In the following narrative passage, what ideas about Maurice Richard are implied?

PARAGRAPH 6

One of the popular indoor pastimes year-round in Montreal is talking over old Richard goals – which one you thought was the most neatly set up, which one stirred you the most, etc. – much in the way Americans used to hot-stove about Ruth's home runs and do today about Willie Mays' various catches. In Dick Irvin's opinion – and Hector (Toe) Blake and Elmer Lach, Richard's teammates on the famous Punch Line, also feel this way – the Rocket's most sensational goal was "the Seibert goal" in the 1945-46 season. Earl Seibert, a strapping 225-pound defenseman who was playing for Detroit that season, hurled himself at Richard as he swept on a solo into the Detroit zone. Richard occasionally will bend his head and neck very low when he is trying to outmaneuver a defense man. He did on this play. The two collided with a thud, and as they straightened up, there was Richard, still on his feet, still controlling the puck, and, sitting on top of his shoulders, the burly Seibert. Richard not only carried Seibert with him on the way to the net, a tour de force in itself, but, with that tremendous extra effort of which he is capable, faked the goalie out of position and with his one free hand somehow managed to hoist the puck into the far corner of the cage.

Ideas in an exposition

An expository piece of writing may contain several ideas, depending on the length of the selection and the fertility of the writer's mind. But in most expositions there is one central and dominating idea, and discovering this is the reader's chief responsibility. Sometimes the decision regarding which idea in an essay or paragraph is really the central one may be hard to make, but the following strategy can be of considerable help in deciding this. This strategy consists of asking two questions: (1) what is the general *subject* of the exposition; and (2) what has the writer said about this subject? What is the main idea of the following expository paragraph?

PARAGRAPH 7

It has yet to be explained why the "Indian race" has so many different languages, cultures and physical traits. Anthropologists are not yet sure, but it is likely that variations both in origin (within Asia) and in the time of migration account for the differences. The Indians did not come as blank slates to be inscribed with a common culture by the environment; however stripped down they were for their journey, they brought the portable goods of language, mythology, and all the other unwritten but firmly established elements of their own way of life. Although they have come to be known as "the Indians", it is more realistic to think of them not as a homogeneous society but as separate nations or groups of tribes, with languages, cultures and economies shaped to their varied regional environments. Physically and culturally they are all of distinct stock from the Eskimos; and yet the differences between Indian and Indian were, at contact [with Europeans], almost as great as the present difference between Indian and Eskimo.

There is no simple rule governing the position of the main idea in an exposition. More often than not it will appear quite early and be supported by the rest of the essay, as is the case with No. 1 in the anthology ("Canadian Regions" by Kildare Dobbs), and No. 20 ("Louis XIV and New France" by Alan Gowans). However, in essays that consist of a logically developed argument, the main idea is likely to be found towards the end. For examples of essays with this type of structure, see No. 27 ("Checks and Balances" by Pierre Elliott Trudeau), and No. 50 ("Overpopulation" by Aldous Huxley).

3. Follow the Development of the Idea

The main purpose of most writing is, then, the presentation of an idea. But good writing does much more than just present ideas in a raw state. Rather it *develops* them with clarity and appropriate fullness so that the reader will be convinced by what he has read. Central to the problem of becoming a skilled reader is the ability to follow closely the way a writer has developed his idea. This is especially true of expository material, for the development in most narrations is relatively easy to follow, consisting as it does of a series of chronological events. It is true that narrations can be more complex than this (they can make use of flashbacks or shifts in the narrative point of view), but as a general rule the reader gets picked up by the flow of events and is carried effortlessly along.

But with expository material, where the basis of the development is psychological, not chronological, the reader must attempt to follow the flow of thoughts within the author's mind, rather than the flow of events in time. Reading an exposition, therefore, demands the ability to define accurately the thought relationships that exist between adjacent sentences, and in order to do this, the reader must have terminology for defining at least some of these thought relationships. No simple list can cover all the possible types of thinking that the human mind is capable of, but there are some types that do occur frequently and an understanding of these will make it possible for a reader to describe the development of expository material. The following are the main types of thought relationships common to prose. One statement may provide an *illustration* for another, or it may introduce a *comparison* or a *contrast*, or suggest a *reason* or a *result*, or introduce a *qualification*, or add supporting facts or *details*. Some statements may ask a *question*; others might answer it. And, inevitably, some statements will carry the *main idea*, while others will note a *conclusion*, provide *transition*, or make a *summary*.

At first all of this may sound overly technical, but it really is not, since these are the normal mental processes that most of us are engaged in every day, even if we don't define them in these terms. In any case, the terms themselves are not of prime importance. They merely provide us with a useful and exact means of describing the way one statement in a paragraph is related to the statements adjacent to it. Through practice, and through learning to follow the transitional words and phrases that most writers provide us with, we can become adept at following the thought relationships that the writer expects us to see as we read. In the following paragraph, the thought relationships between adjacent statements have been indicated. (In each case the explanation in parentheses refers to the preceding statement.)

PARAGRAPH 8

There is a popular notion that the boy or girl who is to become a writer can usually be spotted by certain familiar traits of character (*general statement that serves as an introduction*). He is supposed to be rather shy, non-athletic, fond of going off by himself and reading, very introspective and hardly ever a man of action (*details*); in short, a kind of lame duck (*summary*). If a father has such a lame duck in his family he is led to believe hopefully that the thwarted little creature is going to be a writer (*result*). But as I have found it this isn't the case at all (*contrast that presents the main idea*). Good writers whom I have known – men like Thomas Wolfe, William Saroyan, Ernest Hemingway, or Scott Fitzgerald – have been full of bounce, socially at ease, and often aggressively active (*illustration offered as proof of main idea*). There is only one trait that marks the writer (*a contrast to the opening generalization*). He is always watching (*elaboration of "only one trait"*). It is a trick of mind and he is born with it (*further elaboration*). If his grandmother is dying and tears are streaming down his face while his heart breaks, he is nevertheless watching and recording, and he can't help it (*an illustration*). So there he is in the world with this trait and what he does with it will depend on his intelligence and integrity and the training of his taste (*a result*).

4. See the Total Structure

As was stressed in the two preceding sections, our main purpose when we read is to discover exactly what a writer is saying about his subject. Our first strategy for doing this is to follow carefully the steps by which the central thought has been developed. A second strategy is to recognize that the selection has a particular shape or over-all structure, and to realize that this total structure will often, in its own way, be an expression of the selection's idea.

The structure of narration

The usual order for presenting the flow of events in a narration is chronological: the author begins at the beginning and continues until he comes to the end. In a well-told narration, the events will rise toward a climax, or even towards a climax that is followed by an intentional anticlimax. For an example of a narration with a climactic structure, see No. 14 ("The Birth of Rawhide" by Max Ferguson); for an example of climax followed by a sharp anticlimax, see No. 17 ("Percy Williams at the Olympics" by Ray Gardner).

The structure of exposition

Expositions offer considerably more structural variety than is commonly found among narrations, although there is one common structural pattern that is widely used in expository writing and our attention here will focus primarily on this. This "Basic Essay Structure" has four essential parts: (1) an *introduction* that indicates why the subject of the essay is worth writing about; (2) a statement of the *main idea*; (3) several paragraphs that *develop* this main idea; (4) a *conclusion* that has grown out of the development and does something more than restate in a flat and mechanical way the main idea. This structural pattern can operate in an exposition of essay length, but it also is commonly found in expositions only a paragraph long, and since it is more easily comprehended in the shorter of these two forms, let us illustrate it by the following paragraph. The four sections described above have been indicated in the example.

PARAGRAPH 9

INTRODUCTION: It is customary among many people to think of that comic device called the pun as "the lowest form of wit". Many people respond to a pun not with laughter but with a groan. MAIN IDEA: But not all puns are bad, some of them are very good indeed and bring forth our sincere laughter. DEVELOPMENT: The difference between a good pun and a bad one is not hard to define. The bad pun depends for its effect entirely on the sound of words and not on what they mean. To say, for example, that "George thinks he is funny as all get out and when he tries to be funny most people just want him to get out" is not a very good pun. It doesn't add much to the meaning merely to repeat the phrase "get out" in two different senses. But the good pun plays on the meaning of words and adds a dimension to what is being said. To say, for instance, that a farmer is "a handy man with a good sense of humus" increases our understanding of what a good farmer should be, implying as it does so that a "sense of humor" may also be useful in dealing with the vicissitudes inherent in farming. And there is more than just the sound of words in the double pun about Spring being the "time of year when the boys feel gallant and the girls feel buoyant". Another good example of a good pun was provided recently by the critic who described the comic strip "Peanuts" as "a child's garden of reverses", a pun that not only describes Charlie Brown's world quite accurately, but establishes the contrast with the happier world for children that Robert Louis Stevenson wrote about in his "A Child's Garden of Verses". CONCLUSION: As with any aspect of life that can be classified into "good" and "bad", there is always the territory in between where it is hard to be sure which is which. Everyone has to decide for himself whether the pun contained in a newspaper headline on a recent snowy New Year's Eve – it predicted a "Flurry With A Binge on Top" – is a very good pun or just a wild editorial headhunter out on the loose. In any case, a good pun is a thing of beauty and a joke forever.

This same structural pattern has been used in several selections in the anthology. See No. 11 ("The Canadian Eskimo" by Diamond Jenness),

No. 22 ("Lord Durham and His Report" by Edgar McInnis), and No. 48 ("The Wooden Bucket Principle" by Noel Perrin).

5. Attack the Unfamiliar

In the normal course of his life as a reader, the average person will come across words and allusions with which he is not familiar. The person who wants to become an above-average reader will take the trouble to find out about what he has not understood. It is not difficult to discover the meaning of an unfamiliar word, for dictionaries are easily obtained and most words that are encountered in all except technical writing will be defined in a standard desk dictionary. And even readers who resist the dictionary habit have another resource for dealing with unfamiliar words. They can make use of the hints provided by the context in which a word is found, for often the verbal setting in which we meet new vocabulary will help us to make an intelligent guess about its meaning. This is the case with the word "trauma" in the following sentence from No. 1 in the anthology ("Canadian Regions" by Kildare Dobbs) : "*Je me souviens*, their motto, recalls the national trauma – the conquest of New France upon the Plains of Abraham before the walled city of Quebec." Even though the context may not provide the reader with a *dictionary* definition of "trauma" ("a startling experience which has a lasting effect on mental life; a shock"), it should be clear in a general way that a "traumatic" experience is one that involves the suffering that must be endured by anyone who has a setback of some serious kind. In contrast to "trauma", for which there are clues, is the French motto "Je me souviens", which the context does not explain. Here a dictionary – in this case a French dictionary – is needed.

Allusions

The problem of allusions is slightly more complicated, since not all the persons, places, things, and events that we are likely to find references to will be explained by the average dictionary. Nor is the context likely to be very useful. The reader must therefore be prepared to seek help from reference sources other than the dictionary: from encyclopedias, dictionaries of mythology, books of quotations, and so on. And if these don't provide an answer, he must try to ask someone who knows. In any case, the initial step in dealing with an allusion is recognizing that one has been made. The second step is not being content until its meaning has become clear. Generally, an allusion works as a kind of shorthand, allowing the writer to express a fairly complicated notion in a neat and brief way, as Max Ferguson does in the opening sentence of No. 14 ("The Birth of Rawhide") : "It was somewhere in the dying weeks of December, 1946, that old Rawhide

15

was born and rose, more like a Quasimodo than a Phoenix, from the ashes of the old year." The comic point made by these allusions will be missed by the reader who does not know (or does not take the trouble to find out) why Quasimodo and the Phoenix might rise from the ashes in a different way. What is the difference?

The whole matter of dealing with allusions is a complex one, since writers are free to refer to things that may be known only to people living in a particular place or to people who were alive in an earlier time. For example, someone living outside of the Maritimes may not understand what is implied by a reference to Sable Island; and not everyone born after 1938 is likely to get an allusion to "Wrong-Way" Corrigan.[1] But the problem of understanding allusions is not an impossible one, for it tends to solve itself through the normal process of regular reading. The more a person reads, the greater his general knowledge will become, and the wider will be the range of allusions that he does understand.

Consider the following paragraph in terms of any allusions or vocabulary that might need to be explained. Who, to begin with, was Isaac Moses Barr?

PARAGRAPH 10

Isaac Moses Barr was unfortunate in his name. It gave him aspirations which his talents could not match, set him treading paths he had no staying power to follow. Once, at least, in the course of a long life, he must have felt anticipations of fulfillment – when at the head of a band of the Chosen People he stood in sight of the Promised Land. But like that other Moses, though for far different reasons, he was not allowed to enter it. Nor could he find on the rolling prairies a Mount Nebo on which to leave honourably his bones. There are men who, though a good deal talked and written about, contrive somehow always to elude us. The Reverend Moses Barr is one of these. A villain with no real evil in him; a good shepherd accused of "fleecing" his flock; an empire-builder incapable of coping with building materials more complicated than a child's set of blocks, Barr is a quicksilver character, practical and idealistic, wambling and tendentious, above all elusive – of whom one can say with assurance only that he was born neither to lead nor to follow.

6. Understand Figurative Language

It is characteristic of the human mind to think about one thing in terms of another. Such comparisons may be either literal or figurative ones. A literal

[1]Sable Island is a desolate stretch of shifting sand off the coast of Nova Scotia. It is usually referred to as "The Graveyard of the Atlantic". "Wrong-Way" Corrigan was an American pilot who in July 1938 set out on what was supposed to be a solo flight from New York to California. But he ended up in Ireland.

comparison is one in which the two things compared are actually comparable because they are the same kind of thing. We are making a literal comparison if we write that "Sheep are smaller than cows". Figurative comparisons, on the other hand, bring different kinds of things together for comparative purposes, as when we write that "The people of this city are a bunch of sheep". Figurative comparisons are generally referred to as metaphors, although several other types of figurative statements are often identified, especially *simile, personification,* and *analogy*.[2] But the terminology is not in itself important, since the key to understanding figurative language lies in identifying what two dissimilar things have been brought together, and recognizing what characteristic the writer sees them as sharing in the context in which he has coupled them. It is also important to realize that figurative language enables a writer to convey an idea with more emotional impact than may be possible by means of a literal statement. For when a writer compares two objects, or two situations, he can transfer the emotional overtones associated with one of these to the other, as Farley Mowat does in the following sentence from No. 3 in the anthology ("People of the Sea") : "The merchant class of Newfoundland held the people in a deadly vice." Here the writer has transferred to the life situation of the Newfoundland people the unpleasant associations connected with being caught in a vice, and in so doing has achieved a stronger expression of this idea than if he had stated it literally, as, for example: "Because of the merchants, the people of Newfoundland were not economically free."

The metaphor discussed briefly above is not a complicated one. The average reader would see at once what two dissimilar things were being compared and what attributes they shared in common. But metaphorical statements are often more complex than this, and when they are, the reader must try not to let the idea conveyed by the metaphor elude him. The strategy for dealing with metaphorical statements involves asking two questions: (1) what two things are being compared; and (2) what characteristic does the author see the two as sharing? Apply this strategy to the several fairly complex metaphorical statements in the following paragraph by the American writer John Updike.

PARAGRAPH 11

The afternoon grew so glowering that in the sixth inning the arc lights were turned on – always a wan sight in the daytime, like the burning headlights of a funeral procession. Aided by the gloom, Fisher was

[2]A *metaphor* is a figurative comparison in which one thing is said to be, or implied to be, another. In a *simile*, the two things compared are introduced formally, usually by "like" or "as". *Personification* is a special type of metaphor in which a lifeless thing is spoken of as if it were alive. In an *analogy*, two situations are seen as comparable.

slicing through the Sox rookies, and Williams did not come to bat in the seventh. He was second up in the eighth. This was almost certainly his last time to come to the plate in Fenway Park, and instead of merely cheering, as we had at his three previous appearances, we stood, all of us, and applauded. I had never before heard pure applause in a ballpark. No calling, no whistling, just an ocean of handclaps, minute after minute, burst and burst, crowding and running together in continuous succession like the pushes of surf at the edge of the sand. It was a sombre and considered tumult. There was not a boo in it. It seemed to renew itself out of a shifting set of memories as the Kid, the Marine, the veteran of feuds and failures and injuries, the friend of children, and the enduring old pro evolved down the bright tunnel of twenty-two summers toward this moment. At last, the umpire signalled for Fisher to pitch; with the other players, he had been frozen in position. Only Williams had moved during the ovation, switching his bat impatiently, ignoring everything except his cherished task. Fisher wound up, and the applause sank into a hush.[3]

7. Recognize Irony

Irony is a subtle matter that cannot easily be defined, for no simple statement embraces all the different kinds of irony. But perhaps the best way to begin a definition is by noting that the ironical tone is involved in those situations in which we say or write something that is in some way different from what we really mean, as when a man who has just started off the week by breaking his leg remarks that Monday was always his lucky day. But irony is more than just words. It is also an attitude of mind, an attitude that is likely to express itself in criticism or mockery of the subject being discussed. Perhaps it is through example rather than definition that we can arrive at an understanding of what irony really is. Where is the irony in the following paragraph?

PARAGRAPH 12

The Williams Lake courthouse, two storeys high and square as the cross, was built in the 1920s when the Cariboo had experienced a sudden rush of blood to the head cause by a powerful feeling of prosperity. It may be that it was built ahead of its time. In those years there were not many laws. However, the few they had, the people broke; it was felt that the structure was indeed justified. Of course, the times were good. In those years it was believed that the stock market,

[3]Ted Williams did not disappoint his fans. He celebrated his last time at bat by hitting a home run. The complete story of Ted Williams' last game after twenty-two years as the Boston Red Sox's super star has been told in a brilliant piece of sports reporting entitled "Hub Fans Bid Kid Adieu". This can be found in John Updike's *Assorted Prose*, published in 1965 by Alfred A. Knopf.

beef prices, wages, debts and government hand-outs could increase to infinity without let or hindrance. The money supply was endless, the proof being that the population was increasing every year. It was shortly to be arranged that everybody should become healthy and wise, and there was never going to be another severe winter. Odd, the way people thought in those days.

This example of the ironical tone is the first paragraph of No. 13 in the anthology ("Country Justice" by Paul St. Pierre). Among the several other anthology items that have touches of the ironical tone are No. 1 ("Canadian Regions" by Kildare Dobbs); No. 5 ("The Sensual City" by Peter Desbarats); No. 19 ("Bicultural Angela" by Hugh Hood); No. 38 ("Canada: Case History" by Earle Birney); and No. 53 ("Let's Stay Off The Moon" by Bertrand Russell).

8. Identify the Slant

Closely related to the tone of any piece of writing is its slant, that is, the feeling the writer conveys of being either strongly for or strongly against his subject matter. The word "slant" in this context is often assumed to be pejorative; it seems to suggest that an author has done something vaguely underhand or indecent by failing to maintain absolute neutrality concerning his subject. But such neutrality is not really a requisite of good writing. In fact, it is seldom sought after and even more rarely attained, for most authors who are willing to expend the time and energy to write something worth while are likely to feel strongly about their subject, and this will be revealed in what they write. So the problem of slant from the reader's point of view is not a matter of being critical of a writer who has not maintained neutrality. Rather it is a matter of being alert to recognize writing that has been so subtly slanted that the reader may not realize he is being influenced.

The slant of most writing is revealed in a number of quite specific ways. Three of these are especially worth noting. The first clue is in the kind of *words* the writer uses. Pejorative words will cause the reader to feel against the subject; honorific words, to feel in favour of it. Another indication is the kind of *comparisons* that the writer has made. If the metaphorical statements depend on comparisons with pleasant things, the reader will feel sympathetic; if the comparisons are with unpleasant things, the opposite effect will be achieved. The third determiner of slant is the kind of *details* that have been included or omitted. By consciously omitting or stressing either pleasant or unpleasant details, the writer can effectively influence the way the reader responds to whatever is being described.

Keeping the above criteria in mind, consider the following paragraph. What specific words, comparisons, or details determine its slant?

There are those, however, who think that physical conditions on the moon can gradually be changed by scientific manipulation. I have read a curious recent Russian work containing the kind of very serious science fiction which the Soviet government considers good for its more youthful subjects. In this book it was suggested that, in time, chemical means would be found of turning lunar rocks into gases and gradually creating something that would do as an atmosphere. If once an atmosphere had been created, hydrogen and oxygen extracted from minerals could be made to produce water. Low forms of life might then become capable of living in the newly created pools, and gradually the biologists might coax these forms of life up the ladder of evolution.

9. Be Aware of Style

The ability to recognize stylistic differences opens up a new world of reading pleasure. It is not easy to define the many variations of style in simple terms. Initially the reader should try to identify some quite measurable qualities that make one author's way of writing different from another's. Such qualities may be of several different kinds, but the list below, though incomplete, will help the reader to focus on most of the basic elements of prose style.

The Ideas: Are the author's ideas commonplace or original? Is the material down to earth or abstract?

The Writer's Attitude: How does the writer feel about his subject? Is he sympathetic or critical? How does he seem to feel about the reader? Does he respect him or appear to scorn him? What attitude does the writer seem to take to the reader? Does he chat? Lecture? Argue? Propagandize?

The Development: What type of illustrative material does the writer make use of? Are the illustrations taken from books, from everyday life, or from the writer's imagination? Is the idea developed fully or just sketched in quickly?

Sentence Structure: What type of sentences does the writer customarily use? Are they long, short, simple, or complex? Is there variety? Does the writer employ parallel or climactic sentences to any marked degree? (These terms are explained and illustrated in Section III of this introduction. See pages 48-9.)

Diction: What general level of diction does the writer employ? Is his choice of words formal, standard, or colloquial? Does the writer make use of difficult or unusual words? Is the diction fresh and lively or marked by triteness? Does the writer sometimes employ technical language?

Rhetorical Devices: Does the writer make use of figurative language? Does he use puns? Allusions? Verbal Contrasts? Repetitions? (See pages 54-5.)

Specific answers to some or all of the above questions will help to define most styles, for it is by such means as these that an author consciously or unconsciously reveals his personality, or at least that part of his personality that is involved in the work being analysed. And even though the asking and the answering of such questions will not always make it possible to tag a style with some neat and decisive adjective (such as Formal, Informal, Plain, Comic, Poetic, or Scientific), the application of the principles outlined above will enable the reader to distinguish more exactly and more confidently the difference between one way of writing and another.

In its initial stages, stylistic analysis should be fairly objective, concerned primarily with describing what a particular style is like, and not with making judgments about whether or not it is an effective or suitable one. But evaluation will eventually become a part of analysis, and as a reader becomes familiar with different kinds of writing (as, for example, the many different styles represented in this anthology), he will find that an understanding of the rudiments of stylistic analysis will help him to define *why* he admires one piece of writing and dislikes another.

Below are three paragraphs, each of which has a distinctive style. By finding answers to some of the questions suggested above, point out some of the stylistic differences between the three. Is any one of the styles especially effective or ineffective?

PARAGRAPH 14

Air transport in Canada performs two distinct transport tasks: first, as a mainline aviation function, it provides the means of rapid communication between the widely spread centres and between Canada and other countries, and second, it provides modern transport services in the frontier or northern parts of the county where the establishment of efficient surface transport services is difficult or economically unjustified. These two different tasks have been reflected almost from the beginning in different organizations of the two branches of the industry.

PARAGRAPH 15

Two parallel shafts of steel, nothing else, first joined the little pockets of settlement in a land not yet a nation. They made it a nation.

The Canadian remembers that story, and to him the locomotive is more than a machine. If it is not quite a living thing, it has, like no other machine, the look and energy of life, and it propels the nation's lifestuff. Without it, the national economy is not viable, the Canadian scene is unimaginable, the loneliness of the land is unendurable.

A freight train of fifty cars, wriggling across the prairies, is no larger than a gartersnake against this void of earth and sky.

The longest passenger train is a momentary glint of metal in the Rockies. It bores underground and crawls out again, but is instantly lost.

PARAGRAPH 16

It is hard for us to realize just what the bicycle meant in the nineties. Here was everyone's dream – a speedy, pleasant means of travel available to people who could never afford a carriage and team of horses. Overnight Canada became a nation on wheels. Bicycle clubs sprang up in every town and city. The younger generation pedalled out to the country on picnics; families got out a bicycle-built-for-two, with extra carriers fore and aft for the youngsters, and pedalled to the beach. The man who wanted to prove his strength cycled a "century," one hundred miles, in a single day – no mean feat over the roads of the times. Others raced in bright club sweaters. The "scorcher," or speeder, became a public menace. After the drop frame was introduced to preserve feminine modesty, many women took up the sport. Most wore knickers or long, baggy bloomers under their skirts, but even that wasn't enough to calm the critics, and a few women were arrested for wanton exposure of their ankles. Nevertheless the bicycle, by giving women a new mobility – and an individual and unchaperoned mobility at that – did much to speed their eventual emancipation.

10. Interpreting Fiction

As was pointed out on page 8, a narrative usually does something more than just tell a story. It presents an idea, even though it may do this indirectly. It may even be that the writer of a short story or novel[4] has expressed some ideas unconsciously, so it is not too absurd to imagine a situation in which a reader of fiction sees more in the story than even the author saw. However, the reader of novels and short stories should feel some restraint when "interpreting" a plot. He is not justified in reading between the lines in any way that suits his free-wheeling imagination. To be valid, an interpretation must be supported by all the plot details. Any

---

[4]The difference between a short story and a novel is not just a matter of length; rather it is a matter of focus. The short story is generally concerned with one significant episode in the life of its central character, and its intention is to reveal how this character responds to his moment of crisis. A novel, on the other hand, is more likely to be concerned with *developing* rather than *revealing* character. Under the impetus of a series of related crises, the central character changes and we watch him change.

interpretation that takes into account only part of the story – while leaving major contradictions in other parts – cannot be considered valid.

In learning to interpret fiction, it is important to develop the ability to "stand back from the plot" in order to see the story's larger implications. This technique can be illustrated conveniently by considering this well-known verse narrative:

> Humpty Dumpty sat on a wall;
> Humpty Dumpty had a great fall.
> All the king's horses and all the king's men
> Couldn't put Humpty Dumpty together again.

We can just leave this as a simple nursery rhyme about an "egg" that had a bad break. But we can "interpret" the poem to produce some quite sensible ideas on serious issues. For example, the opening couplet makes the point that no one should go around doing things he isn't equipped to do, things like sitting on a wall if he happens to be an egg. And this first couplet also introduces the basic theme of tragic literature: he who puts himself in a high position is in danger of suffering a fall. The second couplet is equally rich in implications. It says something about power, specifically about the limited power of kings, for in spite of all his horses and men, there are some areas of life where even a king is helpless.

Such an interpretation of a simple plot is not too fanciful; everything that was said in the interpretation can be supported by evidence in the poem. Nor is there any danger that this approach will take away the pleasure we can get from reading the story. We can continue to enjoy this sad and simple tale about a careless egg even when we are aware that it has numerous implied meanings.

Conflict and structure

Short stories and novels can also be enjoyed and understood at levels above the plot, and the main strategy for interpreting fiction is to identify clearly the *conflict* that lies at the heart of the story. The reader of fiction should train himself to see not only the direct confrontations that the narrative describes, but also the implied conflicts that are represented symbolically in the story. For example, in thinking about the conflict in Morley Callaghan's "A Girl With Ambition" (No. 33 in the anthology), the perceptive reader can see that it is not just about Mary Ross and her efforts to move one step up the social ladder, but also about social mobility in general. How does one, the story asks, get ahead in life? What *is* the relationship between our talents and our ambitions, or between our dreams and the realities we must accept? And on an even higher level of abstraction, the plot of Mr. Callaghan's story poses the question of whether anyone is *really* free to choose his path in life.

A second aspect of fiction that will help the reader to see a work's larger implications is the *structure* of the plot, for the structure can often be seen as a symbolic representation of the author's main idea. To illustrate this, let us consider briefly once again "A Girl With Ambition". We will see that the plot is concerned with the several choices of occupation that Mary Ross seems to have when she leaves school. As the plot unfolds, her choices are reduced until she ultimately takes the only "choice" that was ever really hers. The structure of the plot is, in effect, a statement about the fact that people with ambition but no talent have severe limits placed upon them.

There are, of course, other techniques used in fiction that will help the reader make an intelligent interpretation of a novel or a short story. Among these are the story's symbols, its verbal images, and its general tone. But *conflict* and *structure* are the central devices by which the reader of fiction stands back from the plot to discover its larger implications.

II. The Writer's Responsibility to the Reader

The writer's responsibility to the reader is to be as clear and as interesting as he can. For most people this is not a responsibility that can be fulfilled easily, for the ability to write well is the result of understanding some basic rhetorical principles and practising these principles diligently. Mere familiarity with the theory of writing is of little use without the practice; and practice itself may be of little value if the person doing the practising has no real understanding of what is required of him. The student of composition must himself take the responsibility for practising; but the fundamental principles can be set down. This has been done on the following pages.

1. Have Something To Say

Good writing involves more than correct spelling, accurate punctuation, and neat handwriting, although each of these does make its minor contribution to a polished composition. It is of much greater importance to have a worthwhile idea, one that can be developed in appropriate fullness in a paragraph or essay whose structure the reader can follow with relative ease. More than anything else, good writing is the product of clear thinking, and although a certain amount of verbal skill is obviously necessary in order to get an idea down on paper successfully, it is *getting* the idea in the first place that matters most. Curiously enough, many students who have difficulty in expressing their ideas often find that their problems of expression become less serious when they are writing on a subject they know something about and have considered carefully *before* writing. William Cobbett's advice to "Sit down to write what you have thought, and not to think what you shall write" is as true today as it was when he first said it over 150 years ago.

It is not possible to set down absolute rules on where or how a writer goes about finding his idea. But one simple principle is useful: no one can write well about a subject he knows nothing about, any more than, as the folk-saying puts it, he can "come from a place he ain't been at". The two main sources of material for anyone who writes are: (1) observations of his own first-hand experiences (either real or imaginary); and (2) reflections on the vicarious experiences he has had through reading, watching television, talking to other people, and so on. So the simple principle stated above can be extended slightly; we should write on something we already know about, or on something we can find out about in the time available to us.

Assuming that a writer has found a subject he wants to deal with, his next step is to approach it with the conviction that he has something worth while to say, something that he alone can say about the subject. In the unique experience of every human being is ample material for writing, particularly for those who have trained themselves to see what is going on in the world around them. The art of writing is, as was stated above, essentially the art of thinking, but it is also the art of seeing. As C. E. Montague once observed, most people will think most originally and see most clearly when they deal with the "long thought about familiar things" of their experience.

One further principle about effective writing can be stressed at this point. It is related to the writer's attitude to his reader. Perhaps the best comment on this subject was made by Ernest Hemingway when he was asked if he thought he had ever written an unsuccessful book. Hemingway's answer, as it is quoted in A. E. Hotchner's *Papa Hemingway*, was as follows:

> When you first start writing you never fail. You think it's wonderful and you have a fine time. You think it's easy to write and you enjoy it very much, but you are thinking of yourself, not the reader. He does not enjoy it very much. Later, *when you have learned to write for the reader*, it is no longer easy to write. In fact what you ultimately remember about anything you've written is how difficult it was to write it.

2. Know What You Are Trying To Write

Since, as the selections in the anthology will make abundantly clear, there are many different types of writing, and many different ways of shaping an idea in prose or verse, the writer should know *before* he begins to write just what it is he intends to do. He must know, for example, whether he is writing an exposition or a narration; he must know the approximate length that his essay or paragraph is to be; and he must know who his audience is. Such knowledge should have a considerable effect on the writer, forcing him to select, limit, and shape his material in terms of his intentions. He should realize, for example, that the kind of idea that can be handled in a paragraph or short essay will differ considerably from the kind that can be handled in a long essay or book. He should also realize that whether he is writing a paragraph, an essay, or a book, he must be specific. And even though the narrow scope of a short composition may limit him to one or two main ideas, these ideas should be developed in concrete terms. A student should be careful to avoid what is probably the most serious error made by beginning writers: attempting in a short assignment to cover too much ground, attempting – so to speak – to discuss the universe and give two examples, all in one paragraph. Nothing makes for more tedious reading than an endless series of broad generalizations on a subject that is too big for the literary bag that is trying to contain it. Good writing is specific.

3. Understand the Part Played by Usage

To gain confidence in his ability to handle words effectively, a writer should have some understanding of how words work, and especially an understanding of what makes a particular word or construction "correct" or "incorrect". To begin with, he must understand that correct and incorrect are not absolute terms. When we say that a person uses "correct English" we simply mean that he is using it in the same way as those members of the community who are thought of as speakers or writers of "standard" English. The notorious expression "He ain't" is considered incorrect usage not because some absolute authority has stamped it as incorrect, but rather because standard speakers (often referred to as "the educated minority") customarily say "He isn't", not "He ain't". It is *usage* that determines the acceptability of the thousands of choices available in all aspects of language: in word choice, in meaning, in spelling, in punctuation, in sentence structure, and even to some extent in style. It follows, therefore, that the writer who wishes to use the style of the literate minority must make a conscious effort to imitate their usage whenever he writes. And he must remember that language is a living thing, and that usage changes in terms of both time and place. An expression that is standard in England may not be so in Canada; and certainly many expressions that were current usage in Shakespeare's time would be considered unacceptable today. And since usage does play this important role in determining how our language is to be used, the person who wants to write well (or speak well) must develop a good ear for language – not only a literal ear that hears what standard speakers say, but also an inner ear that can tune in on how writers "speak" in print.

Levels of usage

A word or construction that is appropriate on one occasion may not be suitable on another. We can, and often do, express our ideas in varying degrees of formality. For example, we can be quite formal, saying: "This is the hour at which I generally dine." But much the same idea can be expressed *informally*: "I usually eat about now." Somewhere in between these two is what we can call the *standard* level of English, where the above thought would be expressed as "I usually have dinner about this time." It is on this standard level of usage that most published work is written, and it is generally expected that writing assignments in college will also be on this level. There is, of course, a certain amount of flexibility in standard English towards both the formal and the informal. What the student of writing should realize, however, is that when he is writing on the standard level, he should avoid any jarring deviations into either inappropriately formal or unnecessarily slangy diction. To make use of words that are too formal for the quality of the idea ("I took up a sedentary position and began my perusal of the volume") is just as absurd as using words that are too informal for the subject being discussed ("Shakespeare was sure a guy that could string together a wicked sentence").

Something of the range of diction that is found in printed material is indicated in the two paragraphs found below, both of which are from books published recently in Canada. Which specific words help to determine the level of diction in each paragraph?

PARAGRAPH 17

Torontonians still get kidded now and then about their city, of course. But they don't mind – in fact they've rather grown to take a peculiar kind of pride in the way people in other parts of the country – such as those in Toronto's arch rival Montreal – talk about them. They'd feel a little lost if they weren't occasionally getting a ribbing from someone. Yet, even the kidders are no longer quite so sure about the subject of their jokes as they were a few years ago when Toronto was known far and wide in Canada as Hogtown. The Montreal comedian who once described a contest in which the first prize was a one-week trip to Toronto and the second prize a two-week trip, wouldn't roll them in the aisles with this joke today the way he did a few years ago. Something very exciting and profound has happened to Toronto, and it has happened so swiftly that even its own people, leave alone outsiders, are not quite aware of its exact extent or nature.

PARAGRAPH 18

Canadians, French- and English-speaking, are not a military people. Enjoying a sense of security in their geographical position, Canadians within the last century have displayed small interest in the problems of defense, either of the past or present day. And yet, withal, the history of Canada is filled with military and naval exploits: the very fact that Canada exists today as a separate and distinct political entity on the North American continent is the result of military operations of some magnitude. During the first years of its existence this country struggled hard for survival against the assaults of the League of the Five Nations; during the seventeenth and eighteenth centuries the wars of France and England in the old world had their counterparts in the woods and on the rivers and lakes of the New World; during the eighteenth and nineteenth centuries Canada was threatened by the continentalism of the

United States; and within the last fifty years Canada has on three separate occasions sent her sons abroad to fight at the side of Great Britain, first in South Africa and later against the German Reich.

If any exception can be made to this general rule that college assignments should be written on the standard level of English (about like paragraph 18 above), it is that narrations can be slightly more informal than expositions. The writer who is dealing with everyday or comic events is justified in employing an informal style. And if dialogue is introduced into the narrative it should be appropriate for the person who is speaking, whether it be formal, standard, informal, or substandard. In other words, the writer must decide whether it would be more natural for a particular character in his story to say "Certainly", "Yes", "Yeah", or "Yup".

In the anthology, this principle of different levels of diction is illustrated by various selections. See No. 29 ("Building Bee in the 1830s" by Catherine Parr Traill) ; No. 25 ("Clifford Sifton's Medicine Show" by Ralph Allen) ; and No. 52 ("Tickling the Dragon's Tail" by Ralph E. Lapp).

Idiomatic English

One further aspect of usage that is particularly important is idiom. This involves knowing what combinations of words are considered acceptable at a particular level of usage. (In discussing idiom, we need not, incidentally, concern ourselves with what are called "cast-iron" idioms such as "To come in handy" or "How do you do", for these idiomatic expressions, despite the fact that they do not employ usual grammatical patterns, are not the ones that cause trouble. Anyone reasonably familiar with English will use these cast-iron idioms correctly without even noticing their oddity.) But some attention must be given to idiom as it applies to the "usual forms of expression" that are employed by standard speakers and writers. Maintaining these usual forms in standard writing poses some difficulties even for someone who has spoken English all his life. This is because the possible combinations are so numerous, and because *usage* places some quite severe restrictions on which combinations of words can or cannot be employed. If we were to write, for example, that someone in an essay "perpetrated many silly ideas on the reader", we would be unidiomatic, since "ideas" are not among the things that can be "perpetrated", at least not in standard English. Likewise it is unidiomatic to write "From India he made his way *for* Ceylon", since in standard English we usually make our way "to" a place, not "for" it. The important thing to remember is that idiom is a matter of usage, not of logic. There is, for instance, no logical reason why we could not write "In today's world many jobs have become obsolete to computers", but the fact is that the writer concerned with maintaining standard usage would not express the idea in this way, but would write "Many jobs have been taken over by computers", or "Because of computers, many jobs have recently become obsolete".

It might seem that no one could ever learn which combinations of words are correct usage. But the situation is not as impossible as it might at first appear, for we do not have to "learn" all the idioms of our language in a formal way. We can learn them informally by listening to standard speakers and reading standard writers, and paying close attention to the usage they employ. To learn to write correct idiomatic English is not an impossible task, but neither is it something that anyone can take casually. The careful writer continually checks what he has written to see that he has employed only those combinations of words that have an established place in current, standard English.

4. Revise Your Own Writing Critically

Only the exceptional writer can produce a polished piece of prose without considerable editing and rewriting. Learning to *revise* is, therefore, an important part of learning to write well. Many inexperienced writers think of revision merely as a time to correct the most obvious spelling errors, add some punctuation, and make a tidy copy of their essay. But real revision involves much more than this. It must be concerned with all aspects of the composition, beginning with the quality of the *ideas* themselves, and moving through the *development*, the *total structure* of the essay, the *sentence structure*, the *diction*, and the quality of the *figurative statements*, if any of these have been made. While revising his essay, the writer has to work in much the same way as a juggler, for he must maintain control over several separate but related things.

Good revision is impossible unless the writer has clearly established in his mind some standard that will help him to decide which aspects of his writing need to be revised. Such a standard for prose composition is described and illustrated on the following pages. The material has been divided into six sub-sections, each of which represents a major area of concern for the writer who wants to handle words effectively.

(a) A standard for ideas

It cannot be emphasized too often that the aim of most writing should be to present the author's ideas in a clear and interesting way. During revision, therefore, the writer should examine his ideas in the light of this basic aim. More specifically, he should check to see that what he has written does make a true statement about some aspect of reality. Also he should check to see that he has supported his idea adequately and in specific terms, for nothing makes duller reading than an essay consisting entirely of abstract and *overly generalized* statements that forever circle a subject without ever landing on it. There will be, it is true, some abstract or general statements in a composition, but it is a basic principle of composition that general statements must be supported by concrete details or specific examples. (More is said about development in the next sub-section of this introduction.) A third check must be concerned with detecting the presence of *truisms* in what has been written. Truisms are ideas that are so universally known and accepted that there is no point in repeating them. The following is a typical example: "Canada is much less powerful than the United States and has fewer people along its side of the undefended border." The writer who throughout his essay says nothing more original than this is really saying nothing, at least not anything that anyone would want to read. On occasion a writer might use a truism as *part* of an argument he is developing, but a composition that consists entirely of pale statements that would already be known by the audience for whom the essay was written should be revised. Often the only possible revision for an essay that consists entirely of truisms (or of untruths or unsupported generalizations) is to begin again by thinking of an idea that would be worth developing.

Revision exercise

Below are three paragraphs. Consider the quality of the idea that each contains. Which of the paragraphs presents a clear and interesting idea? For what reasons are the other two paragraphs unsatisfactory?

PARAGRAPH 19

The art of smoking is fast becoming nothing more than a distant memory. This statement may possibly under some conditions seem to be a paradoxical one, but it's true. More people smoke today than ever before, but few of these do anything to uphold the dignity of their recreation. The reason for this is simple. Too many people start smoking when they are still young and inexperienced. By "young" I mean below 49. For smoking belongs to the older generation and always has. Just as good tobacco must be aged, so must a good smoker be aged. Examples to support the above hypothesis are prevalent also in older civilizations. Take the North American Indian, he smokes beautifully, with an inscribed and awesome device that cools the smoke as he smokes. People like this put our low chain smokers to shame. It is all enough to cause one to have a wonder whether there is any hope for the future of smoking. Perhaps the big-wigs of big business and nervous tension have finally taken their toll.

The sociologist steps into the historical field at this juncture and points out that the American from the beginning was an individualist who took the attitude that every man must be capable of looking after himself. Canadian frontiersmen, on the other hand, were organization men, held together not only by police and law but by big corporations and enterprises – the Hudson's Bay Company, the Canadian Pacific Railway – which, with state blessing, possessed authority to distribute land and favour. Results of the dissimilar heritages are noticeable today. For one thing, the quieter respect for law and order in Canada is due only partly to British traditions; it is due also to the disciplines learned in the earliest days in a harsh and lonely environment. For another, the American has retained an obsession for "rugged individualism" or personal initiative, while the Canadian, never cognizant of these incentives in the same degree, takes it for granted that society as a whole will share in his protection and welfare. Even the United Empire Loyalists, destitute on their arrival from the Thirteen Colonies, learned the first lesson when the government handed them food, land and tools. One of the striking contrasts between the United States and Canada today is the calm approach a Canadian makes to a subject anathema to an American: socialism. Though, by European standards, Canadians are only now catching up in measures of welfare, by United States terms they are virtually socialists with cradle-to-the-grave security.

There is simply no doubt about the fact that if you want to succeed at something, you will have to work at it, and work hard. This is true of athletics, of business, and of college work. If, in the last of these, you expect to get top marks, you will probably have to be organized and keep up with your assignments, and do the necessary studying before you have an examination, where the emphasis will have to be on reviewing. And since there is the likelihood that college or university will get harder the higher you go, you will have to realize that at the college level of schoolwork you will have to do much more studying than you did when you were in the earlier grades, and will have to learn to work independently.

(b) A standard for development

Even the possession of an excellent idea will not guarantee the success of a composition. The idea must be *developed*, that is, supported convincingly and at appropriate length. In discussing this aspect of prose from the reader's point of view earlier in this introduction (pages 11 to 13), it was noted that among the main ways of developing ideas are the following: *illustrations, examples, reasons, results, comparisons, contrasts, details, qualifications*. When we write, we should make conscious use of such means, singly and in combination, to support our topic statements in a convincing way. And when we revise, we should examine carefully the methods we have used in developing our paragraph's or our essay's main statement. Illustrations should be tested to see that they really do illustrate what they claim they do. Reasons should be checked to see that they are clear, results that they are probable, comparisons and contrasts that they are fair, and so on. In addition, we should, as Hemingway noted, write for the reader. This means providing adequate *transition* between adjacent statements, and seeing that the flow of the thought relationships within each paragraph, and within the essay as a whole, is *immediately* clear. The successful author writes not so that he can be understood if the reader really works hard at it, but so that the reader cannot help understanding.

Revision exercise

Consider the following two paragraphs. In which has a reasonably interesting central idea been developed convincingly? Why should the author of the less satisfactory paragraph have revised the *development* of what he has written?

PARAGRAPH 22

Canada has crammed into the ten decades since Confederation a vast transformation of environment that took as many centuries in most parts of Europe. The buildings which characterized the historic regions of Canada, the architecture which had such diversity and traditional roots, and the original planning of settlements – all have been virtually wiped out, or submerged, or changed out of all recognition, in the urban and industrial revolution of the twentieth century. The traces that remain indicate not one world but several different worlds that have risen and then in their turn been swept aside in the tidal waves of change. In central Canada, it is not uncommon to find a city which is only as old as our Confederation but which has had four or five city halls, of which not a trace remains, except of the latest. In almost every region of Canada, places that were thriving in 1867 have passed away, their former presence now scarcely suspected; new developments attest to the gaps in local historical knowledge, as bulldozers clearing the path for housing unearth Indian burial grounds, or the graves of former heroes. Places that confidently expected great expansion are now quiet backwaters, and every decade new towns are established. The landscape, even in the wilderness, bears witness to the transforming power of the new nation, for good or ill.

PARAGRAPH 23

There hasn't been as much publicity about the laying of a new telephone cable across the Atlantic as there should be. I was reading about this just the other night, and it reminded me of something else I had been thinking about recently. This was about when they put down that earlier cable across the floor of the Atlantic in the middle of the last century. It was a ship called the "Great Eastern" that was used to lay that cable, a ship that has gone through all kinds of misfortunes since it was first built. Actually the "Great Eastern" was a seven days wonder, but everything seemed to go wrong from the very day that it was launched. On that day there was a stampede among the crowd that witnessed the ceremonies. Later the ship was burned and wrecked by storms and suffered most of the calamities likely to be endured by ships. The new cable across the ocean has been badly needed for some time and many people will welcome its arrival.

(c) A standard for structure

The point was made earlier in this introduction (see page 13) that although there are many ways in which an expository essay can be organized, there is one basic type of structure that every writer should be able to handle confidently. This structural pattern consists of four distinct parts, usually placed in the following order: an *introduction*; a statement of the *main idea*; an adequate *development* of this main idea; and a *conclusion*. Such a pattern can be employed at virtually any length: in a paragraph, in an essay, and even throughout an entire book. In a paragraph, each of the parts would occupy only a sentence or two; in an essay each would be a paragraph or several paragraphs; in a book, each would be a chapter or a group of chapters. We have already seen an illustration of this structure at paragraph length (see page 14), and have noted that the structure is employed in several selections of essay length in the anthology. Here is one further illustration of it, this time in an essay of five paragraphs. Notice in this example that the introduction and the main idea are both found in the opening paragraph. (The main idea is stated somewhat indirectly in the final sentence of paragraph 1.) Notice, too, that the idea is then supported by specific illustrations in paragraphs 2, 3, and 4. In paragraph 5 a conclusion developing out of these examples is put forth, and the essay's main idea is restated, this time directly.

PARAGRAPH 24

(1)   Language in Canada, as in most countries, is taken for granted. Unfortunately, however, a great deal of nonsense is taken for granted by many Canadians. Some people, especially recent arrivals from the United Kingdom, refuse to accept the fact that the English spoken in Canada has any claim to recognition. Others, who themselves speak Canadian English, are satisfied with the view that British English is the only acceptable standard. To these people the argument that educated Canadians set their own standard of speech is either treasonable or ridiculous.

(2)   One Canadian I know had his eyes opened in a rather curious way. While shopping in a large Chicago department store, he asked where he might find chesterfields. Following directions to the letter, he was somewhat dismayed when he ended up at the cigar counter. He soon made other discoveries as well. Blinds were "shades" to his American neighbours; taps were "faucets," braces "suspenders," and serviettes "napkins."

(3)   Before long his American friends were pointing out differences between his speech and theirs. He said *been* to rhyme with "bean," whereas for them it rhymed with "bin"; and he said *shone* to rhyme with "gone," whereas for them it rhymed with "bone." In fact, their Canadian friend had quite a few curious ways of saying things: *ration* rhymed with "fashion" rather than with "nation"; *lever* with "beaver" rather than "sever"; *z* with "bed" rather than "bee." Moreover, he said certain vowels in a peculiar way, for *lout* seemed to have a different vowel sound from *loud*, and *rice* a different vowel from *rise*.

(4)   The Englishman is also quick to observe that Canadians talk differently from himself. For example, he doesn't say *dance, half, clerk, tomato, garage,* or *war* as Canadians do; and he always distinguishes *cot* from *caught*, a distinction that few Canadians make. He also finds that many of the words he used in England are not understood by people in Canada. Suppose he gets into a conversation about cars. Says he, "I think a car should have a roomy boot." No headway will be made until somebody rescues him by explaining that in Canada the boot is called a "trunk." Before the session is finished, he will probably learn that a bonnet is called a "hood" and the hood of a coupe is "the top of a convertible." Similarly, he must substitute *muffler* for *silencer, windshield* for *windscreen, truck* for *lorry,* and *gas* for *petrol.*

(5)   The examples I have mentioned suggest, quite correctly, that Canadian English, while different from both British and American English, is in large measure a blend of both varieties; and to this blend must be added many features which are typically Canadian. The explanation for this mixed character lies primarily in the settlement history of the country, for both Britain and the United States have exerted continuous influence on Canada during the past two hundred years.

MORE ABOUT ESSAY STRUCTURE

When revising an essay, the writer should keep in mind the following points about *structure.*

(i) The opening and closing statements of an essay are of particular importance. It is desirable, therefore, to find effective statements with which to begin and end the essay.

There is no simple recipe to guarantee success at beginning an essay. But the principle is simple: the writer should make a real effort to get the reader's attention in the first sentence. If handled well, the following types of *beginnings* can be effective: a short, relevant anecdote or story; a challenging or paradoxical statement; a curious fact or statistic; a rhetorical question. In all cases, of course, the introduction should be closely related to the main substance of the essay. It is unfair to the reader to tempt him through the door with an interesting come-on that leads only to a dull interior.

Consider the following essays in the anthology for examples of effective beginnings: No. 5 ("The Sensual City" by Peter Desbarats); No. 18 ("Success Story" by the Editors of *Time*); No. 20 ("Louis XIV and New France" by Alan Gowans); and No. 50 ("Overpopulation" by Aldous Huxley).

There are a number of over-used and somewhat obvious beginnings that are best avoided. Among these are a dictionary definition ("Webster defines a skunk as . . ."), or a statement that is already too well known ("As Mark Twain said, everyone talks about the weather but nobody does anything about it"). Also weak is opening with a comparison that is not really connected with what follows ("Natural history books tell us of the great rivalry that exists between the cobra and the mongoose. In the modern world there is a comparable rivalry, that between the turned-on and the turned-off generations."). The connection between cobras, mongooses, and the generations is at best vague.

One or another of the following devices may be used for an effective *ending*: a wise saying or aphorism, or one that has been twisted slightly ("A woman's place is in the wrong"); a repetition of something introduced at the beginning of the essay; a rhetorical question; a brief statement of a related idea that might be discussed in a further essay.

Consider the following selections in the anthology as examples of essays that end in a particularly effective way: No. 1 ("Canadian Regions" by Kildare Dobbs); No. 9 ("British Columbia" by Roderick Haig-Brown); No. 17 ("Percy Williams at the Olympics" by Ray Gardner); No. 48 ("The Wooden Bucket Principle" by Noel Perrin).

In ending an essay avoid making a sudden shift in the point of view or a self-contradiction that, even though it gets the writer out of the essay, makes everything said up to that point meaningless ("We have been discussing at some length in this essay what a dull country Canada is, but perhaps on closer examination it's not really such a dull country after all"). If it isn't dull, why discuss at some length that it is?

(ii) An essay should possess *variety* in all aspects of the writing: in the type of development employed, in the length and structure of the paragraphs, in the length and structure of the sentences, in the diction.

(iii) The principle of *proportion* should be observed. Important parts should be treated at greater length than unimportant parts.

(iv) *Transition* between paragraphs should be provided. Sometimes a short transitional paragraph (two or three sentences) can be used as a means of moving from one major section of the essay to another. Whatever transition is used, it should be clear but unobtrusive.

(d) A standard for sentence structure

The sentences in a carefully revised essay will be *correct, clear,* and *varied.*

Correctness will be the result of seeing that no incomplete sentences, or run-on sentences, or faulty parallel structures have been allowed to remain in the writing. (*Note*: the rhetorical terms used in the above sentence, and other terms to be used in what follows, have been defined and illustrated in Section III of this introduction.)

Clarity will be the result of seeing that the internal parts of all the sentences are clearly related: that pronouns have clear antecedents, that modifiers stand close to what they modify, that subordinating and co-ordinating words provide exact relationships between the clauses within each sentence.

Variety will be the result of seeing that different lengths and different patterns of sentences have been used within each paragraph. Anyone writing English has available to him the means of writing prose of considerable flexibility, for in addition to writing sentences of different lengths, he can write sentences of different clausal structures (simple, compound, complex), and sentences of different structural patterns (parallel, balanced, climactic, loose, periodic). Sentence variety is also a matter of paying some attention to the way adjacent sentences begin and end. As a general rule, it is best not to end one sentence and begin the next with the same word or phrase; nor is it desirable to begin or end a number of adjacent sentences with the same word, phrase, or structural pattern.

Revision exercise

Read carefully the following three paragraphs from the point of view of their *sentence structure*. Which of the paragraphs has sentences that are correct, clear, and varied? In what specific ways should the sentences of the other two paragraphs have been revised?

PARAGRAPH 25

Every country in the world has its own language, although some countries have more than one. Canada, for example, has two, although not

37

every Canadian speaks both of them. Because of these two languages, many English schools also teach French. Because the students taking this language, however, don't have much chance to speak it, they never become experts. Although it is unfortunate that this is so, it may not be a complete loss because some students do learn to read the language quite well, although they may never learn to speak it. Because I am not very good in French, I have not learned to read it or speak it, although I wish I could do both.

PARAGRAPH 26

The wind had been blowing across the deep snow for several days. This was something that nobody in the community seemed to like very much, the continual blowing got on their nerves, especially at night, it was also difficult to get into town to get the mail. Out behind the barn the fields had been blown bare of snow, which made them look barren and strange on the otherwise snowy landscape. Next to our fence, the snow had drifted in a high ridge, and looked like a railroad embankment, except that there were no tracks of any kind. Although desolate, the snow gave the landscape a sparkling, magical look in the daytime, and when it was night, the moonlight made the surface of the snow look cratered, like the surface of the moon itself. But after a few days, everyone began to wish it would go away.

PARAGRAPH 27

It is, nonetheless, in the geographic order that Canada ranks as a country of truly exceptional importance and her very vastness sets a characteristic seal upon all her physical features. She is the second largest country in the world, and covers the enormous area of 3,892,390 square miles – virtually the same as that of the whole European continent. Her greatest width is 3,700 miles and the railway journey from Halifax on the Atlantic coast to Vancouver on the Pacific coast takes five days and five nights. Yet over a third of this land area cannot be cultivated. The larger part of these great regions extending north from sixty degrees latitude are quite useless to the farmer, except for certain rare pockets of fertile soil. Mining prospects in this part of Canada are scarcely more promising: production is low and maintains only a small percentage of the white, Indian and Eskimo population; on the other hand, surveys now under way are turning up evidence of new mineral resources. Fortunately, the rest of the country, spread over some 2,000,000 square miles, provides a most propitious environment for human habitation and the progress of modern man.

(e) A standard for diction

In revising the diction of any composition, the writer should be guided by the principles of usage that were discussed on page 27. You will recall that according to these principles, words should be employed only in ways that represent the standard usage of established authors. It must be stressed, however, that this restriction does not mean that originality in the choice of vocabulary is not possible. Originality is not only possible, it is desirable. Any piece of writing will be improved if the author has taken the trouble to use words in a fresh, vivid, and at the same time exact way. However, it must also be understood that the word choice should not be so "original" that the reader cannot understand what is being said; nor should originality be so strained after that the style becomes grotesque.

In addition to this positive aim of using words with lively precision, the author revising his work must see that he has not committed such jarring errors as mixing the levels of diction, or employing incorrect idioms and trite expressions (see page 29).

Two further suggestions concerning diction need to be stressed. First, never make an adjective do what a noun or verb could do better. Although it cannot be said that adjectives should be avoided entirely, they should be used with restraint. It is, for example, more direct to write "He strode into the room" than to express the idea of "strode" by means of a pair of adjectives and a colourless noun: "He entered the room with a firm, steady walk". Second, always strive to express ideas as concisely as possible. One of the most important (and the most difficult) functions of revision is to see that all unnecessary words and needless repetitions have been avoided.

Revision exercise

Read the three paragraphs that follow. Only one of them has been adequately revised in terms of its diction. Which paragraph do you consider satisfactory, and what revisions would you suggest for the other two?

PARAGRAPH 28

Many years ago Charles G. D. Roberts wrote a wonderful book about an unarmed woodsman meeting a bear in the dark. The woodsman had left his gun in his canoe on the shore of a lake and was walking up a narrow path to his camp in the forest. The atmosphere was so heavy he knew a storm was about to break and it was so dark he was feeling his way step by step. Suddenly lightning flashed and in the blaze of light the woodsman saw a huge bear directly in front of him. He stopped dead still his hair prickling. Another flash and the beast was on his haunches with paws raised. Then it was dark again. The hunter listened to the bear breathing. He let out a shout. He began to curse and threaten the bear at the top of his voice. Another flash, and the bear was still before him. In the following darkness the hunter had an idea. He threw back his head and gave a loud peal of laughter. There was a wild crackling of twigs as the bear fled, and when the next flash came the man was alone.

PARAGRAPH 29

Almost every day the newspapers carry some story about someone whose number came up while he was out driving the nation's highways. It is no exaggeration to point out that the prevention of death on our highways is one of the number one problems on this continent. A number of groups are interested in solving this problem. One group thinks that the solution may lie in hiring more traffic cops and getting them out there on the highways with orders to pinch anyone and everyone who breaks the law. But the latest models of cars are so speedy that almost everyone is potentially a traffic violator. Maybe we should just put wings on the things and get cars off the highways completely.

PARAGRAPH 30

As my topic I select to write about my sister's driving experience. I felt sort of sorry and still do for the car whenever my sister lays her hands on the wheel. She was always the kind of gal who thought of herself as being erudite, but she found different after her first interview with the driving examiner. She stepped into the driving office arrogant as can be, thinking she would get her license unerringly. She came home, though, with eyes red from rubbing. So we knew what had happened. For the next few weeks she was willing to accept everyone's contribution to her driving. Finally, she decided in the end that the only way to make herself capable of passing another test would be by taking a driving course from a driving school. This she finally did and though it cost her a fair amount of money, she finally got her driving license unerringly.

(f) A standard for figurative statements

Not everyone has the type of mind that needs to express itself in figurative statements, although most writers at one time or another will use metaphor in some form. It will be worth while, then, to end this discussion of standards for prose composition with a brief look at metaphorical statements.

The purpose of a metaphor is to convey an idea emphatically, as Kildare Dobbs does when he describes the busy life of downtown Montreal as "the whole exciting circus of planned obsolescence and competitive selling". In this context, the word "circus" makes a simple, clear, and emphatic image that conveys an idea forcefully. But if a metaphor is allowed to become so involved that it brings the attentive reader to a wondering halt, then it should be revised. Consider the following sentence: "His was a mind in which the glue of human wisdom had never really enabled him to cement himself to some profound belief without the threat that everything would become unstuck in a week and fall apart." This is, indeed, a metaphorical statement, but not a very clear one. Instead of speeding up communication between the writer and the reader, it slows it down, for if the reader pays attention to anything in the statement, it is to the absurd complexity of the image, and not to the idea that it is supposed to convey.

In addition to being clear, a metaphorical statement should have some basis in reality. In other words, objects that are brought together metaphorically should do in the metaphor only what they are capable of doing in reality. Consider the following metaphorical statement: "Good manners are a fence that we can grow around ourselves in order to keep strangers from poking their noses into our business." This contradicts reality in at least two ways: fences are built, not grown; and fences are unlikely things to use for keeping out noses. The metaphor would have corresponded to reality if it had been revised to read: "Good manners are a fence that we can put up around ourselves to keep strangers at a distance."

The use of that special type of metaphor termed analogy also offers some perils to the writer. Since the proper function of an analogy is to *illustrate* some idea that already has general acceptance, an analogy is used wrongly when it is offered as *proof* of a statement that is open to question. The distinction between analogy used as *illustration* and analogy used as *proof* is discernible in the following pair of examples. In which has the analogy been used as a weak proof of a debatable idea? In which has the analogy been used as an illustration of an idea that would find general acceptance?

ANALOGY A

The difference between Canada and the United States, it has been pointed out, is like that between the upper and lower stories in a house. The Americans occupy the warm and spacious lower floors, while the Canadians find themselves in the attic where there isn't that much living space, and they can't help but notice that there is often snow on the roof.

ANALOGY B

Canada and the United States are such close neighbours and such good neighbours that there is bound to be some problems between them, just as there will be between neighbours in the suburbs. But these problems, like the problems between friendly neighbours, are easily solved, usually by a bit of across the fence or over the border chit-chat.

One final point about metaphor: it should be understood that this aspect of writing is one where personal taste plays an important part. Absolute judgments about the quality of a figurative statement cannot always be made. A metaphor that seems effective to one reader can seem absurd to another. Consider, for example, the metaphorical statement found in the penultimate paragraph of the essay entitled "The First Fourteen" (No. 26 in the anthology).

Revision exercise

Even though metaphor is an area where personal preference does influence judgment, it should be possible to decide quite objectively which of the following paragraphs has made effective use of metaphor, and which has used metaphor only to create confusion. In which should the figurative statements have been revised?

PARAGRAPH 31

Is education a fountain at which youth can drink deeply of knowledge, or is it a filling-station at which children and adults are force-fed facts, in much the same way that the Danish people are said to force-feed geese in order to increase the meat content? I ask this question knowing that its answer will depend on a personal outlook. There are many people who attend college only because they want to stay in the mainstream with their friends. They do no swimming while in this mainstream, but sit idly at their desks waiting for the bell to call them back to dry land again. The professor is to them a mere receptacle of facts whose job it is to pour them out as painlessly as possible. This is the filling-station concept of education. These drive to school in the morning to have the gas tanks of their brains filled up with high-octane knowledge. They are the excess baggage of the system. Opposed to them are the ones who stand quietly in line waiting to drink at the fountain of knowledge. These are the ones who get educated in the true sense of the word.

PARAGRAPH 32

Often in Saskatchewan a man awakens on a winter night hearing a great wind, and his heart sinks at the prospect of more shut-in days, more cold, difficulty, discomfort and danger. But one time in ten, something keeps him from burrowing back under his blankets, something keeps him suspiciously on his elbow, straining his ears for the sounds of hope. Repudiating his hope even while he indulges it, he may leave the warmth of bed and go to the door, bracing himself for the needles of thirty below. And one time in ten, when he opens door and storm door against the grab and bluster of the wind, the air rushes in his face as warm as milk, all but smelling of orange blossoms, and he dances a caper on his cold floor and goes back to bed knowing that in the two or three days that the chinook blows it will gulp all the snow except the heaviest drifts and leave the prairie dry enough to sit down on. Dozing off, he hears the crescendo of drip, the slump of heavied snow on the roof, the crash of loosened icicles under the eaves.

5. Exercises in Critical Reading

Below are a number of paragraphs taken from a wide range of sources.

Some of the paragraphs meet the standard for composition discussed on the preceding pages, but others do not. Consider each of the paragraphs in terms of its *idea, development, structure, sentence structure, diction,* and use of *figurative statements*. Which of the paragraphs would you consider examples of good writing? Which do you find unsatisfactory? Notice that the paragraphs in Exercise B probably demand a more sophisticated type of critical judgment than the paragraphs in Exercise A.

Exercise A

PARAGRAPH 33

Many of the early pioneers in this fair land of ours can bear witness to the fact that when Canada was first opened up as a place, the prospect before them was a heart-rendering one indeed. There were no roads. In many places the country was rough, though beautifully timbered. Development materials such as lumber and brick were unheard of. And above all, at this time, tractors and motor cars and other mechanical devices had not come to the help of man. It was because of this that the horse became such a valuable essential. Without the horse this country would not have become the great country that it now has become today. In spite of summer heat and winter cold, in spite of the dangers of drought, fire and flood, in spite of the indescribable discomforts of pioneer life in this new land, because of the horse, man was able to win through and make a wilderness shine.

PARAGRAPH 34

Take the people of any great city if you want to find diversity of occupation. Within the streets of any town you may no longer find the candlestick-maker, but the butcher, the baker and the cop on the beat are still there, along with the salesgirl, the store owner and the bus driver. Not all of these people may like their jobs, but even those who don't enjoy their work show up every day ready to put in another eight hours on the job. And some of them are good at their jobs. The average bus driver can wend his way through traffic day after day with consummate ease. Cities are, indeed, filled with such a variety of things that we should all be, as Robert Louis Stevenson once noted, happier than kings.

PARAGRAPH 35

Years ago, when I was hunting along a chain of lakes and swamps, I heard a party of deer hunters fire several shots a mile or so away from me. I went over to the sound and found a little lake with three dead swans floating on its surface. There was no sign of the hunters and it was still day, so I swam out and brought in the swans. They had been killed by rifles, for "sport" presumably, though they were protected birds even at that time. Less than a month ago a friend of mine was fishing in a lake when a lone swan lit not far from him. Almost at once two men pushed off from the shore in a power boat, came near the swan and shot at it with a rifle. It was wounded, so they chased it with the power boat, caught it, dragged it in and killed it. The swan was protected by law from hunting of any kind; all migratory birds are protected from hunters with rifles or in power boats. But the swan is dead. Multiply this by all the thousands of brutal, thoughtless, ignorant individuals who carry firearms in the name of "sport" and it is easy to see why a residue of five hundred or a thousand trumpeter swans may be too few to perpetuate themselves in spite of all the protection they can be given.

PARAGRAPH 36

Why in the wide world there must be these battles and warring exploitations is something I have never understood. War, the sound of the bugle blaring, the guns raging, the men dying is an abomination that no devout person could possibly have wishes for. Napoleon is a case in point. His behaviour is an indication of the kind of tyranny I wish to discuss. And what finally happened to him at Moscow and at Waterloo is an example in my mind of governing justice in the plan of things. Other examples abound. Korea, World War I, the Riel Rebellion, and now the present war being fought by the states. If this is what causes some to become an objector to war, then I don't mind who sees me stand up to be counted on this issue when I say I don't agree. "Let there be light" the prophet says. And I say let there be no more of the darkness of war. For a war is the human race reaching most blindly into the dark.

PARAGRAPH 37

As you advance in college, you will probably notice that there is a difference between "learning" something and really "understanding" it. The difference is a subtle one, but it is nonetheless real. Learning is what others might be able to make us do; understanding is what no one can stop us from doing, even if they wanted to. Take, as one example, the difference between learning and understanding certain details of mathematics. Most students can learn what Pythagoras had to say about the sum of the squares of a certain kind of triangle, but how many really understand why it works out as Pythagoras said it does and what its implications are? Or, for a second example, consider the difference between learning about and understanding the rhetorical device called metaphor, a subject that is often discussed in English classes. Most students can learn what a metaphor is ("A comparison between two unlike things"), but how many really understand why a writer will use this particular form of expression in order to express his most deeply felt ideas? Perhaps there is a kind of lesson to be

44

drawn from this difference between learning and understanding. Perhaps we can use what we really understand to provide us with a clue to our real interests.

The development of several separate talents is necessary if you are to become a good golfer. One must learn how to drive the ball from the tee, how to make controlled shots from the fairways, and putting on the greens is also necessary. Since the objective of the game is to sink a small white ball into a hole on the green with as few strokes as possible, it is essential that a golfer become proficient in all kinds of shots. Before reaching this perfection, many long hours must be spent in practice sessions on all parts of the course. All the great golfers have had to do this, Arnold Palmer and Jack Nicklaus are not exceptions and they are among the greatest golfers of our time. I am convinced that the world's best game is golf, because of the high degree of accuracy needed for all its parts.

Exercise B

On the frosty, sunshiny morning of Thursday, December 6, 1917, a telegraph operator named Vincent Coleman, idly sitting in his Richmond Terminal Office overlooking the piers, happened to glance out at Halifax Harbour. He was startled to see two tramp steamers, the *Mont Blanc* and the *Imo*, collide in midstream. The shock of their collision shook the whole world.

But Coleman was one of the few who seems to have realized the horrible portent as he saw tongues of ice-blue flame snaking from the shattered hull of the *Mont Blanc*. He reached for his telegraph key and tapped out his last message on earth.

"Ammunition ship is on fire and is making for Pier Eight," he signalled. "Good-bye."

Soon there was a sound like the crashing of a million chandeliers, and Coleman's head was blasted from his body. All they ever found of him were his brass watch and his telegraph key.

"We must be free or die." "Of old sat freedom on the heights." "To no man will we deny justice." These great phrases have always rung in my ears. They seem to embody the very essence of that which makes life worthwhile. To annoy them into thinking things out, I often used to tell my students that few of them, especially the women, wished to be free; most of them longed for the security and irresponsibility of the slave. This did annoy them and then they would half-prove my point by copying down religiously every word that fell from the mouth of –

one of their lecturers! But some I expect got a glimpse of that which had been bed-rock for people of English speech – freedom. So I put freedom, which must be squared somehow with a just society, high up on my list of values – free men, a free society, a free environment – yet in all things circumscribed and ordered by law, that is, by collective wisdom. I want nothing of the freedom that is mere anarchy – you can have that in any one of a dozen badly governed countries.

PARAGRAPH 41

There are many people who feel that governmental control of censorship is to an extreme on what can and cannot be viewed or published. On the other hand, there are individuals and groups who do not take the position that there is no need for measures of control. Articles are often labeled "risque" and "sensational" and are restricted from newsstands on the pretense that they contribute to pervert society and promote delinquency. For the most part, opponents of censorship feel a loss of personal freedom rather than a moral sense of corruption for the nation. Through constant changes in political makeup and social structures, arguments concerning censorship and freedom have shown remarkable progress to the present age. The general argument for censorship runs, whatever contradicts or endangers one's mind should be controlled. The main purpose in this theory would be that censorship's intention is to protect the media from information which might lead to immorality with the direct result of lessened individual respect for governmental institutions and control. I am therefore inclined to believe that censorship is a proven practice, and suppressing immorality has a definite role in our society.

PARAGRAPH 42

During the past few weeks I have had chats with several young men and women who think they would like to get into the trade of which I am a humble practitioner. What amazes me about them all is their frankness. "I'd like to get some practice in a little joint like yours before trying for a job in the Big City," they all say, or words to that effect. As they all come to me without previous experience, this gives me something of the feeling of a professor in a kindergarten, whose job it is to set the feet of beginners upon the upward path, soon to be left behind and patronized by my former pupils. And yet, they do not want to work for beginner's pay, nor do they seem to sense the painful fact that for six months or so they will be more of a hindrance than a help. I hope that I may be forgiven in heaven for some of the bittersweet answers which I return to their demands. It seems odd to me that in our present educational system, in which virtually everything else is taught or half-taught, nobody teaches these young hopefuls how to behave when looking for a job. I do not ask for grovelling humility, but some hint of modesty, and some offer of honest service would be welcome. Does any man like to be told that he is a given point which beginners in his trade soon hope to pass?

PARAGRAPH 43

When a ship in harbour is ready to sail, outward bound, she hoists the "Blue Peter". Every spring, all across Canada, there are imaginary "Blue Peter" flags fluttering over universities and schools to signal the launching of students upon the sea of life.

These young people have been equipped with formal education, which is comparable to a set of charts. In itself, knowledge is like a chart – of no value except as it is used to steer your ship with understanding and judgment.

Steering is necessary because you can't sail everywhere at once. Life is a voyage during which one touches at many ports. A happy outcome is due largely to the skill with which you pilot your craft from one harbour to another.

Men have progressed all through human existence because of a fundamental drive, a constant pressing against boundaries, and an enterprising spirit that drove them into adventurous searching for what lay over the horizon.

Every young person can look forward to the day when, instead of the cautious coasting which never ventures to lose sight of land, he will turn his helm and hazard a bolder navigation. But he must have provided himself with the required charts and with wisdom in their use.

PARAGRAPH 44

Most communities in North America still have to come to grips with the problem of air pollution. There may still be time for them to do so, but the experts say that time is rapidly running out. One reason is that North America may eventually lose its source of clean air, for the air that now streams across the Pacific from Asia is clean when it arrives on the west coast. Pushed by the prevailing winds, this air crosses the coastal cities where it picks up its first pollution. It loses some of this over the Rockies, but becomes dirty again as it passes over the highly populated, highly industrialized areas of the eastern seaboard. But at least one meteorologist has wondered what the situation would be like if a large percentage of the 800 million Chinese drove a gasoline-powered automobile – as most adult North Americans do. And the fear is that many of them soon will. Then the Chinese autos will pollute Asian skies, dirtying the air currents before they even reach this continent. If this happens, meteorologists claim, air pollution may well increase beyond the capacity of the atmosphere to cleanse itself. Then smog will encircle the earth and civilization will pass away, not from a sudden cataclysm, but from gradual suffocation of its own effluents.

III. Some Technical Matters

1. The Structure of Sentences

(Some of the terms used below inevitably overlap. For example, a simple sentence may also be periodic; a complex sentence may be loose; a climactic sentence may be simple, compound, or complex. This overlapping need not be confusing, since each of the terms does illuminate a significant aspect of sentence structure, and the illustrations reveal something of the *variety* possible in writing English sentences.)

A simple sentence consists of one main clause.
EXAMPLE: About two-thirds of all the people in Canada live in either Ontario or Quebec.

A compound sentence has two main clauses joined co-ordinately.
EXAMPLE: Each of Canada's first fourteen prime ministers made his special imprint on national history *and* each changed in some way the very nature of the prime-ministry.

A complex sentence has at least one main clause and at least one subordinate clause.
EXAMPLE: If language tends to separate Quebec from the other provinces, does it follow that language tends to bind together the nine English-speaking provinces?

A periodic sentence is one in which the thought is not complete until the end of the sentence.
EXAMPLE: In essence the troubles associated with the name of Louis Riel were the manifestation, not of traditional rivalries of French-Catholic Quebec and English-Protestant Ontario, but of traditional problems of cultural conflict, of the clash between primitive and civilized peoples.

A loose sentence is one in which a complete idea has been stated long before the end of the sentence.
EXAMPLE: *In the afternoon the ships opened fire,* while the troops entered the boats and rowed up and down as if looking for a landing place. (It should not be assumed that periodic sentences are necessarily better than loose sentences, even though the term "loose" might seem to imply an unfavourable judgment. The term is descriptive in this context, not critical. Most good prose is a blend of both loose and periodic sentences, generally with a higher percentage of loose than periodic.)

48

A parallel sentence is one in which ideas of equal value have been expressed in the same grammatical form and have been joined co-ordinately. EXAMPLE: *When you have had a few more lessons* and *when you have had several more hours of practice,* you will be quite a good tennis player.

A climactic sentence is one in which three or more parallel elements have been arranged so as to create a rising movement within the sentence. EXAMPLE: Dozing off, he heard *the crescendo of drip, the slump of heavied snow on the roof, the crash of loosened icicles under the eaves.*

A balanced sentence is one in which the parallel elements joined co-ordinately are approximately equal in length and are similar in phrasing. EXAMPLE: Today it is fashionable to say unkind things about suburbia; fifty years ago it was fashionable to say unkind things about cities.

2. Common Sentence Errors

An incomplete sentence is a group of words that has been punctuated as if it were a sentence, even though it does not contain a main clause. An expert writer may occasionally use such a sentence fragment to gain emphasis, but only in a context where the meaning is clear. Sentence fragments that occur through carelessness should be made into complete sentences during revision.
CARELESS: His grandfather who for many years had been a fisherman in Nova Scotia.
REVISED: His grandfather, who for many years had been a fisherman in Nova Scotia, later moved his family to Ontario.

A run-on sentence occurs when two main clauses are joined together with a comma. Main clauses, unless they are very short, require a stronger type of connection than a comma. A period, a semicolon, or a conjunction should replace the inadequate comma.
CARELESS: He then began to tell a long story about his interesting life in the Northwest Territories, at least he thought it was interesting, it certainly did not interest his audience.
REVISED: He then began to tell a long story about his interesting life in the Northwest Territories. At least he thought it was interesting, but it certainly did not interest his audience.

Faulty parallelism occurs when two unequal grammatical elements have been joined co-ordinately.
CARELESS: If asked why he disliked living on the farm, he would have said *it was the loneliness* and *that you could never be sure that your labours would be rewarded.* (A main clause has been made co-ordinate with a noun clause.)

49

REVISED: If asked why he disliked living on the farm, he would have said it was *the loneliness* and *the uncertainty* of being rewarded for your labours.

Faulty subordination occurs when, for one reason or another, the relationship between two clauses is inexact, loose, or misleading. Since subordination is an important aspect of mature writing, the relationship between clauses should be examined carefully during revision.

CARELESS: The use of the television replay gives a person a second look at what's going on *which makes the game more exciting.*

REVISED: The use of the television replay, which gives the viewer a second look at important moments in the game, can make watching sports doubly exciting.

A misplaced modifier occurs when a modifying word, phrase, or clause is not placed as close as possible to what it modifies.

CARELESS: I could tell that the car had just come from Ontario *by its licence plates.*

REVISED: I could tell by its licence plates that the car was from Ontario.

A dangling modifier occurs when the object a phrase or clause is supposed to modify has been omitted from the sentence.

CARELESS: *As a result of playing football for several years,* my nose was broken several times. (The player and not just his nose did the playing.)

REVISED: As a result of playing football for several years, I had broken my nose several times.

Faulty pronoun reference occurs when the antecedent of a pronoun is ambiguous.

CARELESS: When the bridge across the river was completed, it was not long before it was filled with cars. (Does "it" refer to the bridge or the river?)

REVISED: Soon after the bridge across the river was completed, traffic was moving over it in a steady stream.

A split construction results when closely related sentence elements are needlessly interrupted by a long qualifying statement.

CARELESS: It is one of the fascinations of history that certain individuals of little historical significance in the eyes of the world manage to *now and then, whether through doggedness or by sheer luck or the force of events,* become legends.

REVISED: It is one of the fascinations of history that certain individuals of little historical significance manage now and then to become legends, and whether they do this by sheer luck, or the force of events, or just plain doggedness does not seem to matter.

3. Basic Sentence Punctuation

There are probably several hundred "rules" of punctuation, but no writer needs to carry them all around in his head. However, there are some basic principles of punctuation that should be so well understood that they will be applied automatically. This is especially true of punctuation *within* sentences. The basic sentence punctuation that a writer should learn to use automatically has been outlined below. The statements made about punctuation and the examples given here are meant to define and illustrate *principles* that should be understood, and not *rules* that should be memorized. And the writer should realize that the purpose of using punctuation is not just to satisfy a rule, but to help a sentence become immediately clear to a reader.

Use a comma after a long phrase or clause at the beginning of a sentence.
EXAMPLE: *When the first farmers settled in the wilderness of Ontario,* they had to be virtually self-sufficient.

Use a comma following a participial phrase at the beginning of a sentence.
EXAMPLE: *Flying to Calgary from Vancouver,* the pilot lost his way over the mountains.

But note that when a phrase at the beginning of a sentence functions as a noun rather than as an adjective, no comma is required.
EXAMPLE: *Flying to Calgary every year for the Stampede* was something he always looked forward to.

Use a comma to prevent any ambiguity in meaning.
EXAMPLE: Halfway across, the country began to take on a more rugged appearance. (If the comma after "across" had been omitted, the reader would have thought that the sentence began with the phrase "Halfway across the country".)

Use a comma to separate long co-ordinate clauses, especially when they are joined by "but" or "for".
EXAMPLE: He kept telling us what a wonderful idea it was, but no one really took much interest in what he said.

Use a comma to separate a subordinate clause from the main clause it follows, especially when the subordinate clause is not closely related in meaning.
EXAMPLES: So far he has spent most of his adult life away from his home province, *although he has returned for visits occasionally.* (The comma is

useful here because the thought in the subordinate clause is additional rather than essential to the meaning.)

A number of people travelled to Montreal during centennial year *because they wanted to visit Expo 67.* (No comma is necessary here because the subordinate clause is essential to the meaning of the sentence.)

Use a semicolon to separate two main clauses that are not joined by a conjunction such as "and", "but", or "or".
EXAMPLE: By definition the absolute ruler reserves all authority to himself; he delegates only responsibility and blame.

Use a colon to separate two main clauses not joined by a conjunction if the second clause offers an explanation of the first.
EXAMPLE: The weather this year has been unusual: *the snow came a month early and stayed a month longer than usual.*

Use a semicolon to separate two main clauses that are joined by a conjunctive adverb (such as "however", "therefore", "consequently"). The comma following the conjunctive adverb is optional.
EXAMPLE: Last summer he set out to visit all ten provinces in the dominion; *however,* his car broke down and he only got to five of them.

Note that when such words as "however", "therefore" and "consequently" are used in the middle of a clause, they are marked off by a pair of commas, not a semicolon and a comma.
EXAMPLE: There should, *however,* be no doubt about the major issues that now face this country.

Use a comma to mark off a word, phrase, or clause that interrupts the main flow of the sentence, especially when the interrupting element is fairly short or is closely connected with the main idea of the sentence. However, there is no fixed rule here. More remotely connected interruptions can be separated either by dashes or parentheses. The following examples will illustrate the difference.
EXAMPLES: It is, *as a matter of fact,* not worth bothering about.
Cars, *which are now fairly expensive to buy,* are still purchased by people of nearly all social classes.
Cars *which have defective brakes* should be taken from the highway. (When the subordinate clause is indispensable to the meaning of the sentence, *no commas* are used.)
Montcalm sent to Ramezay, *the commander of Quebec,* for twenty-five cannon which were not being used in the town.
He told me – *but that was something that happened yesterday* – that his opinion on this subject would never change.

The prairie provinces (*especially Manitoba where the summer has been exceptionally dry*) benefited greatly from last week's rainfall.

4. Common Diction Errors

Wrong level of usage occurs when the writer makes a needless shift into inappropriately formal or informal diction.

CARELESS: The music that the *assembled musicians* were playing on this *particularly auspicious occasion* wasn't exactly the *type I go for*.

REVISED: The music that the orchestra played during the concert was not the kind I enjoy.

Incorrect idiom occurs when the writer uses combinations of words that do not have an established place in standard English.

CARELESS: Although I was *unmindful* of what he had told me, I *reflected back* on what I had read about the subject and decided to *proceed in my own discretion.*

REVISED: Although I had forgotten what he had told me, I thought about what I had read on the subject and decided to use my own discretion.

Triteness is the result of using expressions that were once thought bright and lively but which have become flat and stale through over-use.

CARELESS: He made up his mind that he would get up *at the crack of dawn* and *seize every opportunity* to deal with his problems in *no uncertain terms.*

REVISED: He made up his mind to get up early and deal decisively with his problems.

Careless repetition results from failing to find synonyms for unimportant words. Although the repetition of words can be an effective rhetorical device (see page 55), verbal repetition that draws attention to the word rather than to the idea should be avoided.

CARELESS: The only job he could get that summer was a part-time job in a gas-station, but he did not find this as pleasant a job as the job he had had the summer before.

REVISED: The only job he could get that summer was part-time work in a gas-station, but he didn't enjoy working there very much.

In attempting to avoid repeating a word, the writer should not fall into the opposite error of "*elegant variation*", a fault that is illustrated by the following revision of the sentence cited above.

CARELESS: The only *job* he could get that summer was part-time *employment* in a gas-station, but he did not find this as pleasant an *occupation* as the *work* he had had the summer before.

Redundancy is the unintentional repetition of an idea that has already been adequately expressed.

CARELESS: One night when he was in a violently drunken mood, he *killed* her by *cutting off her head*.

REVISED: One night when he was in a violently drunken mood, he cut off her head.

Circumlocution is the expression of an idea "the long way around", either accidentally or through the mistaken notion that pomposity makes for impressive writing.

CARELESS: The potential for prospective job opportunities in tomorrow's world may not be as certain of realization as is now the case.

REVISED: In the future, job opportunities may be fewer than at present.

Weak use of the passive voice results from using a passive construction where the active one could have been used. (In the active voice, the subject of the clause is the *doer* of the action; in the passive, the subject is the receiver. *Active*: He read the book. *Passive*: The book was read by him.) As the preceding examples show, the active voice offers a more concise style of expression than the passive, and is, therefore, preferable. The passive does, however, have some legitimate uses, particularly in situations where the doer of the action is not known ("Our car was stolen last night"), or when scientific objectivity is described, as, for instance, in laboratory reports or some types of research essays. Otherwise the passive is best avoided.

CARELESS: Every morning on waking *it was discovered* that our firewood was soaking wet despite the precautions that *had been taken* the night before to see that *it would be kept dry*.

REVISED: When we woke in the morning, we found that the rain had once again soaked our firewood despite our efforts on the previous night to find a way of keeping it dry.

5. Rhetorical Devices

Rhetoric is usually defined as "the art or science of effective discourse". Illustrated below are some of the most frequent methods prose writers employ to make their writing effective.

Simile and *metaphor* are two of the most widely used rhetorical devices. In both cases a comparison is made between two unlike objects that, in a particular context, have at least one characteristic in common. In a simile, the comparison is stated explicitly and is usually introduced by "like" or "as". In a metaphor the comparison is implied.

EXAMPLES: The mid-winter hoar frost hung on the fences and telephone lines *like strung popcorn*. (Simile)

Montreal is a choir of two million voices singing a continual hymn of gratitude. (Metaphor)

Verbal repetition involves the repetition of a word or phrase in order to stress an important idea.

EXAMPLE: In fact, the place of Sir John Macdonald *in this country* was so large and absorbing that it is almost impossible to conceive that the political life *of this country*, the fate *of this country*, can continue without him. His loss *overwhelms* us. For my part, I say with all truth, his loss *overwhelms* me. It also *overwhelms* this parliament.

Verbal contrast is the juxtaposing of two words of opposite (or nearly opposite) meaning so that each intensifies the meaning of the other. This device is used with greatest effect in sentences containing parallel or balanced structure.

EXAMPLE: This kind of government not only makes successful long-term planning *impossible*; it makes disastrous mistakes *inevitable*.

A pun is a verbal device that focuses on two or more meanings of a word in a single context. Although puns are usually employed for comic reasons, they can be used to convey a serious idea.

EXAMPLE: The student complained that too much of the literature he had been reading was about death. Most of it seemed to be straight from *the hearse's mouth*.

6. Mechanics

In the general category of "Mechanics" are matters related to the *form* in which numbers, dates, sums of money, and certain words are written. The guiding principle in dealing with these matters is to use the form that will be most immediately clear to the reader. Some suggestions related to mechanics are made below, but the student should realize that the form used is influenced to a considerable degree by the circumstances in which the writing is being done, and that "styles" change from circumstance to circumstance.

Capitals: In standard prose, capitals should not be over-used. The writer should have a good reason for every capital he employs. It is usual to capitalize the following:

(i) The names of specific institutions and organizations.

EXAMPLE: He attends the University of Toronto. (But: He attends university.)

(ii) The first word in a direct quotation.

EXAMPLE: Authorities in Saskatchewan told me: "We have less oil than Alberta, but more wheat."

(iii) The main words in the title of a book, song, film, magazine, and so on.

EXAMPLE: Ramsay Cook is the author of a book entitled *Canada and the French-Canadian Question*.

Abbreviations: Abbreviations should be kept at a minimum. As a general rule, the non-abbreviated form of any name is used the first time it is employed; following this the abbreviated form is used. It should also be noted that in standard prose it is customary to avoid making use of such abbreviations as *gov't, dept, prof, etc.* When abbreviations are used, they are generally capitalized.

Numbers: *(i)* Numbers of *less than three digits* should be spelled out; numbers that would require *three or more words* are usually represented by figures.

EXAMPLES: There are *ten* provinces in Canada.

The House of Commons has *265* members.

(ii) Round numbers should be spelled out, but figures should be used when the number is not an approximate one.

EXAMPLES: Canada now has a population of just over twenty million people.

The total area of Canada is 3,851,809 square miles.

(iii) The usual forms for writing sums of money are as follows: $3.98; 35 cents; $15,489; one million dollars.

(iv) Dates can be written in a variety of ways but the usual style in standard prose is *July 1, 1967*. In referring to a particular date, the usual form is March 15. (The form March 15th is more or less out of fashion now.)

(v) The customary way of writing the time of day is either *3 p.m.* or *three o'clock*. (*But not*: *3 o'clock* or *three p.m.*)

Italics: In standard prose, italics are used for the following purposes (in typed or handwritten material, italics are indicated by underlining):

(i) To indicate titles of books, magazines, films, and so on.

EXAMPLES: *Never Cry Wolf, The Tamarack Review, Bonnie and Clyde*. But note that quotation marks, not italics, are used for anything that is part of a larger work (e.g. a section of a book, an article or a story from a magazine).

EXAMPLE: The short story "Bicultural Angela" was originally published in a book entitled *Around the Mountain*.

(ii) To differentiate a particular word or phrase, especially if it is of foreign origin.

EXAMPLE: The words *cultus* and *skookum* were borrowed from the language of the West Coast Indians.

(iii) To show that a word is being referred to as a word.

EXAMPLE: Although *already* is considered standard English, *alright* is still felt to be colloquial usage.

Note: Quotation marks are sometimes used instead of italics for the purposes described in *(ii)* and *(iii)* above.

(iv) To show that a word is being emphasized. This device should be used sparingly.

EXAMPLE: I'm not blaming him, but I am blaming *them*.

7. Conventions of Scholarship

Over the years, certain conventions have developed regarding the use of names, titles, quotations, footnotes, and bibliographies in essay-writing. Since this is an aspect of composition that involves numerous small details and a wide range of possible styles, no attempt has been made here to cover the subject fully. But some fundamental concepts related to the conventions of scholarship are touched on below. The student who wishes to know more about this aspect of writing should provide himself with one of the many books or pamphlets in which scholarly conventions are described comprehensively. Two such works are Edward D. Seeber's *A Style Manual For Students* (published by Indiana University Press), and W. R. Parker's *The MLA Style Sheet* (published by the Modern Language Association of America).

Names and Titles: It is important to use names and titles accurately. When referring to an author by name, use the form of his name that the author himself generally employs or employed. For example, use "E. J. Pratt" rather than "Edwin Pratt", and "Earle Birney" rather than "A. E. Birney". When referring to an author a second time in an essay, the convention is to use only the last name.

Titles of books (or of essays, poems, or short stories) should be exactly right. If a book is called *Sunshine Sketches of a Little Town*, it should be called this, and not something nearly right, such as *Sketches of a Small Town*.

57

Quotations: A quotation from any source should be indicated by one of two means. If the quotation is relatively short (a line of verse or a sentence of prose), it is retained within the body of the text and marked off with quotation marks. If the quotation is longer, it is separated from the body of the paragraph and marked off by additional spacing above and below, and by wider margins on either side. When this is done, quotation marks are not used. The fact that some of the selections in the anthology section of this book may not follow this prescription illustrates the fact that not all authors or editors employ exactly the same stylistic conventions. See No. 8 ("Saskatchewan" by Edward McCourt) and No. 51 ("The Human Price" by Rachel Carson) for examples of professional writers using quoted material.

Whenever a quotation is used, it should be quoted accurately. Nearly right is not good enough. And quotations should be fitted into, rather than just dropped into, the normal flow of the writer's own prose. It is, for example, very weak style to use a quotation in the following way:

> Earle Birney makes use of a figure of speech called simile in his poem "Maritime Faces". "Smashing the slate with unappeasable fists."

It is preferable to introduce a quotation more clearly than in the above illustration. This can be done as follows:

> Earle Birney makes use of a figure of speech called metaphor in his poem "Maritime Faces" when he speaks of the "boxer waves" as "smashing the slate with unappeasable fists".

Whether or not such a quotation is to be followed by a footnote will depend on the nature of the quotation and on the kind of essay that is being written. In a short, informal essay dealing with only one literary work, footnotes would probably be omitted. In a longer, more formal essay concerned with several different selections, a footnote identifying the source of the quotation would probably be expected. (See the section on footnotes below.)

Footnotes: In essay-writing that is done in college, footnotes are used appropriately for two purposes. First, to add information that is relevant to the essay but does not fit into the general flow of the material being presented. (Footnotes of this kind should be used with some restraint.) Second, to indicate the source of quoted material. In doing this, it is customary, the first time a quotation is made from a particular work, to give the reader the following information: the author's full name, the full title of the book, the place of publication, the name of the publisher, the date of publication, and the page or pages on which the quoted material can be found. This is usually presented in the following manner:

Ramsay Cook, *Canada and the French-Canadian Question* (Toronto: Macmillan, 1966), pp. 143–50.

When the same book is referred to in subsequent footnotes, a simpler form is used. This is usually the author's surname, followed by the phrase *op. cit.* (for "work cited") and the page reference. For example: Cook, *op. cit.*, p. 168.

Just one further example out of the many that could be given for dealing with different kinds of publications will be included here. If the quotation has been taken from an article in a magazine, the form of the footnote is as follows:

M. J. Arlen, "After Progress, What?", *The New Yorker*, Oct. 24, 1959, pp. 38–9.

Bibliographies: As the term is used here, a bibliography means a list of books included at the end of an essay to show what works have been referred to during the preparation of the essay. It is customary to include not only the works referred to in the footnotes, but also all the books, articles, and pamphlets consulted though not actually quoted from. The items in the bibliography are listed alphabetically and contain the following information: author's name, title of the book, place of publication, and date of publication. Here are two examples of the form used when listing items in a bibliography; the first is for a book, the second for a magazine article.

Cook, Ramsay. *Canada and the French-Canadian Question*, Toronto, 1966.
Arlen, M. J. "After Progress, What?" *The New Yorker*, Oct. 24, 1959, pp. 38–9.

PART TWO

Canadian Themes and Styles

I. People in a Landscape

The immensity and grandeur of the Canadian landscape has been one of
the main sources of inspiration for the Canadian writer. It is not difficult,
therefore, to take a trans-Canada journey along the verbal lines laid down
by Canadian poets and essayists. Gathered together in this opening
section of the anthology are eleven perceptive comments on the Canadian
scene, both landscape and cityscape, and on some of the people who
call Canada home. It is not, of course, possible by means of only eleven
selections to visit every Canadian district and town, or to pay homage to all
the capes and bays in this the most watery of the world's landscapes. But
cumulatively these selections do suggest something of the variety that is to
be found within Canada, this country of nearly four million square miles
that is occupied by only twenty million people. And, like the country
they describe, the selections themselves offer considerable variety. Four are
in verse; seven are in prose. The first two – an essay by Kildare Dobbs and
a poem by A. M. Klein – present an overview of the entire country,
while each of the other nine touches down on a particular city or region.
The trans-Canada journey that can be taken via the authors represented
here runs from east to west, beginning with Farley Mowat in Newfoundland
and ending with Roderick Haig-Brown in British Columbia. A poem by
F. R. Scott and an essay by Diamond Jenness offer a side trip to the north
at the end of the trans-Canada journey. If any one characteristic dominates
the style of these varied selections, it is the use that so many of the authors
have made of metaphor in their desire to capture and perhaps tame this
immense and powerful land.

1. Canada's Regions

KILDARE DOBBS

Kildare Dobbs is a free-lance writer who currently lives in Toronto. He has travelled widely and written entertainingly of his travels; his Running to Paradise *won a Governor General's award in 1962. Mr. Dobbs' most recent work is* Reading the Time, *a collection of essays published in 1968. The selection that follows is part of an essay which accompanied a collection of photographs of Canada by Peter Varley. It was written in 1964.*

This discussion of Canada's main geographic regions illustrates the principle that a well-written essay should have a clear overall structure. The writer has stated his main idea early in the essay, and has then supported it with specific (and often ironic) comments on each of the six regions he identifies. The over-all structural pattern is further strengthened by the fact that the development follows a consistent spatial movement, in this case from east to west.

The truth is that the thought "Canada" is impossible to think all at once. Love of country is difficult when, like Aristotle's "creature of vast size", its unity and wholeness are lost to imagination. And so the patriotism of Canadians tends to be – in a perfectly respectable and human sense – provincial, and even parochial.

The people of each region have their own character.

Maritimers are a seafaring race whose roots are deep in history. Canada is sometimes thought of (quite wrongly) as a "new" country. The Maritime provinces belong essentially to the Old World. The things that surprise, enchant, and sometimes distress North American travellers in Europe are also to be found here: craftsmanship, tradition, cheerful poverty. A sense of history clings about the silvery weathered shingles of fishermen's huts; the vivid colours of boats and lobster floats – red, blue, ochre, green – and the black-and-white dazzle of painted wooden houses are affirmations of life and vigour against the hard grey weather and the dangerous ocean. Men have been here a long time; they have come to terms with the forests, the rocks, the tides. It was in 1605 that Samuel de Champlain planted Canada's first settlement at Port Royal – now Annapolis Royal, Nova Scotia. Not far away, at Pubnico, there are some eight hundred French-speaking Nova Scotians named D'Entremont. Most of them have the ascetic features of the family face: they are all descended from the Sieur D'Entremont who landed here in 1650. St. John's, Newfoundland, was first settled in 1613: its people retain the Jacobean turns of phrase, the ballads, the hearty manners of their ancestors.

Maritimers, many of them with the quick pride of Scots Highland descent, are touchy about the chronic depression of their region. Aware that their economy is to some extent subsidized from Central Canada, they resent "Upper Canadians" and are fond of denouncing the frantic pace of life in Ontario compared with the pleasant, lethargic tempo of their own existence.

French Canadians cherish their own mythology and defensive folklore. "*Je me souviens*", their motto, recalls the national trauma – the conquest of New France upon the Plains of Abraham before the walled city of Quebec. Since that fatal day, September 13, 1759, they have seen themselves as beleaguered champions of the Catholic faith and its guardian the French tongue in a continent predominantly American and Protestant. Henri Bourassa, most eloquent of Canadian orators, spoke for his nation when he cried out passionately at the Montreal Eucharistic Congress on September 6, 1910: "Providence has willed that the principal group of this French and Catholic colonization should constitute in America a separate corner of the earth, where the social, religious, and political situation most closely approximates to that which the Church teaches us to be the ideal state of society. . . . But, it is said, you are only a handful; you are fatally destined to disappear; why persist in the struggle? We are only a handful, it is true; but in the school of Christ I did not learn to estimate right and moral forces by number and wealth. We are only a handful; but we count for what we are; and we have the right to live. . . ."

More than fifty years later the "ideal state of society" of the devout *habitants* has disappeared and the French Canadians have become an urban proletariat. While the fragrant spirit of John XXIII has sweetened their faith, they have discovered their political strength and a new sense of purpose. By a paradox they have become most sharply aware of their distinctness at the very moment when they are becoming most "American".

The crooked streets of Quebec City cast their old spell, delightfully French-provincial in the shade of old trees in summer, antique as a Christmas-card under winter snow. In the citadel, redcoats of the 22nd Foot wheel and stamp to orders shouted in the curiously nasal French of the province. *Monsieur le Président* (Mr. Speaker) sits under the crucifix in the legislative assembly. A spectacled nun appears at the grille through which visitors are interviewed at the ancient Couvent des Ursulines; a moment later she returns to display with shy pride the skull of General Montcalm. But such impressions can be deceptive. The dark-haired girls, demure in their little black dresses, are North American women, capable, energetic, adventurous. And under the sober jacket of the young *séparatiste* hurrying to early Mass beats the heart of an automobile salesman.

65

All this is much more obvious in Montreal, the world's second biggest French-speaking city. This is the city which, above all others, has seized the affection of Canadians. Novel after novel has explored the intricate life of its streets and parks. Despite the bilingual signs and the brooding presence of huge, prison-like religious institutions, Montreal is plainly a New World city. Everyone here is cheerfully on the make. There is that sense (strong too in Toronto) that nothing is permanent. Buildings are constantly being torn down to be replaced by taller and richer ones, streets being ripped open for new sewers or subways, ambulances racing to the rescue of accident victims, sirens screaming, signs dazzling, merchandise being sacrificed to make way for the new line, the new model, the new chain-store – the whole exciting circus of planned obsolescence and competitive selling.

French Canadians are awakening to the knowledge that this is their world and their country. They have recognized their enemy in the "Anglo-Saxon" *élite* who dominate Canada's economy. This *élite*, though stoutly entrenched in Montreal, whose commercial life it controls, has its spiritual home in Toronto.

One of the few shared sentiments of all regions of Canada is an unreasoning dislike of Toronto. Unreasoning, because the Toronto loathed throughout Canada has pretty well ceased to exist. The dour, philistine Orangemen who earned the city its unpleasant reputation have long been outnumbered by swarms of immigrants from Europe and from other parts of Canada. True, there's still a great parade down University Avenue on the glorious Twelfth of July, with drums and bands and orange sashes and even King Billy on his white charger. But the crowds who turn out to cheer are mostly Italians – everyone, after all, loves a band. For if Montreal is bicultural, Toronto is multicultural – an expanding, expansive metropolis which will soon have a population of two million. As Montreal is the centre of French-speaking Canadian life, Toronto is the hub of English Canada. Here are centred its publishing and communication industries, its commercial and financial empires, music, art, and theatre. Heavy industry is close by in Hamilton, and a third of Canada's population is concentrated in the rich farmlands and small cities of southern Ontario within a radius of three hundred miles.

Ontario people are sober, hard-working, orderly; as if to insist on their difference from the Americans they resemble so closely, they are strong for the Queen. The men tend to be serious about their work to the point of solemnity; at the same time they cherish the image of Huck Finn and are boyishly eager to head out for the bush. They are decent people, if – as they often complain themselves – a bit dull. And they are not nearly so hostile to French Canadians as the latter imagine: their reaction to Separatist agitation is to organize classes in French. Normally, of course, they do not think about Quebec; it simply doesn't impinge on their consciousness any more than Canada itself does on the mind of a New Yorker. For the only evidence of French Canada in Ontario (outside a few border communities) is the bilingual food-package: "snap, crackle, pop" on one side of the cereal-carton becomes "*cric, crac, croc*" on the other. It's hard to build understanding on evidence as flimsy as that.

The West begins at Winnipeg, a mystique of white Stetsons, "man-size" beefsteaks, and back-slapping hospitality. There is a tendency, too, for the necktie to atrophy into a sort of halter of bootlaces. Ontario and Quebec and the Maritimes suddenly recede to a great distance not only in space but in time. Here they are "the East". The cities of Central Canada, which seem to the people who live in them so new and raw, from here take on the aspect of ancient centres of privilege and decorum, crusted with culture and learning. Wide, empty landscapes of bald prairie, oppressed by the enormous sky, wait at the limits of prairie cities. The company of fellow-men becomes vital. And in Alberta, as the flat prairie begins to undulate in ever shorter and steeper waves to the foothills of the Rockies, the company of God himself is sought by the people of the "Bible belt"; not only in theocratic colonies of bearded, black-clad Hutterites, but in small, bleak churches and conventicles of innumerable fundamentalist sects.

British Columbia, cut off from the rest of Canada by range beyond range of enormous, uninhabitable mountains, lives its own life. British Columbians are the most American Canadians, farthest removed from bicultural compromises; they are also the most British. Life is pleasant in the mild green climate of the Coast. The mist comes down on the mountains and silent forests, the Pacific glimmers below – who needs Canada? "As far as I'm concerned," a British Columbian told me not long ago, "the Atlantic Ocean might just as well be washing at the foot of the Rockies." In the remote valleys of the Interior – as the hinterland of Vancouver is gallantly called – a few pilgrim souls, the last puritans, live by the light of conscience: Quakers, anarchists, pacifists, the unhappy Doukhobor Sons of Freedom. Cowboys ride the range on the high, semi-arid plateau of the Cariboo country. Loggers, miners, and fishermen earn the provincial income. But a good two-thirds of British Columbians are concentrated in the cities of Vancouver and Victoria where the living is easy, summer and winter.

People who do not know Canada sometimes think of it, as Voltaire did, as a few acres of snow.

It is, of course, a northern country. Over most of it the climate is one of violent extremes – swelteringly hot summers and Siberian winters. Arctic Canada – the true North – is almost uninhabited. There are only some eleven thousand Eskimoes. The other people of a few small, scattered communities like Churchill, Inuvik, and Aklavik live a frontier life with, at

Inuvik, every modern convenience, including heated sewage. (Because of permafrost, drainpipes are above the surface, and have to be heated to avoid freezing.) Northerners regard the rest of Canada and indeed the rest of the world as "Outside".

There is still a powerful myth of the North. Against all evidence, Canadians sometimes like to think of themselves as a hardy, frugal race of *hommes du nord*. For the farther north one goes, the farther one is from the United States and from supermarkets, super-highways, and advertising-men in crew-cuts and two-button suits. One must suffer to be a Canadian (says the myth): here incomes are lower and prices higher than in the republic to the south: go north, young man. Canadians may not be particularly hardy, but they are hard-headed. They indulge this dream only at election-time and when they are on vacation.

---

2. The Provinces

A. M. KLEIN

A. M. Klein was born in Montreal in 1909. He has continued to live in that city where he has practised law and engaged in a considerable amount of literary activity as editor, scholar, critic, and poet. His poem "The Provinces" was included in The Rocking Chair and Other Poems, *the book for which he won the Governor General's Award for poetry in 1948. The poem deals with only nine of Canada's ten provinces because it was written before Newfoundland entered Confederation in 1949.*

The poem employs personification as a means to developing its main idea. Each of the provinces is seen as a member of the same family; the country's unity lies in "the not unsimilar face". Structurally, this overview is the opposite of that found in the preceding selection by Kildare Dobbs, for the movement here is not from the main idea to the supporting details, but through the details to the main idea, which is not stated until the final stanza.

> First, the two older ones, the bunkhouse brawnymen,
> biceps and chest, lumbering over their legend:
> scooping a river up in the palm of the hand,

a dangling fish, alive; kicking open a mine;
bashing a forest bald; spitting a country to crop;
for exercise before their boar breakfast,
building a city; racing, to keep in shape,
against the white-sweatered wind; and always
bragging comparisons, and reminiscing
about their fathers' even more mythic prowess,
arguing always, like puffing champions rising
from wrestling on the green.

Then, the three flat-faced blond-haired husky ones.

And the little girl, so beautiful she was named –
to avert the evil of the evil eye –
after a prince, not princess. In crossed arms cradling her,
her brothers, tanned and long-limbed.
(Great fishermen, hauling out of Atlantic
their catch and their coal
and netting with appleblossom the shoals of their sky.)

And, last, as if of another birth,
the hunchback with the poet's face; and eyes
blue as the glass he looks upon; and fruit
his fragrant knuckles and joints; of iron marrow; –
affecting always a green habit, touched with white.

Nine of them; not counting
the adopted boy of the golden complex, nor
the proud collateral albino, – nine,
a sorcery of numbers, a game's stances.

But the heart seeks one, the heart, and also the mind
seeks single the thing that makes them one, if one.
        Yet where shall one find it? In their history –
the cairn of cannonball on the public square?
Their talk, their jealous double-talk? Or in
the whim and weather of a geography
curling in drifts about the forty-ninth?
Or find it in the repute of character:
romantic as mounties? Or discover it
in beliefs that say:
this is a country of Christmas trees?
                Or hear it sing

from the house with towers, from whose towers ring
bells, and the carillon of laws?
Where shall one find it? What
to name it, that is sought?
The ladder the nine brothers hold by rungs?
The birds that shine on each other? The white water
that foams from the ivy entering their eaves?

Or find it, find it, find it commonplace
but effective, valid, real, the unity
in the family feature, the not unsimilar face?

---

3. People of the Sea

FARLEY MOWAT

The author of this essay is a writer with a considerable power to command and retain a reader's attention. This ability Farley Mowat has made use of in several brilliant and occasionally controversial books, among which are People of the Deer *(1952),* The Dog Who Wouldn't Be *(1957),* Never Cry Wolf *(1963), and* Westviking *(1965). Mr. Mowat was born in Ontario in 1921, but has lived in several other parts of Canada. Recently he returned to Ontario after living for several years in Burgeo, a Newfoundland outport. The essay on Newfoundland included here first appeared in* Century 1867-1967, The Canadian Saga, *a collection of essays by several writers published in 1967.*

The over-all pattern of development of Mr. Mowat's essay is chronological. The writing also has a unifying theme: the struggle against desperate odds that has always been at the centre of life in Newfoundland. Two other stylistic aspects of "People of the Sea" are worth noting. One is the consistent use that the author makes of specific detail; the second is the smooth and varied flow of his sentences. Both of these devices contribute greatly to Farley Mowat's ability to retain a reader's interest.

Discovered in 986 by Greenland Norse who made an abortive settlement in the north part, Newfoundland began to take shape as a European entity in the west as early as 1450, by which time Basque and Portuguese whalers and fishers were regularly sailing to the Grand Banks, into Belle Isle Strait, and probably to most of the good harbors that ring the island. The early history is dim, principally because until the 1700's it was illegal to settle in Newfoundland. The wealthy west coast fish merchants of England had engineered such laws in an attempt to prevent the establishment of a native fishery in the "New Land". But laws are mostly made to be broken. By 1510 runaways from fishing ships – the Masterless Men, as they are known in tradition – had spread like a slow, silent tide into remote Newfoundland bays. They lived hard lives in a hard land – but they lived. There were six thousand miles of rock-ribbed, sea-roaring coasts to hide them, and here they built their little "tilts" of sod or logs, concealing themselves from strangers and passing ships, getting a little "country meat" from the land, but subsisting mainly on the fish they caught from open boats. Historians have ignored these early planters, remembering only the grandiose attempts of men like Lord Baltimore, which mostly failed. Nevertheless by 1550 a large part of the Newfoundland coast was occupied and these early "liveyers" (people who "live here" – a name still in use on the Labrador coast) slowly increased in numbers.

The odds against them were terrible. Starvation was the common lot through the first three centuries of Newfoundland's recent history, and chronic hunger filled most of the fourth. But a steady flow of new blood came in from Ireland, the Southern Counties of England and the Channel Islands, in the form of indentured labor brought over by great English and Jersey merchant companies to man their fishing factories. These indentured people, men and women both, were practically slaves and a good many of them slipped quietly off to seek freedom in the secret little coves. The English outporters met French fishermen-settlers and Micmac Indians and, since all men were equal before the sea, marriages took place freely across the lines of race and blood.

So the Newfoundlanders early evolved into a unique people – a true "People of The Sea" who eventually ringed the island with more than thirteen hundred outports, ranging in size from two or three families to as high as fifty. Most of these settlements had no contact with one another or with the world outside except by water.

They struggled for survival as few human beings in our time have had to struggle. In small open boats the men fished the year round, with time off for grueling voyages in small schooners carrying salt cod to Europe and the West Indies; while the women "made" (dried and treated) the salt cod which was the great product of the northern seas. Every September at "settling up time" the salt fish was carried to the merchant who bought it, at his price – not for cash, but as payment against the debts, the endless debts, of the fisherman and his family.

The merchant class of Newfoundland held the people in a deadly vice; as inescapable and as ruthless a trap as any that was ever devised by a trader to ensnare a simple Indian. From its beginnings until as late as the 1950's in some remote outports, a man was born, grew up and died in debt to the merchant.

The long centuries slipped by and a score of times Newfoundland became a battlefield, usually between French and English, during which the outporters often lost all they possessed and had to start again with nothing but their hands. During all those years nothing really changed. The system remained the same. The poor stayed desperately poor, and the rich grew fabulously rich. St. John's was the only real town the island boasted, and it was the home of the great merchants – the "Water Street men". Even as late as 1950 St. John's had more millionaires per capita than any other city in North America, including the capital of Texas! And in 1949 the majority of the people of Newfoundland still knew grinding poverty.

Here is the way it was [according to Newfoundlander Harvey Pink]: "In the thirties – the 'Hard Times', we called it – there was nothing to be had. The merchants would give out no more credit and the people had no money, of course. Fish was a glut. Nobody would buy our fish. People all up and down the coasts were starving. Nobody will ever know how many children died, but a good many grown men starved to death. If there happened to be a doctor handy, he'd write it down as heart failure, which was true enough. The government gave out the dole – six cents a day for a family and you took it 'in kind', and the kind, often enough, was rotten or weevily flour. My people were a little better off than most, and many's the time neighbors would come to our kitchen for a feed. I mind how they smelled. My mother told me: 'Son,' she says, 'That is the smell of poverty. Don't you forget it.' I knew one man, poor fellow, set out to ask for help from the relieving officer one day in winter time. But he froze to death on the way. When we found him, all he was wearing was a pair of trousers and a jacket made of wore-out flour sacks. He had no socks – only a torn pair of rubber boots on his feet. . . ."

Hard times! Yes. But a Newfoundlander was used to hard times, having known little else for centuries. He begat immense families, often fifteen to eighteen children, but it was rare for more than a handful of them to reach maturity, and when they were grown-up the sea would take its toll of the men – "Bridegrooms of the Sea", they called the drowned – while tuberculosis took a toll of the women – a heavy toll.

It was like that right up until Confederation in 1949. And yet when union with Canada was mooted, the "Water Street men" fought a bitter battle to prevent it. They preferred things to stay as they were. But they lost. One day in April of 1949 Newfoundland ceased to be the oldest European settlement in North America and became the youngest of the ten Canadian provinces. And an ancient mold was shattered, almost overnight – not by a bomb or by a similar catastrophe, but . . . by the baby bonus!

The baby bonus accomplished in a few years what the merchants had been able to prevent through three or four centuries. It brought cash, and therefore a measure of freedom to the people. The change was unbelievable. My neighbors in the outport of Burgeo, where I now live, never tire of recalling what happened.

"Before my wife got her first bonus money," one of them told me, "nobody in our family had ever seen a five-dollar bill. If we saw five dollars in silver in a year – that was a lot. Everything we sold went to one merchant, and everything we bought had to come from him. He owned us, do you see?"

Here is how things now stand in this old Island after 18 years of being part of Canada. Nobody starves to death anymore, not even children. Nobody, or at least not many people, die because of a lack of medical services. For the first time, every child can learn to read and write, even if the educational standard is much lower than on the mainland. Men who never had anything to lean on except their own strong muscles, can now draw unemployment insurance, sick benefits, or relief assistance, while their wives gather in the baby bonus cheques. Old people, who used to survive (or try to), on a government pension of $120.00 a year, are now so relatively affluent that they hardly know what to do with their money. The population is exploding; not because more children are being born, but because a lot more of them are surviving.

It all looks very good indeed. And yet there is a shadow over the paradise created by Confederation. Having tasted the fruits of the Canadian way of life, more and more and more Newfoundlanders are turning their backs on the pitiless grey sea which made them what they were. The Newfoundland merchant fleet, mostly under sail, was so impressive that as late as 1939 about five hundred sailing vessels were operating out of Newfoundland ports, many of them engaged in the trans-Atlantic salt fish trade, while others carried cargo to and from Canadian and Caribbean ports. Employment in the fisheries has fallen sharply as, indeed, it must. Where once fifty men, working for starvation wages, could land a certain weight of fish, now four or five men, better paid and operating a modern dragger, do the same job.

Standards of living go up, and the number of acceptable jobs at these new standards go down. The birth rate goes up, and there are not enough jobs available even for those presently employable. And so Newfoundland, once noted as the greatest exporter in the world of salt fish, is now exporting men and women as its major produce. They go because they must, and because the new generation will not accept the kind of life their fathers knew.

But more than the physical presence of the new generation is being lost. The tough, impervious core of courage, resourcefulness, ability, endurance, and personal pride that was a product of the evolution of the outport man and woman – the byproduct of adversity – is disappearing in the interval between one generation and the next.

Newfoundland demonstrates with pitiless clarity the terrible paradox of our times: as we make life easier, more tolerable, less demanding, so do we weaken the sustaining fabric of pride and strength which made us men in the first place.

In Burgeo, as in most of Newfoundland, the older men still go fishing in their little boats, although there is no longer any need for men of sixty or seventy to endure the cold seas and the cutting gales. They go because they love the life, not for the money that is in it. But they know they are the last of their kind – that the young fellows who are their sons and grandsons will soon be gone from the little outports; from Heart's Ease, Pushthrough, Fransway, and all the others. They know that in the past ten years more than three hundred outports have died, or been abandoned. They know that the young people will go to the Mainland, where they will become real Canadians – whatever that may be; but they have a feeling that these men of a new age will somehow be less than the men their fathers were.

4. Maritime Faces

EARLE BIRNEY

This poem by one of Canada's best-known poets was written in 1945 when the author, as the subscription to the poem states, was "Approaching Halifax" from Europe. Earle Birney is not a Maritimer. He was born in Calgary (in 1904), and has lived most of his life in British Columbia, where for many years he was a professor of English at the University of British Columbia. Since his first book, David and Other Poems, *was published in 1942, Earle Birney has written two novels, several books of verse, and a wide range of assorted prose. His* Selected Poems, 1940-1966 *was published in 1966.*

Structurally, "Maritime Faces" moves from the sea to the land in four stages, past the gulls and the bergs, and in towards the shores and the hills. Each of these stages is described by a metaphor that helps to develop the main idea of the poem. What is this main idea?

As the waters grey   grace meets you
but only in gulls that hook on the wind
are shaken easily loose
curve to the curving wave

Not these the mark of Canada
nor yet the sentry beat of bergs
around the fading palaces
of fog your ship salutes
but here where heads of Hebridean mould
toss in crusted dories   hard Saxon fingers
sift dour living from the drowned
and drowning Banks

Smell now the landsmell   sweet spruce in the air
but note   remember   how boxer waves
bully these shores   battling and billowing
into the stone's weakness   bellowing
down the deepening caverns
smashing the slate with unappeasable fists

See at last the crouched hills
at bay with Boreas
the old laconic resourceful hills

Something of this in the maritime faces

Approaching Halifax 1945

5. The Sensual City

PETER DESBARATS

The author of the following essay on Montreal is a bilingual journalist who writes for the Montreal Star, *usually as a political reporter. As he states in his essay, he has approached his subject with subjective passion, rather than with objective analysis. And, although he doesn't say this, he has also approached it with a considerable amount of sardonic wit. Like the essay by Farley Mowat, this selection first appeared in* Century 1867-1967, The Canadian Saga.

Several characteristics of vivid writing are illustrated by this selection, most notably the use that the writer has made of metaphorical comparisons in painting his picture of Montreal. He sees incense as "the exhaust of a hundred churches hauling at the city like helicopters", and the city itself as "a choir of two million voices in a continual hymn of gratitude". What other metaphors are found in this selection?

First of all, a confession: I love this city.

I was born here, in the shadow of the mountain; and I know exactly the few square feet reserved for me in the vault on the same mountain where my ancestors watch, behind wrought-iron gates, the island, the river and the low gray swell of the Laurentians on the northern horizon.

No day passes that I am not consciously grateful to this city and whatever providential quirk cast me upon this island. So don't expect me to describe her in statistics, to measure the depth of her new subway or the height of her latest skyscraper, to punch her population into this essay as if I were a computer, my memory a mere collection of tapes and reels activating the keys of this typewriter. Nor am I an artist portraying an unknown model. I have lived with her for the better part of three decades.

There is no comparison with other Canadian cities. Montreal is sensual. It might have something to do with the contours of the mountain, really two mountains separated by the gentle cleft of Cote des Neiges; or the St. Lawrence River whose current gives the island shape and movement. Montreal is a river-city like London, Paris, Prague, Vienna. It also can draw an almost physical response from its writers and artists.

I think of the early streetscapes of John Little, the ones that he painted about ten years ago when he lived in a small apartment somewhere near St. Marc street and the only still-life subject he could find was his own toilet bowl, the most eloquent toilet bowl anyone ever painted. Some collector in New York now has it. In most of his paintings, almost always in his paintings of Sherbrooke street before the new buildings spoiled it for him, there was a blonde in a red coat walking away from the viewer toward infinity. She was John Little's spirit of Montreal. I remember, two summers ago, Roussil and Vaillancourt welding and casting their sculptures on top of Mount Royal as if it had been created to pedestal their work. Montrealers have this sense of owning the whole city. I think of the choreography that explodes from the small studio of Les Grands Ballets Canadiens on Stanley street sandwiched in a narrow building between an association of war amputees and a karate salon.

Where is the comparison? Halifax and Quebec City have character. Toronto, recently and strangely, a kind of bounce. Vancouver has the sea and mountains, a kohinoor setting occupied by a chunk of paste. The others are hesitant proposals for cities.

I am not alone. Montreal is a choir of two million voices in a continual hymn of gratitude. They are not heard only in Westmount where the millionaires live rank upon rank, the poorest of the rich at the bottom of the mountain and the unbelievably wealthy at the narrow top of the pyramid, a diagram of aristocracy by income or birth or both displayed above the city for the edification, emulation and envy of all. No, they are heard also along The Main, in the steamed hot dog parlors (Leonard Cohen returned from Greece the other day and immediately spent a week in these relish and mustard gas chambers seeking native nourishment and inspiration), in the three-feature cinemas and the cheap dance halls where angular Negroes and arrogant French Canadians frug with a fierce escapist intensity. You can hear them in the dark streets of the east end, in summer, when women rock and talk on their iron balconies and every corner seems to have a small store, teen-agers in a patch of light on the sidewalk, the smell of potatoes, hot grease, vinegar and salt.

I know, the *patates frites* imagery is no longer fashionable; nor is one supposed to savor the smell of incense in our streets, the exhaust of a hundred churches hauling at the city like helicopters. One is expected to ignore the nightly radio rosary, the Sorrowful Mysteries a few kilocycles away from beep-beep-zing-a-ling news bulletins, the Top Ten and open-line programs enabling the mute to converse with the deaf. All in glorious bilingualism.

Don't look at:

newsstands buried in pulp: crime, perversion, how to improve your personality, astrology, she hungered for the wrong kind of love (with black grease pencil smeared across the right places on the cover), confessions of a sexpot *chanteuse* from Chicoutimi; basement halls filled with white

77

capes and berets, the "original" Créditistes, celebrating the union of the Virgin and Major Douglas; limousines parked illegally before dress shops on Sherbrooke street, their chauffeurs chatting amiably with traffic constables;

nuns gliding through office buildings putting the bite on, sweetly, for orphanages in Formosa, still praying for the little adopted ones ransomed years ago from paganism to run things today in Peking.

Even to mention these things, now, is quaint. Perhaps even dangerous for a journalist who wants to appear "with it." It is what we were writing about 20 years ago: the city of churches, vice capital of North America, Westmount barons, outdoor staircases and chips with Pepsi. But they remain, after all the uproar of the "quiet" revolution, the basic ingredients of the city, the mud that has been poured into the mould of the new Montreal.

I know, it is unfashionable to discuss the "patois" spoken by east-end Montrealers. Joual? *B'en why, tabernacle,* just because a few uneducated people speak French that sounds like Iroquois to a Parisian, is that any reason to . . . to what? Is it wrong to treasure the patchwork French spoken by many Montrealers? Have not the *chansionniers* themselves worked poetically in this rich vein of popular language? Will not something die in Montreal if the day arrives when every "hot dog steamé" becomes an impeccable *chien chaud?*

I know, it is à la mode today to overlook Catholicism. You can hardly get into the Archbishop's Palace now without a rabbi on one arm and a Jehovah's Witness on the other. But where are those lines of school children going on the first Thursday of every month if not to confession and to cram nine First Friday communions into the school year to guarantee a happy death? Is the crucifix in every Catholic classroom of no more magic than a Greek coin? This remains an intensely Catholic city, from the pre-stressed concrete churches of new French-language parishes to the dark downtown "Irish" churches which still remain closer to the fervent piety of 19th-century Kilkenny than the swinging ecumenicism of contemporary Rome.

The modern concept of Montreal as a city with an international rôle is grafted on to the old idea of an "elect" city favored by Heaven. The original "Ville Marie" grew under the Virgin's special care, and still the illuminated steel cross on the east flank of Mount Royal, facing the "French side" of the city, is a symbol of dedication.

Catholicism gave Montreal the gift of sinfulness. Other Canadian cities in other provinces received a Protestant tradition of puritanism. Montreal was blessed with a religion of warmth, color, drama and suffering – a sensual religion which emphasized not the cold virtues of self-denial but the emotional delights of confession and repentance. "There is more joy in Heaven over one sinner who repents . . ." I am not certain of the quotation, but neither are other Montrealers who joyfully go about the necessary preliminaries. Like Latins, Montrealers draw a kind of suppressed and compressed sensual vitality from their Catholicism, as well as a gift for pageantry. It is no accident that the annual St. Jean Baptiste parade every June is the only major Canadian parade held at night, when illuminated floats and torches create a medieval and almost mystical atmosphere.

There might even be a relationship between this Catholicism and the creativity of the Jewish community in Montreal. This is the only Canadian city where European Jews, particularly those from eastern Europe, were surrounded by a familiar European Catholicism complete, at rare times, with an element of conscious anti-Semitism. Is this why the Jewish writers, poets and artists of Montreal are among the best in Canada, because their fathers did *not* celebrate Brotherhood Week at the local Rotary Club?

I know, it is anti-revolutionary in the new Montreal to discuss the cultural influence of "les Anglais." French-Canadian historians have carefully noted the slow retreat of the English from Quebec City and the Eastern Townships, have wondered if Westmount is a crumbling citadel, have imagined the fleur-de-lis fluttering over the bird and wildflower sanctuary atop Westmount mountain above the house of Bronfman. In a few more decades, will the French Canadians in Montreal win the final skirmish of the battle that began so badly on the Plains of Abraham more than 200 years ago?

Not likely, for a variety of reasons: the equal birth rate between French and English in Quebec, even before the first French-Canadian housewife crossed herself hastily and gulped down the first pill; the undiminished importance of English-speaking Montrealers in the city's national, international and even local trade; the depth of English-language popular culture in Montreal, including radio, television, newspapers, films and magazines, domestic and imported; and the English-speaking community's tendency to absorb most of the city's new arrivals from Europe and other parts of North America.

The sprawling Victorian heart of McGill University's campus is as dominant a feature of the city as the monumental French-language degree factory that stands on the other side of Mount Royal. The empirical solidity of the Mount Stephen Club, where even the soap in the washrooms is British, is as important to the flavor of the city as the zinc bar and sidewalk tables of the Bistro a block away, where even the oysters are French. And in the Bistro, many of the untidiest writers and artists are descended from the bluest strata of Westmount society, as Westmount in recent years has acquired a class of prosperous French Canadians fonder of stately homes and tree-shaded lawns than the noisy native culture of the outdoor staircase and corner store.

79

I know, I know, this is not the new Montreal. I am forgetting about the Place des Arts and remembering the Rodeo, the Mocambo, the Centre Grand National, Fawzia's and the more expensive places where the daughters of the daughters who used to flourish on deBullion street ply their trade according to the new rules. I am forgetting about Expo '67 and thinking of bingo in church basements. Why do I dwell on hot dog parlors instead of Café St. Martin, Auberge St. Gabriel, Magnani's, the Continental and the glass gourmets' playpen atop Place Ville Marie?

Because I know that Montreal herself has not forgotten. She, too, is a bit cynical about her new *politique de grandeur*. Maybe that is one reason for her recent success as a "grande dame" of international society. Beneath the mink stole, she still cherishes the old bawdy.

---

6. The Attitude

PIERRE BERTON

As one critic noted not long ago, it is difficult at present to find a Canadian book that wasn't written by Pierre Berton. Mr. Berton has, it is true, been associated in recent years with a seemingly infinite number of broadcasting and publishing ventures, including a column in the Toronto Star, *his own interview programs on radio and television, and two controversial best-sellers,* The Comfortable Pew *(1965), and* The Smug Minority *(1967). The author of all this industry was born in the Yukon in 1920, was educated and began his newspaper career in British Columbia, and now lives in Toronto. The following selection is an introduction he wrote for a collection of photographs by Henri Rossier published in 1961 under the title* The New City, a Prejudiced View of Toronto.

Mr. Berton's essay demonstrates how a wide-ranging collection of factual details can be unified around a central theme, in this case the notion that it is "The Attitude" that makes Toronto a distinctive North American city.

Every city has its legends, but few cities live a legend. Toronto *is* a legend.

This is Toronto the Good – smug, solid, respectable. This is Hogtown, where money talks. This is where the Dullest Sunday in the World was invented.

There is, in short, a certain Attitude toward Toronto which gives it distinction. Without that Attitude it might be considered just another North American community, growing too fast for its own good, jammed with strangers from both sides of the water, struggling with the inevitable traffic problem, its physical face changing almost year by year, its boundaries exploding in ever-widening circles, its people in constant ferment – a yeasty, culture-happy, money-directed, somewhat disturbing, yet oddly exciting society with an undistinguished façade and a confused inner spirit.

But with The Attitude, Toronto has an image, clear-cut and distinct. It does not matter that the image is all wrong; it manages to hold Toronto together and to give it some direction.

The Attitude to Toronto takes two forms. There is first the attitude of the non-Torontonians, who live in places like St. John's, Maple Creek and Vancouver; and then there is the Attitude of the Torontonians themselves.

The Attitude of the outsider is compounded of envy, malice and pity in about equal quantities. It is admitted that Torontonians make large sums of money but not much else; certainly they never have any fun. There is none of the leisurely Gracious Living that is to be found in Montreal, say, or Halifax or Okotoks, Alberta. When a young man sets out for Toronto (and, sooner or later, all young men set out for Toronto) he is surrounded by a covey of friends – all loudly commiserating with him and whispering to him to look about for a job for them in the big city. It is generally acknowledged that the bereaved young man will return, but he rarely does. If he sees his friends again, he sees them in Toronto where they all have a good cry, and talk over the grand old days when they were poor in Pelvis or West Webfoot.

The Attitude of the Torontonians is that they simply do not care what people think of them. They live in Toronto and that is good enough for them. For years a host of magazine articles, newspaper editorials and commentators have baited Toronto. Toronto refuses to swallow the bait. One mayor tried to launch a campaign to make the city popular but it fizzled out after a few days. Torontonians do not really care about being popular; in fact, about half the criticism about the city comes from its own people. Nobody baits Toronto quite as much as those who live there.

I once heard a visitor from the U.S. praise Toronto in an unguarded moment. He said that Toronto was the nearest thing to San Francisco he'd yet encountered on the continent. There was a shocked silence and look of disdain on the faces of the Torontonians who heard this traitorous remark. They began to argue with the man from the U.S.: Toronto was *nothing* like San Francisco! Why, San Francisco had charm, beauty, good food, sophisticated people and an earthquake! What had Toronto got? They spoke with a warmth and a sense of pride that is supposed to be unusual among Torontonians. For the moment at least The Attitude had made them comrades.

Without The Attitude it would be difficult to put the city into focus since Toronto is now so mercurial that you can say almost anything you want about it and make a case for it.

To a U.S. tourist, the city has a fussily English look. The hotels, theatres, streets and cheap restaurants are Kingly, Queenly, Royal, Regal, Princely, Ducal or Alexandrine. No less than eight streets, lanes, avenues, terraces, places, park lanes, crescents and squares enshrine the name of Queen Victoria. The streets are narrow, in the British colonial tradition, "built by narrow colonial minds" as Arthur Lower, the social historian, has said.

Yet, to any European, Toronto is scarcely distinguishable from any similarly sized U.S. city. The hustling men on Bay Street, brief-cased and crew-cropped, the coiffured ladies on Bloor, minked and mannered, may just as easily be spotted in Detroit, Buffalo or Cincinnati. Save for the occasional grotesqueries of a Casa Loma, the architecture is equally indistinguishable from that of neighbouring U.S. towns. It is The Attitude that is distinctive. In Toronto, not long ago, the most successful skit in a successful satirical revue, poked fun at this same architecture to the audience's and the city's delight. In Toronto, the most ambitious architectural contest in the world was held to choose a design for a new city hall. And when one dragon-killing candidate for mayor announced he'd scrap the whole idea if elected, he was roundly defeated.

His successful opponent, who racked up the record for longevity among Toronto mayors, was a Jew, though that was not even a minor issue in the campaign. This sort of thing confuses the Toronto Image, for the city has long been considered solidly Anglo-Saxon and Protestant – part Methodist, part Family Compact Anglican, part United Empire Loyalist, part Orange Lodge.

It is nothing of the sort. Within the city limits proper, largely because of post-war immigration, every second Torontonian is now a Roman Catholic. In the general Metropolitan area, one out of three is a Roman Catholic. Half of all the immigrants who come to Canada come to Ontario and half of these come to Toronto. They have helped transform the city.

It is this constant, seething change that makes Toronto such a confusing city. If the Torontonians themselves do not understand what is happening to their town, how can anybody else?

In the eyes of many good burghers Toronto is still The Good. "When Christ reappears on this earth we want to make sure he makes his first appearance in Toronto," one minister cried from the pulpit a few years ago. He was attacking the wicked proposal that the public should be allowed to view baseball games on Sunday afternoons. The attack failed, however, and

Toronto became the first English-speaking city in Canada to vote for both Sunday sports and Sunday movies. Torontonians have reluctantly had to stop quoting the famous remark that "Toronto is perhaps the finest city in the world in which to die especially on Sunday afternoon when the transition between the living and the dead is so gradual as to be almost imperceptible". The statement no longer holds.

7. Lake Erie

JAMES REANEY

Something of a sense of the heavy concentration of population in southern Ontario is suggested in these lines by poet and playwright James Reaney, who was born in Ontario in 1926 and is at present a professor of English at the University of Western Ontario. "Lake Erie" is one of the poems that makes up "The Great Lakes Suite", published originally in The Red Heart, *the collection of verse for which Mr. Reaney won a Governor General's Award in 1949.*

In addition to the somewhat sarcastic comment that the poem makes concerning the restlessness of the "Crowds of the cities / That line her shores", "Lake Erie" is stylistically interesting for the rapidity of its movement towards a climactic ending.

Lake Erie is weary
Of washing the dreary
Crowds of the cities
That line her shores.
Oh, you know
The dirty people of Buffalo
And those in Cleveland
That must leave land
To see what the water's like.
And those that by bike,
Motor car, bus and screeching train
Come from London in the rain
To Port Stanley where they spend

The day in deciding whether Grand Bend
Might not have been a nicer place to go.
Up and down in thousands
They walk upon Lake Erie's sands.
Those in Cleveland say, "Plainly,"
As they gaze across the waters
Where swim their sons and daughters,
"That distant speck must be Port Stanley."
Those in Port Stanley yawn, "Oh,
That lump in the mist
Over there really must
Be populous Cleveland in Ohio."
But Lake Erie says, "I know
That people say I'm shallow
But you just watch me when I go
With a thump
And a plump
At the Falls of Niagara into Lake Ontario.
When you see that you'll admit
That I am not just a shallow nitwit
But a lake
That takes the cake
For a grand gigantic thunderous tragic exit."

---

8. Saskatchewan

EDWARD McCOURT

In this lyrical description of Saskatchewan, Edward McCourt, who is a professor of English at the University of Saskatchewan, says something about all three of Canada's prairie provinces. This selection is taken from the prologue to his book Saskatchewan, *published in 1968. Mr. McCourt, who was born in 1907, is the author of several other books including a novel,* Music at the Close, *a travel book,* The Road Across Canada, *and a work of literary criticism,* The Canadian West in Fiction.

Several aspects of the writing in this selection are worth noting. It illustrates, for example, the technique of beginning an essay by contradicting "a popular misconception", in this case the notion that Saskatchewan is a flat and barren land. Also it demonstrates how a writer can develop his central idea by means of material quoted from a variety of sources.

The Indians, and after them the white men, came late to the great central plains area of Canada which today forms the southern part of the province of Saskatchewan. Their reluctance to establish a permanent home on the naked plains will not surprise visitors to Saskatchewan, particularly if they make their visit in the dead of winter; indeed they may be moved to agree whole-heartedly with the embittered early homesteader who expressed his distaste for his surroundings in a verse-portrait of a lady neither sweet nor fair:

> Saskatchewan, you always seem to me
> A woman without favour in your face,
> Flat-breasted, angular, devoid of grace.
> Why do men woo you? naught is fair to see
> In that wide visage with thin unkempt hair,
> And form that squarely stands, feet splayed apart.

The lines express what is in fact a common misconception; the truth is that the Saskatchewan landscape is never barren (except in times of prolonged drought) and in few places flat. The great southern plains are seamed deep by gullies and creek beds and frequently ridged by low hills which at a distance appear bathed in a romantic blue-green haze; two hundred miles north of the border the plains merge into pleasant, rolling parkland which in turn yields after another two hundred miles or more to a vast forest-lake-and-muskeg belt impinging on the subarctic terrain of the barren lands. And everywhere there are things to be seen and felt that exalt or sooth the sensitive spirit: crocuses spreading a mauve mist along railway embankments before the last patch of dirty grey snow has melted; wheatfields merging into a wave-surfaced green or golden ocean, unbounded save for an incredibly remote horizon rim at times indistinguishable from the sky itself; autumn days when the wind is miraculously quiet and premonitions of winter-death impel a man to look on a landscape of muted greys and browns with the passionate intensity of a lover parting from his beloved; mid-winter hoar-frost hanging on fence and telephone wires like strung popcorn; and the occasional vista – from the top of a ridge or butte or even a grain elevator – when a man sees all the kingdoms of the earth stretched out at his feet and feels himself a creature of utter insignificance in the sum of things or else the very centre of the universe.

But in spite of her very considerable scenic variety Saskatchewan is likely to impress the stranger with an awareness of encompassing natural forces more hostile than benevolent. This to a far greater degree than does either of her sister provinces. For Manitoba is only halfway plains country; great forests line her eastern flank, northward her land surface is engulfed by inland fresh-water seas; and her heart – so many truculent true-blue westerners affirm – yearns towards Ontario. West of Saskatchewan amply endowed Alberta floats on a lake of oil and snuggles comfortably into the protective embrace of the Rockies; and even her most exposed parts feel from time to time the caress of the genial chinook. But Saskatchewan stands defenceless, no forest belt or mountain range along her flanks to hold the wind at bay. Nowhere else in the west does the stranger feel himself more exposed to the wrath of the gods and the fury of the elements than in the middle of the Saskatchewan prairie.

Even though he may be sheltered behind walls. A sign in each unit of a Maple Creek motel reads thus: *When the wind blows please hang on to the door.*

The wind blows almost without intermission. The Earl of Southesk, in 1859 struggling through "the glittering white intensity of the cold", reported gloomily that "our fate seems to be that to which prophecy dooms a certain ancient family,

<blockquote>
'The Tracies
Shall always have the wind in their faces.' "
</blockquote>

And a writer of more recent date, Anne Marriott, has encompassed within a poet's lines the frustration and heartbreak experienced by men and women battered by the searing winds of the dust-bowl years when the lamp at noon was the symbol of a wind-and-drought-tormented wasteland:

<blockquote>
God, will it never rain again? What about
   those clouds out west? No, that's just dust, as thick and stifling
   now as winter underwear.
No rain, no crop, no feed, no faith, only
   wind.
</blockquote>

Any attempt to explain why the Saskatchewan man differs to a noticeable degree in personality and outlook from the Albertan or Manitoban who should logically be his counterpart must take into account the consequences, both physical and psychological, of the dust-bowl years. The world-wide economic depression that began in 1929 affected all of Canada; Saskatchewan bore an additional and dreadful burden – nine successive years of drought and crop failure. "The people of Saskatchewan have suffered a reduction of income during the last decade which has probably been unparalleled in peacetime in any other civilized country," the Royal Commission on Dominion-Provincial Relations reported in 1939. (Incredibly, the net agricultural incomes for 1931 and 1932 were reported in *minus* figures.) "The land was a landscape of almost incredible desolation," a Regina newspaper reporter wrote after driving through southern Saskatchewan in the midsummer of 1934, "as lifeless as ashes, and for miles there was scarcely a thing growing to be seen. . . . Gaunt cattle and horses with little save their skins to cover their bones stalked about the denuded acres, weakly seeking to crop the malign Frenchweed which seemed to be maintaining some sickly growth. When the miserable animals moved it seemed as if their frames rattled. The few people in evidence in the little towns appeared haggard and hopeless."

At first Saskatchewan was an object of concern and charity to her sister provinces, most notably Ontario; but as the long years continued to weave the unvarying tragic design with no end in sight the charitable impulse weakened – as it always does over the long stretch – and government relief alone kept many Saskatchewan people alive. Captain John Palliser had been right, it seemed, when he reported in 1859 that the southern plains area of the North-west was unfit for cultivation, and there was talk in eastern Canada of moving the Saskatchewan farm population to the northern Ontario bush.

The year 1937 brought the worst disaster of all. No rain fell, the wind blew what little topsoil remained in the fields into roadside ditches; dust-clouds – black, sinister, shot through here and there with eerie shafts of light – wavered all day and every day between earth and sky, and the heat was appalling. In Weyburn on a July day the temperature rose to 114 degrees above zero – a record which still stands. On the Moose Mountain Indian Reserve old Chief Sheepskin, nominally a Christian, summoned his braves to perform a rain dance. He died shortly afterwards, no doubt confirmed in the faith of his fathers, for the day before he died a heavy shower fell on Moose Mountain. In Regina, bathers in Wascana Lake found themselves unable to reach the bath-houses from the water without being coated with dust and in the end went home to scrape the mud off themselves in their own bath-tubs; and in a small town near by a baseball player – now an archetypal dust-bowl figure – lost his way running round the bases and was later found three miles out on the prairie.

The wheat crop that year averaged two and one half bushels to the acre.

But there was little thought of quitting – and none at all of moving to the Ontario bush. The bewilderment and despair of the earlier years had by 1937 given way to a sterner emotion, and the people now took a kind of defiant pride in showing the world their strength to endure, without flinching, the worst that nature could do to them. "The country is dismal, scorched, smashed," the mayor of Assiniboia said, "but the people are magnificent." He was right. No one could survive nine years of hell without courage. Nor without faith – not in a benevolent god but in one's own capacity to endure.

Nor without scars. The rains fell at last and the erstwhile desert rejoiced and blossomed like the rose; but no amount of rainfall could ever wash away dreadful memories of the agonizing struggle to survive. For the people of Saskatchewan that nine years' sojourn in a dust-darkened wilderness was a genuinely traumatic experience which has left its mark not only on those who actually lived through the Dirty Thirties but to some degree on their descendants.

The Saskatchewan man has thus been shaped by a sterner physical environment than that of most Canadians. Having been compelled to adapt himself to that environment, he has made his own rules for survival and looks with suspicion on traditional values cherished in softer lands. He tends to take a less optimistic view of life than do his neighbours, particularly those who live in Alberta. He is less ebullient and more independent. To the stranger, Saskatchewan cities may appear dull and colourless, and in many respects they are, but at least what character they do possess is honestly their own. (In this they are to be distinguished from Calgary, now an outpost of Texas, and from Edmonton, striving frenetically to become a suburb of Dawson City.) The Saskatchewan man is politically-minded but distrustful of all political parties, remembering that no government did more than keep him barely alive during his time of greatest need – hence his willingness to indulge in far-out political and social experiments and his refusal to conform to any voting pattern that makes sense to the orthodox outsider. What, after all, is one to make of an electorate which for twenty years returned a socialist government to power, supported the introduction of Medicare, replaced the socialist with a government of Liberals led by an ex-socialist, and at the same time sent a solid phalanx of Tories to Ottawa?

9. British Columbia

RODERICK HAIG-BROWN

Roderick Haig-Brown was born in England in 1908 and now lives in Camp-
bell River, British Columbia. As well as being a magistrate, an expert sports
fisherman, and a part-time farmer, he is a noted writer on themes related
to outdoor life. This comment on British Columbia is from a book entitled
The Face of Canada, *published in 1959, a book in which Mr. Haig-Brown*
shared with several other writers the task of describing the look of the
Canadian land.

By means of numerous specific details, this essay develops the idea that
British Columbia is "many things in many forms among its mountains by
the Pacific". Another of the qualities of effective writing that this selection
illustrates particularly well is the use of transitional *words and phrases to*
maintain a smooth sentence flow, and to establish clear thought relation-
ships between adjacent ideas. What are some of the transitional phrases the
author makes use of?

British Columbia is many things in many forms among its mountains by the
Pacific. In terms of land and population it could be said that it is still a
frontier province. The total area of the province is about three hundred
and fifty thousand square miles, the total population about one and a
quarter million people;[1] and nearly two thirds of the people live in and
around Vancouver on the southwest corner of the mainland or in and
around Victoria on the southeast corner of Vancouver Island. The rural
population of the province averages less than one person to the square mile.

Against this, it is important to remember that nearly three quarters of the
province is three thousand feet above sea level or higher, and only three
per cent of the total land area is under crops or potentially arable. Another
six or eight per cent is either open or forest range land. Some forty per cent
is rated as productive forest land and more than half of every dollar produced in the province comes from the forests. Settlement is concentrated
in the cities and along the valleys, but men must go out to the forested hills,
to the sea and to the mines, if wealth is to be produced. Only a few can live
on and from the land.

[1]According to the 1966 census the population was 1,873,674. By 1968 the population was said to have passed the two-million mark.

This is not a frontier in the sense that the great plains were a frontier of vast, usable but unused land spaces open to everyone. It is a frontier that now opens only slowly, to heavy modern machinery and great expenditures of capital. Yet even this frontier has been largely opened in British Columbia. The grazing lands have been taken up. Vast areas of forest land are privately owned or privately held under some form of government control. Provincial governments still offer the control of great land areas as inducement to large investors, as they did in the days of the railroad charters. It is unlikely that the heavy postwar investments in pulpmills, for instance, would have been made without such inducements.

For these reasons, in spite of seemingly great open land spaces, British Columbia is no longer a frontier province in the old sense of one that offers an opportunity for the ordinary individual who has little or no capital. There are still homesteads to be taken up, especially in the Peace River country; a small operator can still find his way into logging and work up to bigger things; a man can still invest his money in a fish boat and go out and make a living. But these things are neither so simple, nor so promising, nor so exciting as they once were. It is far easier and safer to make a living by working for someone else.

This sets a limit, even though not a close one, on a dream that has brought so many men and women west: the dream of independence. With the dream limited, the people who come to the province and the people who grow up in it are likely to be different, and they are likely to guard less closely a second dream, that the land belongs to everyone, that everyone has a claim and a share in its yield.

So far this claim has not been lost in British Columbia, only reduced; and only, I hope, temporarily reduced. It is a right to use of the land, and the water, for recreational purposes: for hunting, fishing, skiing, swimming, climbing, camping, riding, walking or any form of peaceful enjoyment. It means above all right of free and unhindered access to the woods and the mountains, to lakes, streams and salt water. It fits perfectly well with the basic philosophy of land tenure within the province. The logger holds his land for one purpose, timber; the miner holds his for minerals, the farmer holds land for crops, the cattleman for the grazing and growth of his beasts. The land produces many other crops at the same time: fish, fur and wild-life, space and scenery, wind and rain, fresh air and freedom. It is a part of western living to use these things, a part of western character to value them and grow on them.

It is true that freedom to use the land for these purposes must not work to the detriment of the priority crop, the timber, minerals, grain or cattle. In fact, it seldom does and never needs to; but the alienation of great blocks of land for special purposes, especially in forest management licences, has tended to work against the right of access. Cities and industries have worked against it by polluting streams and beaches. Almost every aspect of modern life tends to curtail it. So far British Columbians have shown enough of the pioneer spirit to fight for this freedom and the province is still a great outdoor country; its spaces still have meaning for everyone who lives in it and everyone who comes to it.

Like most Canadians and most North Americans, British Columbians take themselves much too seriously. We cannot relax and enjoy, we must always be getting and doing. We become serious and tiresome even in boasting about our province, though none of us has had much to do with making what we boast of. The best things were here, or just happened. And the best things, even the most characteristic things, are different, I suppose, for every one of us. When I think of British Columbia I think of such things as waiting in the rain for a ferry, any one of a dozen or a score of ferries. I think of the powerful, pitchy, sapwood smell of fresh-cut Douglas fir timber, of the silvery bodies of fresh-caught salmon lifted in the brail from the purse to the hold of a boat, of the open hills of the Douglas Ranch and little lakes among them, of golden tamarack among the dark green of the Kootenay hills.

I think also of Vancouver's Georgia Street hung with centennial decorations, of walking up the shallow steps of the Parliament Buildings, of little churches like Father Pat's at Windermere, the stone church at Duncan and the one beside the Chemainus River along the old Island Highway. I think of the patterns of Cariboo fences, of the stony Chilcotin, of mountains always in sight. I remember the hoot of blue grouse through the hills and the drum of ruffed grouse on the flats in spring, the cry of the wavey goose in the fall and the bob of sea brant in April whitecaps along the beaches. I feel the gloom of midwinter rainforest in rain, hear the squeal of dry snow underfoot at forty below in the northern interior, feel the blast of a summer day's heat in the Thompson valley. I look for the bloom of fruit trees in the Okanagan Valley and the blaze of azaleas in city gardens, the leap of a Kamloops trout against a still lake surface, the plunge of a steelhead in the white water of a river. I remember narrow canyons and steep rock bluffs and endless trails.

The list could go on forever, in shifting and repeated patterns. It could be changed to cover shining, rainbeaten city streets, the flare of neon signs, crowded parks on sunny days, Saturday night dance halls, holiday traffic jammed from Blaine and Chilliwack clear down to Granville and Georgia. It could include the Howay-Reid Room at the University library, the Emily Carr Room at the Vancouver Art Gallery, the Cavalier Room at the Georgia Hotel, a group of young lawyers called to the bar in the Court House or young internes hurrying to work at St. Paul's or Shaughnessy or

Vancouver General. It should certainly include girls in summer dresses on all the city streets and Indian babies playing on wharves and floats where the fish boats tie up. But it doesn't really matter what goes into the list. It means only that there is no single key to the province, no simple evocation of its quality. For evidence of this, read only the writings of Earle Birney and Roy Daniells, of Bruce Hutchison and Ethel Wilson; look at the paintings of Emily Carr, Lawren Harris, Jack Shadbolt, B. C. Binning, John Korner, the Bobaks.

I could say of the people of British Columbia that they are friendly, hospitable, unassuming, and uncritical. I might equally well say that they are hostile, withdrawn, and intolerant. I could say that we are industrious, serious, and determined: or lazy, pleasure-loving, and irresponsible. The truth is that we are just people and, like people anywhere, a splendid mixture of virtues and vices, moods, nationalities, influences and characteristics. Perhaps it begins to mean something that nearly three quarters of us were born in Canada. Perhaps, in spite of the mountains and the balmy breath of the Pacific, we are Canadians and part of Canada.

---

10. Laurentian Shield

F. R. SCOTT

Until his retirement in 1964, F. R. Scott was Dean of Law at McGill University. In addition to his writing on legal and political themes, Mr. Scott has produced a considerable amount of poetry. Often his poems are satirical in tone, although the one by which he is represented here is lyrical rather than satirical. He was born in Quebec City and now lives in Montreal.

The Laurentian or Canadian Shield is the largest physiographic region in Canada, covering about forty-seven per cent of the total land mass of the country. To make his point about this as yet undeveloped land, Mr. Scott has used a unifying metaphor that runs, with several variations, throughout the poem. This metaphor is introduced by the word "silence" in line 2, and is sustained by such words as "repeating", "language", "syllables", and "cry".

Hidden in wonder and snow, or sudden with summer,
This land stares at the sun in a huge silence
Endlessly repeating something we cannot hear.
Inarticulate, arctic,
Not written on by history, empty as paper,
It leans away from the world with songs in its lakes
Older than love, and lost in the miles.

This waiting is wanting.
It will choose its language
When it has chosen its technic,
A tongue to shape the vowels of its productivity.

A language of flesh and of roses.

Now there are pre-words,
Cabin syllables,
Nouns of settlement
Slowly forming, with steel syntax,
The long sentence of its exploitation.

The first cry was the hunter, hungry for fur,
And the digger for gold, nomad, no-man, a particle;
Then the bold commands of monopoly, big with machines,
Carving its kingdoms out of the public wealth;
And now the drone of the plane, scouting the ice,
Fills all the emptiness with neighbourhood
And links our future over the vanished pole.

But a deeper note is sounding, heard in the mines,
The scattered camps and the mills, a language of life,
And what will be written in the full culture of occupation
Will come, presently, tomorrow,
From millions whose hands can turn this rock into children.

11. The Canadian Eskimo

DIAMOND JENNESS

Diamond Jenness is one of Canada's leading anthropologists. He was born in 1886 and gained much of his knowledge of Eskimo culture as a member of a Canadian expedition to the Arctic between the years 1913 and 1918. The essay included here was originally presented as a talk over the CBC radio network. Later it was published in a book entitled The Unbelievable Land *(1964), a collection of radio talks by a number of specialists on life in the Canadian north.*

Diamond Jenness's essay provides an example of what can be described as "Basic Essay Structure". This is the type of structure that consists of a relevant introduction, a central idea that is stated early in the essay (in this case it is stated as a series of questions in paragraph 3), an appropriately full development of the central idea (covering several paragraphs), and a relevant conclusion in the final paragraph.

Fifty or sixty centuries ago, about the time when a few wise men in the eastern Mediterranean were inventing the art of writing to preserve the memory of things past, and the inhabitants of Egypt began to immortalize their illustrious dead by raising above them those majestic pyramids that draw so many tourists to the Nile today, in a far distant corner of the world a tiny fragment of the human race – the Eskimos – wandered along the shores and over the barren wastes of Canada's Arctic, seeking a peaceful home where they could live their allotted span and unobtrusively pass on the torch of life to their children.

The world forgetting, by the world forgot – as the poet says – they clung to that remote region through 4,000 and perhaps even 6,000 years, despite the harshness of the climate, the darkness and the cold of the long, blizzardy winters, and the ever-present danger of death from freezing or starvation. No other race, white, yellow or black, has ever wrestled with the polar region as they did and survived. No other people has ever settled there for more than a few days or weeks without constant assistance and support from the milder and richer world to the south.

How was it, we wonder, that only the Eskimos succeeded in overcoming the arctic environment? What advantages did they possess over other races? What qualities, physical or mental, that other people lacked? Had nature perhaps endowed them with certain peculiar traits that helped them in their struggle?

With some qualities, we know, nature did not endow them, although she bestowed them on other living things that dwell in the Arctic. She did not shield them from the bitter cold by depositing an abnormally thick layer of fat under their skins, as she did on the seals and the polar bears. She did not protect their bodies with a dense warm coat of hair or fur such as she wraps around the caribou and the fox. The Eskimo does, or did, wear a coat of fur, but it was an ersatz one that he stole from those animals, and from the seal and the bear. He himself is more hairless than a white man, and seldom grows even a thin beard to protect – or endanger – his chin. He cannot store up fat and hibernate like the bear and the marmot, much as a few natives today might wish to. The majority really prefer the winter season to the summer, for grown-ups as well as children love to romp in the snow.

It is true the Eskimos are a little different from other people, even though they are sometimes mistaken for Chinese. The long arms of a Negro reach to his knees, and occasionally lower. A white man's rarely touch his knees, and an Eskimo's extend only about half-way down his thigh. His hands and feet, too, are smaller than ours, as you quickly discover if you try to put on his gloves or sealskin slippers. Is this because in a very cold climate it is easier for the heart to pump warm blood into short limbs than into long ones? Then again, the nose cavities through which an Eskimo breathes are smaller than the cavities in other races. Is that to protect his lungs from freezing when the wind is howling, and the thermometer registers fifty degrees below zero fahrenheit? We feel as perplexed as a traveller in Africa who asked his guide, "Does the giraffe strip the leaves from tall trees because his neck is so long? Or has his neck become phenomenally long from the habit of stripping tall trees?"

I am unable to answer these troublesome questions. I do know, however, that although the Eskimo's hands and feet will freeze almost as quickly as my own, he is a tougher individual than I am and will struggle on without a moan. I know, too, that he has an unusually sensitive funny-bone, and will plod doggedly along a seemingly endless trail until he drops from sheer exhaustion, provided I keep tickling that funny-bone with remarks that he finds amusing. He is a loyal and cheerful companion on a hard journey, and if his eyes should slant a little more than mine, if his cheek-bones show up more prominently, why should I care? The companion I need is a man who will march steadily beside me when the going is rough and a blizzard is lashing our faces. And the Eskimo is just such a man.

It has taken more than toughness, however, and a lusty sense of humour, to win a livelihood and raise up families in the Arctic, generation after generation, without any help from the outside world. It has required great adaptability and inventiveness to cope with the strange and exceedingly difficult environment, where no trees grow because the ground is forever frozen below the top few inches; where berries seldom ripen on the rare bushes because the summer is too short; where all birds except three species, one of them the useless raven, flee the region for eight months of every year; and where the sea hides nearly as many animals as roam the land. How could man feed and clothe his family in such an environment? What sort of house could he build that would shelter them during the long, dark nights of winter? How could he heat his house? How illuminate it during the weeks, in some places months, when the sun does not rise above the horizon?

We know from travellers' descriptions how the Eskimos contrived to do all these things. Some of us have seen them with our own eyes. I have stalked the wild caribou with Eskimos who were armed only with bows and arrows: I have watched them practise those clever tricks to which every primitive hunter must resort if his family is not to die of starvation. In northern Alaska I have helped Eskimos build small cabins from driftwood which the Mackenzie River carries down to the Arctic Ocean, and to insulate those crude dwellings with clods of earth; and farther east, where driftwood is lacking, I have learned from them to erect a dome-shaped house of snow – the igloo – which melts away under the rays of the spring sun, and even in mid-winter drips water on your head if too many warm-blooded visitors crowd into your home. In my own snow-hut I could fry bacon, and boil rice and oatmeal, over a kerosene-burning primus stove; but the only food many of my Eskimo friends had ever tasted was the meat of the caribou, the seal and other wild game that they killed, and the fish they caught in the lakes and in the sea. Sometimes, through lack of fuel, they ate their food raw, but generally they cooked it in stone pots heated by stone lamps that burned the animal's fat or blubber. A trained economist would have observed how they practised in their kitchen the same division of labour as we do. It was the men who manufactured the pots and the lamps, but only the women knew how to use them – or so at least they claimed. A ten-year-old girl could trim a lamp to perfection, but any man who dared to disturb its wick invariably smoked up the whole dwelling.

As in the kitchen, so too in the art of tailoring, women displayed a marked superiority over men – as, of course, they do in every civilized society. Of all the world's people outside Europe and part of Asia, only the inventive Eskimos ever made separate coats and trousers tailored to fit their wearers. The ten-year-old girl who had learned to keep the lamp smokeless, and to preserve all the flavour of caribou tongues by boiling them with the tips upward, could cut out and stitch a perfectly fitting suit of caribou fur artistically adorned with inset patterns; but the man who attempted to make or to mend his own clothes looked like a hobo. We need not wonder, then, that before the white man entered the Arctic, no one ever heard of an Eskimo youth or an Eskimo maid reaching the age of eighteen unmarried. Each needed the other. Might we not bring about this same happy condition in southern Canada if we sternly abolished all men tailors and all men cooks?

In many other ways the Eskimos have revealed more than usual adaptability and ingenuity. It was from them that we Europeans learned to speed over the frozen sea with dog sleds and to capture great whales and walruses with hand-harpoons. The light fold-boats, in which some of our holiday seekers explore the inland waters of Europe and a few of our North American rivers, are but imperfect copies of the Eskimo's *kayak*, the skin-covered boat from which he harpooned the seals in the ocean, and speared the caribou as they swam the rivers and the lakes during their spring and autumn migrations.

Nevertheless, for arctic living the Eskimos needed more than short limbs and narrow noses, adaptability and resourcefulness. Their stern environment, where throughout nearly half the year cold and darkness confined them for sixteen and eighteen hours each day to one-roomed dwellings, which every neighbour entered at will, and into which every stranger or chance visitor squeezed for shelter and rest; an environment whose innumerable dangers, seen and unforeseen, limited their average span of life to only twenty years, forcing them to cling to one another for safety, to share every hardship of fishing and the chase, and to hold all food in common; that environment imposed upon them a deep social consciousness, strong social bonds which man elsewhere has generally worn very loosely, but which the ants, the bees, cattle and many other forms of life hold inescapably tight. The Eskimos had to abrogate all privacy; to submerge, yet at the same time to preserve, their separate individualities; and to acquire an endurance of each other's company, and a tolerance of each other's idiosyncracies, far beyond the capacity of most Europeans.

We of old world descent, who through our superior knowledge of nature's forces have long held the rest of the world at our mercy – we incline to be mavericks, weaker than other peoples in the social consciousness that holds human communities together. But now that this atomic age, with its fantastic powers of destruction, links together all mankind in a common fate, we must either develop a more profound sense of our obligations towards our fellow-men than even the Eskimos possessed, or prepare to follow the dinosaur and the mammoth into total oblivion.

II. Canadian Characters of Several Kinds

It has been said so often that Canadians are a dull people that most Canadians are now willing to believe it. But like so many generalizations about national character, this one is open to debate. It has never been proved that *all* Welshmen can sing, that *all* Irishmen have nasty tempers, or that *all* Canadians are dull. This myth of the colourless Canadian can be seriously questioned by anyone who reads widely in Canadian biography or autobiography. For here he will find any number of eccentric or exceptional characters, ranging from such humble men as Rufus Kimpton, the respectable storekeeper who stole a church, to Bobby Hull who each year makes a fortune playing Canada's national game for an American team. The first three of the eight narratives assembled here are selections from autobiographies, suggesting perhaps that Canadians aren't even as modest as they are said to be. These three autobiographers have in common the fact that each was blessed with the gift of self-laughter, and each has made a singularly Canadian contribution to the art form in which he worked: the comic sketch for Stephen Leacock, landscape painting for A. Y. Jackson, and radio broadcasting for Max Ferguson. Among the other five selections in this gallery of Canadian characters, the reader will find some stories that are true, some that are fictitious, and some that are probably a mixture of both. But whatever they are, they challenge the myth of Canadian dullness.

12. The Autobiography of Stephen Leacock

STEPHEN LEACOCK

Stephen Leacock (1869-1944) is one of the few Canadian writers with an international reputation. This fragment of "autobiography" was written as a preface for his third and best-known book, Sunshine Sketches of a Little Town, *published in 1912. (A longer, though never completed, autobiography,* The Boy I Left Behind Me, *was published posthumously in 1946.) Stephen Leacock wrote over fifty books. Most of them were comic entertainments, but several were serious works on economics, political science, and history, subjects that Leacock taught at McGill University.*

The analysis of humour is always a potentially unrewarding activity since the operation might kill the patient. But it is worth noting that Leacock gets a good part of his comic effect through his use of the unexpected word, as, for example, when he writes of "the policemen, postmen, street-car conductors and other salaried officials of the neighbourhood". And it may also be worth noting that the Leacock brand of humour is not without a somewhat abrasive and bitter edge.

I know no way in which a writer may more fittingly introduce his work to the public than by giving a brief account of who and what he is. By this means some of the blame for what he has done is very properly shifted to the extenuating circumstances of his life.

I was born at Swanmoor, Hants, England, on December 30, 1869. I am not aware that there was any particular conjunction of the planets at the time, but should think it extremely likely. My parents migrated to Canada in 1876, and I decided to go with them. My father took up a farm near Lake Simcoe, in Ontario. This was during the hard times of Canadian farming, and my father was just able by great diligence to pay the hired men and, in years of plenty, to raise enough grain to have seed for the next year's crop without buying any. By this process my brothers and I were inevitably driven off the land, and have become professors, business men, and engineers, instead of being able to grow up as farm labourers. Yet I saw enough of farming to speak exuberantly in political addresses of the joy of early rising and the deep sleep, both of body and intellect, that is induced by honest manual toil.

I was educated at Upper Canada College, Toronto, of which I was head boy in 1887. From there I went to the University of Toronto, where I graduated in 1891. At the University I spent my entire time in the acquisition of languages, living, dead, and half-dead, and knew nothing of the outside world. In this diligent pursuit of words I spent about sixteen hours of each day. Very soon after graduation I had forgotten the languages, and found myself intellectually bankrupt. In other words I was what is called a distinguished graduate, and, as such, I took to school teaching as the only trade I could find that needed neither experience nor intellect. I spent my time from 1891 to 1899 on the staff of Upper Canada College, an experience which has left me with a profound sympathy for the many gifted and brilliant men who are compelled to spend their lives in the most dreary, the most thankless, and the worst paid profession in the world. I have noted that of my pupils, those who seemed the laziest and the least enamoured of books are now rising to eminence at the bar, in business, and in public life; the really promising boys who took all the prizes are now able with difficulty to earn the wages of a clerk in a summer hotel or a deck hand on a canal boat.

In 1899 I gave up school teaching in disgust, borrowed enough money to live upon for a few months, and went to the University of Chicago to study economics and political science. I was soon appointed to a Fellowship in political economy, and by means of this and some temporary employment by McGill University, I survived until I took the degree of Doctor of Philosophy in 1903. The meaning of this degree is that the recipient of instruction is examined for the last time in his life, and is pronounced completely full. After this, no new ideas can be imparted to him.

From this time, and since my marriage, which had occurred at this period, I have belonged to the staff of McGill University, first as lecturer in Political Science, and later as head of the department of Economics and Political Science. As this position is one of the prizes of my profession, I am able to regard myself as singularly fortunate. The emolument is so high as to place me distinctly above the policemen, postmen, street-car conductors, and other salaried officials of the neighbourhood, while I am able to mix with the poorer of the business men of the city on terms of something like equality. In point of leisure, I enjoy more in the four corners of a single year than a business man knows in his whole life. I thus have what the business man can never enjoy, an ability to think, and, what is still better, to stop thinking altogether for months at a time.

I have written a number of things in connection with my college life – a book on Political Science, and many essays, magazine articles, and so on. I belong to the Political Science Association of America, to the Royal Colonial Institute, and to the Church of England. These things, surely, are a proof of respectability. I have had some small connection with politics and public life. A few years ago I went all round the British Empire delivering addresses on Imperial organization. When I state that these lectures were followed almost immediately by the Union of South Africa, the Banana Riots in Trinidad, and the Turco-Italian war, I think the reader can form some idea of their importance. In Canada I belong to the Conservative party, but as yet I have failed entirely in Canadian politics, never having received a contract to build a bridge, or make a wharf, nor to construct even the smallest section of the Transcontinental Railway. This, however, is a form of national ingratitude to which one becomes accustomed in this Dominion.

Apart from my college work, I have written two books, one called "Literary Lapses" and the other "Nonsense Novels." Each of these is published by Dodd, Mead & Company, New York (and in London by John Lane, The Bodley Head, Ltd.), and either of them can be obtained, absurd though it sounds, for the mere sum of one dollar and fifty cents. Any reader of this preface, for example, ridiculous though it appears, could walk into a bookstore and buy both of these books for three dollars. Yet these works are of so humorous a character that for many years it was found impossible to print them. The compositors fell back from their task suffocated with laughter and gasping for air. Nothing but the invention of the linotype machine – or rather, of the kind of men who operate it – made it possible to print these books. Even now people have to be very careful in circulating them, and the books should never be put into the hands of persons not in robust health.

Many of my friends are under the impression that I write these humorous nothings in idle moments when the wearied brain is unable to perform the serious labours of the economist. My own experience is exactly the other way. The writing of solid, instructive stuff fortified by facts and figures is easy enough. There is no trouble in writing a scientific treatise on the folklore of Central China, or a statistical enquiry into the declining population of Prince Edward Island. But to write something out of one's own mind, worth reading for its own sake, is an arduous contrivance only to be achieved in fortunate moments, few and far between. Personally, I would sooner have written "Alice in Wonderland" than the whole Encyclopedia Britannica.

In regard to the present work I must disclaim at once all intention of trying to do anything so ridiculously easy as writing about a real place and real people. Mariposa is not a real town. On the contrary, it is about seventy or eighty of them. You may find them all the way from Lake Superior to the sea, with the same square streets and the same maple trees and the same churches and hotels, and everywhere the sunshine of the land of hope.

Similarly, the Reverend Mr. Drone is not one person, but about eight or ten. To make him I clapped the gaiters of one ecclesiastic round the legs of another, added the sermons of a third and the character of a fourth, and so let him start on his way in the book to pick up such individual attributes as he might find for himself. Mullins and Bagshaw and Judge Pepperleigh and the rest are, it is true, personal friends of mine. But I have known them in such a variety of forms, with such alterations of tall and short, dark and fair, that, individually, I should have much ado to know them. Mr. Pupkin is found whenever a Canadian bank opens a branch in a country town and needs a teller. As for Mr. Smith, with his two hundred and eighty pounds, his hoarse voice, his loud check suit, his diamonds, the roughness of his address and the goodness of his heart – all of this is known by everybody to be a necessary and universal adjunct of the hotel business.

The inspiration of the book – a land of hope and sunshine where little towns spread their square streets and their trim maple trees beside placid lakes almost within echo of the primeval forest – is large enough. If it fails in its portrayal of the scenes and the country that it depicts the fault lies rather with an art that is deficient than in an affection that is wanting.

13. Landscape Painters

A. Y. JACKSON

The Group of Seven, which was Canada's most original force in art during the 1920s, has been written about widely and often ponderously. However there is nothing ponderous about A. Y. Jackson's reminiscences of the Group of Seven's first ventures into new geographic and artistic territory. In this excerpt from A Painter's Country *(A. Y. Jackson's autobiography, published in 1958), five of the original members of the group are mentioned: Jackson himself, Lawren Harris, J. E. H. MacDonald, Frank Johnston, and Arthur Lismer. The two not mentioned are Frank Carmichael and Frederick Varley. The events described took place in 1919.*

Canada's most famous landscape painter writes prose in a headlong and vigorous style that can best be described as "discursive". It moves rapidly from one event to the next without going into any considerable detail.

I had little desire to paint, but it was good to get back to Georgian Bay again that summer, to paddle and swim, to go fishing and exploring. Then, in the autumn, Harris arranged a sketching party in Algoma and had a box car fitted up with bunks and a stove to accommodate us. In addition to a canoe, we had a three-wheel jigger, worked by hand, to go up and down the tracks.

There were few trains on the Algoma Central Railway at that time. The railroad runs north for two hundred miles from Sault Ste Marie to Hearst on the C.N.R., crossing the C.P.R. at Franz. It passes through country heavily wooded with birch and maple, poplar, spruce and white pine, a country of big hills that drop down steeply to Lake Superior. The rivers cut through the hills and fall down in a series of rapids and waterfalls to the lake. In October it is a blaze of colour. The box car became a studio, and the party consisted of Harris, MacDonald, Frank Johnston and myself. Our car was hitched to the passenger train or the way freight. When we reached a place where we wished to paint it was left on a siding where the only inhabitants were the section men.

I always think of Algoma as MacDonald's country. He was a quiet, un-adventurous person, who could not swim, or paddle, or swing an axe, or find his way in the bush. He was awed and thrilled by the landscape of Algoma and he got the feel of it in his painting. He loved the big panorama; "Solemn Land", "Mist Fantasy", "Gleams on the Hills" were some of the titles of his paintings.

The nights were frosty, but in the box car, with the fire in the stove, we were snug and warm. Discussions and arguments would last until late in the night, ranging from Plato to Picasso, to Madame Blavatsky and Mary Baker Eddy. Harris, a Baptist who later became a theosophist, and Mac-Donald, a Presbyterian who was interested in Christian Science, inspired many of the arguments. Outside, the aurora played antics in the sky, and the murmur of the rapids or a distant waterfall blended with the silence of the night. Every few days we would have our box car moved to another siding.

Since this country was on the height of land, there were dozens of lakes, many of them not on the map. For identification purposes we gave them names. The bright sparkling lakes we named after people we admired like Thomson and MacCallum; to the swampy ones, all messed up with moose tracks, we gave the names of the critics who disparaged us. It was during this trip that MacDonald made studies for "October Shower Gleam" and I got the sketch that I later painted into a large canvas, "October, Algoma"; both paintings were acquired by Hart House, University of Toronto.

The following year we rented a cottage in the same district, at Mongoose Lake. We asked a trapper how such a name got up there. He didn't know;

all he knew was that a mongoose was a kind of a bird!

The Algoma country was too opulent for Harris; he wanted something bare and stark, so at the conclusion of one of our sketching trips he and I went to the north shore of Lake Superior, a country much of which had been burnt over years before. New growth was slowly appearing. The C.P.R. main line follows the north shore of Lake Superior from Heron Bay westward to Port Arthur. I know of no more impressive scenery in Canada for the landscape painter. There is a sublime order to it, the long curves of the beaches, the sweeping ranges of hills, and headlands that push out into the lake. Inland there are intimate little lakes, stretches of muskeg, outcrops of rock; there is little soil for agriculture. In the autumn the whole country glows with colour; the huckleberry and the pincherry turn crimson, the mountain ash is loaded with red berries, the poplar and the birch turn yellow and the tamarac greenish gold.

There were few places to stay in this country, so we took with us a tent and camping equipment. We chose our camp sites with great care, always near water, protected from wind, and on ground that sloped away from the tent. In poor painting weather we built a big stone fireplace where we could sit and gossip until it was time to turn in. Whisky jacks soon found our camp, and came to it to pick up food; they would even swoop down and fly off with a slice of bread or bacon. A weasel came to the tent once and tried to steal our eggs; he refused to move and we had to push him out. We had no stove in the tent, so we dug a trench between our sleeping bags, which we filled up with hot embers from the fire. Then we would close up the tent and turn in comfortably even on cold nights.

When we camped near a sand beach we went in swimming although the water was very cold. Harris, who liked to have a system for everything, worked out one for bathing in cold water. We would start off far up on the beach, then run at the lake, waving our arms and yelling like wild Indians. This procedure was supposed to distract our attention from the cold water.

It was a strenuous life. Harris was up before daylight, making a lot of noise with pots and pans as he got breakfast. The rain would be pattering on the tent when Harris would call, "Come on, get up."

"What's the use of getting up," I would growl. "It's raining."

"It is clearing in the west," was Harris' invariable reply.

So I would get up, breakfast, and we would go off in the rain. Three days later when it stopped raining, Harris would say, "I told you it was clearing."

One of Harris' fads was for Roman Meal. He claimed it made us impervious to wet and cold, and we had a large bowl of it each morning. At a later date we got a folding stove for these expeditions; it was practical, it kept the tent dry and warm, but we couldn't see a glimmer of light from it. Harris dubbed it the gloom box.

Then the approach of winter sent us back to Toronto. The newspapers had been busy with our paintings in our absence, and had a great many unpleasant things to say about us and our work. One of them, commenting on Harris' painting, said that if it was allowed to continue it would discourage immigration to Canada.

The year I made my first trip to the Arctic, Lismer went with Harris to Lake Superior. It rained continuously. Harris carried a large sketching umbrella, and he kept on working while Lismer sulked in the tent. He had thrown his pack-sack in a corner; as he looked at it with half-closed eyes, it began to assume the form of a big island lying off the mainland; the straps became a ridge of rock in the foreground and the light coming through the folds of the tent became an intriguing sky. When Harris returned there was a sketch in Lismer's box.

"Gosh, Arthur," said Harris, "where did you get that? It's a beauty, the best thing you've done."

There is a large canvas of Harris', entitled "North Shore, Lake Superior", which won the gold medal at an exhibition in Baltimore; it shows a big pine stump right in the centre of the canvas and Lake Superior shimmering in the background. Among the members of the Group it was known as "The Grand Trunk". I was with him when he found the stump, which was almost lost in the bush; from its position we could not see Lake Superior at all. Harris isolated the trunk and created a nobler background for it.

14. The Birth of Rawhide

MAX FERGUSON

The 1967 winner of the Leacock Medal for Humour was Max Ferguson. And Now . . . Here's Max, the autobiography for which he won the award, was Mr. Ferguson's first book, although for twenty years prior to its publication he had been one of Canada's best-known humorists. Max Ferguson's usual medium is radio where, for many years in the guise of "Old Rawhide" and recently under his own name, he has been a one-man producer of satirical sketches that make fun of most things Canadian. In addition to his considerable skill in comic invention, Mr. Ferguson is a versatile mimic, creating not only the voices of his many imaginary characters, but imitating as well a wide range of public personages. The following account of how Old Rawhide came into being is from And Now . . . Here's Max.

This selection provides an especially good example of the use of literary and historical allusions. The reader who does not understand what is implied by the reference to Quasimodo, the phoenix, Devil's Island, Dreyfus and Zola will miss not only the humour, but also the point of what the author is saying.

It was somewhere in the dying weeks of December, 1946, that Old Rawhide was born and rose, more like a Quasimodo than a Phoenix, from the ashes of the old year. As the newest addition to the announcer staff of CBC Halifax, I took my turn at all the various assignments in the normal program day – newscaster, host of record shows, farm broadcast announcer, wet nurse to women commentators and, of course, surf and gull man on Harmony Harbour.[1] At the end of my second week, I reported for duty on a Saturday morning, checked my schedule of duties and found to my horror that they included a half hour of cowboy records called *After Breakfast Breakdown*. With the exception of a very few legitimate songs which were actually sung by cowboys and have come down to us from the old frontier days of the American west, I loathe the entire field of Tin Pan Alley hokum loosely termed "cowboy music". Moreover, at twenty-one I was a good bit more impressionable than I am now and being a fully fledged CBC announcer was to me, at least in those days, only a rank or two below beatification. I had already blabbed all over Halifax to any who would listen the long list of vital and indispensable duties with which I had been entrusted by the CBC. What on earth would these people think now if they should hear me feigning an enthusiastic introduction to some guitar-twanging drugstore cowboy singing, "I Rapped On the Hearse Window, Granny, But You Did Not Look Out", or something of similar inspiration.

With a desperation born of despair and with just twenty seconds to air time, I hit on the idea of disguising my voice by dropping the register, thrusting out my jaw, and clamping my back teeth together. As I pushed down the microphone switch, out came the words, "Howdy! Welcome to *After Breakfast Breakdown*," in a low, aged, hard, flat, sloppily sibilant voice that surprised even myself. "This is your old pal Rawhide," I continued, pulling the name out of the air on the spur of the moment, although I'd heard it used once or twice in my life to denote a type of tough, un-tanned leather. I then proceeded for the next half hour to introduce each cowboy record in the most insulting fashion I could devise, popping in at

---

[1]Announcers were assigned the duty of controlling the appropriate sound effects for this program of song and narrative about Maritime seafarers. Mr. Ferguson describes his misadventures with this duty in an earlier chapter.

the close of each song to thank the artist and bid him farewell as he "mosied off down the canyon, headin' tall in the saddle into the flaming sunset, whose glare would no doubt prevent him from seeing in time that 400-foot sheer drop into the chasm below waiting to claim him for that great Studio in the Sky . . . and not a moment too soon."

The names of the various cowboy singers were all strange to my ears (as were the voices) and so, when I cued up the second last record that morning and noticed that the performer was billed as the Yodelling Ranger, I didn't think it would be too indiscreet to good-naturedly change this in my introduction to the Yodelling Idiot. The record finished, and I thanked him, sending him on his way to the Great Studio in the Sky via the 400-foot chasm I'd so felicitously invented. Suddenly the studio door opened slightly, and there was Syd Kennedy's panic-stricken face mouthing some message which, though I couldn't decipher it, nevertheless seemed quite urgent. The thought crossed my mind as I was trying to lip-read Syd and at the same time verbally despatch the Yodelling Idiot that perhaps the studios were on fire. I quickly sent the Yodelling Idiot over the cliff, released the last record of the program without any introduction, and cut my microphone.

At last I was able to ask Syd what the problem was. He took two full minutes to babble out his message, but when I'd mentally pruned all the extraneous and profane prefixes and suffixes it was reduced to a rather concise skeletal form – "The Yodelling Ranger is not only a local Halifax boy but also the most popular idol in the Maritimes." Syd further advised that, to avoid being lynched the moment I stepped out onto Sackville Street, I should hastily make the most abject apology I could think of. There wasn't much program time left, so I faded down the record that was playing, opened my microphone, and said, still in the Rawhide voice, "I just made a very unfortunate mistake in calling that previous singer the Yodelling Idiot. I certainly didn't mean to be disparaging and was obviously confusing him with *another* Yodelling Idiot I once knew in Upper Canada. This is the Canadian Broadcasting Corporation."

Kennedy showed great restraint, waiting till the very last word of the corporation cue was finished and the microphone cut before he clasped both hands to his head, emitted an anguished groan, and vanished from the studio. His fears were quite unfounded. It must have been my juxtaposition of the words "idiot" and "Upper Canada" which appeased the aficionados of the cowboy idiom in Halifax. At any rate the apology was accepted as a complete and penitent catharsis, and I was to reach my little rented room that day without being set upon by an unruly mob.

The chief danger to my well-being was to come a few days later from a different and totally unexpected source, S. R. Kennedy. I was called into his office at the beginning of the following week to face what I presumed would be nothing more than a mild lecture on the importance of being kind to local cowboy singers. However, it turned out that Syd had completely forgotten my faux pas in the excitement of a brilliant idea he'd conceived over the weekend and which was now beginning to spring fully formed, mirabile dictu, from his mouth. "I like the idea of using that old guy's voice. Starting next Monday, we're scheduling a half hour of cowboy music, six mornings a week, to the Maritime network with you as host doing the old guy's voice!"

I can remember, once my speech returned, trying to reason with Syd. I was being quite serious when I offered to do extra announce shifts and even give the CBC one night a week janitorial service if he'd only abandon this insane idea. But it was like asking a mother to abandon her first-born, and though I continued to plead and protest, Syd merely sat, smiling smugly like a balding Mona Lisa, gazing out through his office window at his favourite landmark, the red funnels of the old *Aquitania* thrusting up from the harbour. The following Monday I reluctantly launched the first program in a series that was to run for seventeen consecutive years.

Whereas most broadcasters strive either to entertain or inform, my motivation during those early weeks of incarceration on the Devil's Island to which Kennedy had sent me was considerably more selfish. It was simply to make that half hour of cowboy music each morning pass as quickly and painlessly as possible. Not knowing or caring who might be listening and strictly for my own amusement, I brought into the studio with me each morning a little sound-effects door. Between cowboy records I would open and close this door to signal the arrival of mythical characters and, one by one, I would people my little cell with quite an assortment of warped figments of my imagination to keep me company.

There was Granny, her sweet little eggshell voice giving no indication of the thoroughly rotten, corrupt, and malicious personality which lurked behind it. There was Marvin Mellobell, a sickeningly irritating embodiment of all the adenoids, pomposity, and self-adulation that the world of show-biz had to offer. Then there was my favourite, the unnamed pest and constant thorn in Marvin Mellobell's flesh, whose wild, semi-literate speech poured out in the raucous voice of Doug Trowell's old Scott C. Mulsion. He was a sort of Rousseau's natural man carried to the extreme, unfettered by even the thinnest veneer of social decorum. What he lacked in polish and mentality he made up for in enthusiasm and in his time played all the major roles in the Rawhide Little Theatre Company. From Tarzan of the Apes to the brooding Prince of Denmark, they all rolled out with the same raw gusto and paucity of dramatic insight.

There were also the Goomer Brothers, rural entrepreneurs who operated an illicit hard-cider operation in the Gaspereau district of Nova Scotia's lovely Annapolis Valley. They hated the RCMP and were constantly and angrily campaigning on the program to get the CBC to include, along with road and weather reports, Mountie Reports designed to keep the little man in their particular field posted on the latest whereabouts of the federal law. They also purveyed as a sideline 155 over-proof eggs derived from a flock of semi-stoned White Leghorns which they fed on fermenting apple mash. Their steady customers included world-famous personalities who unwittingly bit into the free trial samples which the Goomer Brothers mailed out all over the world and became hopelessly hooked. The only sample egg ever to be returned unopened was the one they sent Princess Margaret Rose, and she was immediately lumped in with the RCMP as their favourite objects of scorn and dislike.

Rawhide often feigned horror at some of the things all these characters came out with, but secretly he, and certainly his creator, welcomed these morning visits and prolonged them, knowing full well they were eating up valuable time which otherwise would have to be devoted to the cowboy records. Although these little interludes with character voices served as welcome and selfishly devised breaks in the monotony, I never for a moment lost sight of my main objective in those early weeks. I continued to wait patiently for the opportunity to get myself taken off the air.

It was a good six weeks before the golden moment arrived in the form of a nasty letter from some lady in New Brunswick who was taking violent umbrage at what she alleged was my blatant partiality toward Wilf Carter and the shameful neglect of Hank Snow. These men were the two top favourites in the Maritimes in the field of cowboy music. Like a mother striving to avoid sibling rivalry, I meticulously played one record of each singer every single morning, except on one occasion while possibly wool-gathering, when I allowed a second Wilf Carter aria to slip in at the expense of Hank Snow. It was this occasion to which she was referring in her letter. I read the letter through to myself twice, scarcely able to believe, from the strength of the language, that it had been penned by one of the weaker sex. However, for what I had in mind she'd do nicely. Dreyfus had found his Zola.

The very next morning, instead of opening with the usual camaraderie, I asked the operator in the control room to play a particularly heartrending version of *Hearts and Flowers*. Then I came in over this as Rawhide, with much sniffling and noseblowing, to say in a shaken voice, "In the short time I've been living in these parts, I've come to look upon Marimtiders as a friendly, warm-hearted bunch, and it saddens my old heart this morning to realize there's one among you who is trying to cut my throat behind my back." I then read the letter verbatim (omitting only the pungent parts) and ended with the writer's name, street address, and home town. Then I went on, "You realize, of course, Mrs. ———————, of ——————— Street in ———————, New Brunswick, that I would be quite within my rights to say something nasty to you in return. But somehow, deep down inside, I'm . . . well . . . I'm just not built that way. Instead, I'm merely going to turn the other cheek and ask you, in the spirit of true Christian friendship to (here I paused for dramatic effect) . . . *drop dead!*"

The expression in those days was just coming into vogue and had not yet lost its freshness and shock value through later overuse. It must have sounded particularly fresh when boomed over a 50,000-watt transmitter to a CBC customer who at the time was no doubt paying her $2.50 licence fee to help keep the likes of me on the air. There was no doubt in my mind that she would be justifiably outraged and would contact her local MP in Ottawa who, in turn, would contact the Minister of Transport. Next in the chain of command would be A. Davidson Dunton, then chairman of the CBC Board of Governors, who would call W. E. S. Briggs, who would take me off the program. Like the old lady's cow, I'd be over the stile and home free. Two days later my house of cards collapsed when the woman wrote me again to say, "Well, Rawhide, old pal, you sure gave it to me over the air the other day and by golly I asked for it. No hard feelings."

Along about this time the Rawhide program had begun to bring in a rather steady flow of mail from all over the Atlantic provinces. From these letters I began to realize that there was an encouraging percentage of the audience who were listening for the skits I was doing and not the cowboy records. My morale picked up. Earlier, the mail had consisted almost entirely of requests for cowboy songs, usually of the more morbid variety. One lady, writing with soft pencil in a most laborious and semi-legible hand, had requested *We Shall Gather By the River* sung by the Carter Family, "in memory of my daughter that was drowned there six years ago."

The mail each day would invariably bring several parcels, sometimes chocolates or home-made cookies, but most often sturdy knitted mittens or tuques from Newfoundland. Among the many pairs of heavy-duty white wool socks that were knitted and sent in by ladies in Newfoundland was one pair which came in with the instruction, "Wear these over your shoes to save the leather." On my CBC salary of nineteen hundred dollars a year I can assure you that none of these gifts was sneezed at.

15. Bell, Book, and Scandal

ALEC SHAW

This narrative by a little-known author tells of events that took place about 1899 in the East Kootenay district of British Columbia. It was first published in the British Columbia Centennial Anthology *in 1958.*

The effectiveness of Mr. Shaw's story is due primarily to the mock-heroic style in which it is written. Through the conscious use of elevated language ("merits its small but permanent footnote in the robust annals of pioneer days"), and hyperbolic statement ("a theft the like of which has not been known, before or since, on the entire North American continent"), Mr. Shaw has given to the events of "Bell, Book, and Scandal" a comic quality that a straightforward narration of the events would not have possessed.

If the name of Rufus Kimpton merits its small but permanent footnote in the robust annals of British Columbia's pioneer days, it is not merely for singular devotion to his wife, but because of the remarkable manner in which he expressed it. True, in frontier communities like the town of Donald at the turn of the century, esteem for a wife, even one's own, was not unusual; scarcity added value to woman's natural charms. But even by the standards of those heroic days the unique deed performed by Rufus Kimpton to please his lady ranks among the prodigies of a Paul Bunyan.

Yet Rufus Kimpton was not a man from whom his fellow-citizens could have expected such a feat. In 1899 he was forty years old, a time of life not ordinarily associated with romance or daring. Moreover, he was of only average height, plump and bald – although a hint of suppressed bravado might have been betrayed by his flowing blond moustache. He owned the general store and a small hotel at Donald and had other interests at Windermere – and prospering merchants are not usually inclined to recklessness. He was an exemplary father, a warden of St. Peter's Anglican Church, and altogether one of those dependable citizens dedicated to prosperity and respectability who are the very sinews of an orderly society.

Yet this model burgher, this paragon of husbands and fathers, committed a theft the like of which has not been known, before or since, on the entire North American continent. It was no commonplace bank-looting, or train robbery, or theft of gems, motivated by greed or the hope of gain. Such are the vulgar deeds and sordid motives of little souls, of the petty desperadoes of the Old West whose names are legion. Rufus Kimpton was cast in a larger mould.

His inspiration was his wife, a woman of estimable character and virtue, and the object of his malfeasance had to be worthy of the object of his affections. Therefore – he stole a church. An entire church: building, altar and pews, books and Bible and the 600-pound bell in its belfry. By wagon, train, and barge, he carried them through a hundred and fifteen miles of wilderness and assembled his loot into a church again. And all this was a labour of love, so that in the village of Windermere, to which they had moved, his wife might continue to worship in her old familiar surroundings.

A shrewd observer of human foibles once declared, "Society prepares the crime; the criminal performs it." Certainly Rufus Kimpton's brilliant coup would have been impossible if the stage had not been properly prepared. In the 'nineties Donald, nestling in the foothills of the Selkirk Range in Eastern British Columbia, was the mountain divisional headquarters of the Canadian Pacific Railway. It was a small but lively community, and consisted almost entirely of railroad-workers and their families and the business and professional men who catered to them.

Situated among its homes and stores, and modestly dominating the railroad shops, the school, and the Odd Fellows' Hall, was St. Peter's Anglican Church – an ample wooden structure of simple architecture, and already distinguished in many ways before Rufus Kimpton lifted it, so to speak, to greater fame.

It was the first church of any denomination in a vast wilderness, the creation of that famous Anglican missionary, the Rev. Henry Irwin, known affectionately throughout the Kootenays as "Father Pat." Its great bell of exceptional tone had been sent from England by the Baroness Burdett-Coutts, and its handsomely bound Bible was a gift from the venerable Theological College of Litchfield. When a Bishop journeyed to Donald from distant New Westminster to consecrate this edifice in 1889, it was rumoured that the good Anglicans in the larger town of Revelstoke shed bitter tears of envy, for they had to worship in a school-house.

As the warp is to the woof, so became St. Peter's Church to the lives of Rufus and Celina Kimpton. In it they knew many of their most joyous and most poignant moments. Here they were married and their two sons christened, and from it their first-born was buried. Rufus served it as warden, and never was there a social, or a party to raise funds, or a service, that did not find Celina foremost among the workers in this vineyard of the Lord.

Then came a fateful day in 1897 when the Canadian Pacific announced that Revelstoke, sixty miles to the west, was to be the railway's new divisional headquarters and that Donald must be abandoned. The company obligingly offered to move the homes and household goods of all railway employees to Revelstoke, together with any other buildings they might want. Eventually even the large Odd Fellows' Hall was knocked down, carried to Revelstoke, and re-erected there.

By this time Revelstoke had built an Anglican church of its own, but when its energetic vicar, Dean Paget, heard that Donald was about to become a parish without parishioners, he wrote to the Synod requesting the Donald church, to be added as a chancel to his own. In due time the Synod replied, granting the abandoned church to the Anglicans of Revelstoke, provided they went to Donald and fetched it. But when Dean Paget's crew of voluntary workers arrived at the deserted village, the gilded Celtic cross above the gabled belfry no longer dominated the landscape. The stone foundation supported only a large and empty space. The church had vanished. It had, in fact, been stolen.

Meanwhile, Mr. and Mrs. Kimpton had not accompanied their fellow-townsmen to Revelstoke. Instead, they had decided to move to Windermere, where Rufus had other interests. Sadly they had watched the demolition of the town about them, the disappearance of house after house, the departure of old, familiar faces – until the church was almost the only remaining mark of Donald's brief day.

Together they went to pay one last visit to this shrine before leaving for their new home. Amid surroundings that evoked many tender memories, Celina Kimpton burst into tears. The thought of abandoning the church to emptiness and neglect seemed unendurable; the prospect of a good life away from it seemed impossible. What place would ever be home without it?

History fails to record the exact words spoken on this memorable occasion. Perhaps the devoted Rufus, like many another strong man, could not endure the sight of feminine tears and gallantly exclaimed, "Weep not, Celina! You shall have your church – even if I have to steal it for you."

Or perhaps it was she, seeing that her tears had softened his manly heart, who put her hand in his and cajolingly whispered, "Rufus, dear – can't we take it with us?"

Nor does this last seem unlikely, for we have the word of their son, Vaughan Kimpton, himself a venerable and respected citizen of Windermere: "Father stole it, but Mother was the moving spirit."

Would this be the first time that an Eve had been not only the rib but the backbone of a man?

Now working with great haste, as though either the Devil or Dean were in his mind, Rufus Kimpton dismantled the church and moved it by rail to Golden, where it was transferred to barges and towed a hundred miles up the Columbia to Windermere. There it was erected again on a site prepared for it. The happy Celina not only had her church, but now it was on property adjoining her very home.

Rufus had indeed been as good as his word. Almost, but not quite. When the church was reconstructed, something was found missing: the large, silver-toned bell! It was quickly located, it is true, but – of all places – in the belfry of the Anglican church at Golden! While it had awaited barge transportation at Golden, the good churchmen of that community, no doubt inspired by Kimpton's example, had stolen the bell for themselves.

Rufus did not accept this larceny with equanimity. Perhaps his old mercantile prejudice against petty pilfering momentarily assailed him; or he may have been loath to think that he had led his brethren into temptation, and wished now to deliver them from evil. In any case, he offered to take upon his own broad shoulders the burden of their guilt, and wrote demanding the return of the bell.

To this the Anglicans of Golden replied that since Windermere's possession of the whole church was illegal, it had no rightful claim to its bell. And now Dean Paget, supported by the Synod, entered the fray from Revelstoke, accusing them both of wrong-doing and demanding both church and bell. Sharp exchanges between the churches soon involved all three communities. Editorials, both lay and clerical, fanned the flames of recrimination. After all, if a church and a church bell could be stolen, then what was safe?

For five years the controversy raged, and if most of the Synod's letters to Rufus Kimpton went unanswered, no doubt it was only because Kimpton now had the government contract to carry the mail to Windermere, and simply refrained from delivering letters to himself.

Finally Dean Paget, with a wisdom born of weariness, built his own chancel for the church at Revelstoke and renounced all claim to the church stolen from Donald. In turn the Windermere congregation, with Kimpton's charitable assent, renounced claim to the stolen bell in Golden. The Synod bestowed forgiveness on all and sent a Bishop to reconsecrate the stolen church. Once again Christian harmony ruled the three towns.

St. Peter's still serves the parish of Windermere. And there the church stands today, a monument to the iniquity of Rufus Kimpton, who had the moral courage to silence his conscience, and the strength of character to overcome the good habits of a lifetime, and by his one bold gesture this frontier merchant achieved the stature of a hero, and the village innkeeper became a legend.

16. Country Justice

PAUL ST. PIERRE

Paul St. Pierre's novel, Breaking Smith's Quarter Horse, *has its setting in British Columbia's Cariboo country. The novel's central event, the trial for murder of Gabriel Jimmyboy, is mentioned only incidentally in this excerpt, which describes the setting in which the trial takes place. Prior to his election to Parliament in 1968, Paul St. Pierre was a columnist with the* Vancouver Sun. Breaking Smith's Quarter Horse *was published in 1967.*

This novel fragment provides an illustration of the ironic tone. *Which statements in the selection mean something quite different from what they at first might appear to mean?*

The Williams Lake courthouse, two storeys high and square as the cross, was built in the 1920s when the Cariboo had experienced a sudden rush of blood to the head caused by a powerful feeling of prosperity. It may be that it was built ahead of its time. In those years there were not many laws. However, the few they had, the people broke; it was felt that the structure was indeed justified. Of course, the times were good. In those years it was believed that the stock market, beef prices, wages, debts and government hand-outs could increase to infinity without let or hindrance. The money supply was endless, the proof being that the population was increasing every year. It was shortly to be arranged that everybody should become healthy and wise, and there was never going to be another severe winter. Odd, the way people thought in those days.

The Williams Lake courthouse compared to Vancouver's much as is suggested by the politicians' joke about the Pacific Great Eastern Railway – not as long as the CPR, but just as wide. There were no stone lions on the Williams Lake courthouse steps. Even the steps were of wood. A sign at the door said WIPE YOUR BOOTS OFF. The colour of the Williams Lake courthouse was not grime grey, like Vancouver's, but grime mustard. The paint for it had been chosen by a decorator then recently come from the mustard-plaster district of Bavaria, specifically München, home of mad King Ludwig, who apparently favoured that shade. Such is the proof of the power of artistic impulse, spanning continents and oceans to link Bavaria with the Cariboo.

Within the clapboard walls of the Williams Lake courthouse were repeated in form if not in substance most of the features of the big city's justice dispensary. In the big city the floors were of red tile, here they were grey battleship linoleum. Vancouver courthouse had corridors. Williams Lake had hallways. Both buildings contained many offices full of lead-faced civil servants, but at Williams Lake these were people in their sixties instead of in their forties.

The courtroom was also considerably smaller than any one of Vancouver's, though just as just, of course. In Williams Lake the jurymen sat on bar chairs beside the windows that face on Oliver Street and they had been known to rise from these chairs to watch something interesting on the street outside, even though the court might be in session at such a time. There were three doors. One was for the judge, one for lawyers and officials, policemen and prisoners, and the third for spectators. Spectators were separated from the main scene of action by a low railing. There was a small witness box, another small prisoner's box, a table and the Bench.

The Williams Lake courthouse has other features than clapboards and paint from mad King Ludwig. It has also many small offices, old desks, dust and rats big as badgers.

(On consideration, it must be said that there are a lot of damn lies in the above. The courthouse is pretty much Mid-Thirties CPR Railway Station Architecture. Also, the Cariboo Assizes are not held in Williams Lake. Some years ago, when the Assizes were being held in unfortunate conjunction with the annual stampede, a Supreme Court justice of B.C. said to his sheriff, "Mr. Sheriff, I think your jury is drunk," to which the sheriff replied, "I am God-damned sure they're drunk. We lock them up in their hotel room every night but their friends are sorry for them because they're locked up during stampede and they pass them bottles down from the roof, on ropes." Shortly after this the Assizes were transferred seventy miles up the highway to Quesnel, a town of notable sobriety.)

At the moment this building contained several characters of note. The judge was one. He was a mixed man. He had been a politician who had become a political liability, fit only for minor diplomatic posting abroad or for the Senate. At the time that his exclusion from the political apparatus became necessary, neither of these areas of the national life had any vacancies. It was finally decided that he should be elevated to the Bench, the decision being made by a typical political hierarchy, composed of a high-society White Anglo-Saxon Protestant who had been cashiered from the militia for stealing from the mess fund, another less noticeable man who had married well, a loan shark and two faceless young men who wore Homburg hats.

This judge proceeded to astonish and dismay his peers by exhibiting a native inflexibility, an occasional stupidity and an infuriating mixture of compassion, brilliance and exotic flashes of emotion that make a man simply impossible. Even those confident of their own unshakable righteousness came to be fearful of the day when they might be thrust in front of him. He had been, at this time, a County Court judge in Kootenay for thirty years and, by some miscalculation of the Justice Department, a justice of the Supreme Court of British Columbia for five. This was his first Assizes in the Cariboo.

He had been born a devout Christian of Baptist and something like Quaker origins and had some years previously turned agnostic – well known to be the worst kind. However, he had told no one of his conversion, not even his wife, with whom he went each Sunday that he was in Vancouver to the First Baptist Church of Kerrisdale. In that, as in other things, he was outwardly a man of the highest probity. He drank nothing stronger than table wine, raised dachshunds, and read at least one hundred and fifty new books every year. He slept with his window open and exhausted much of his salary with secret charities to the bafflement of his family and his investment counsellors.

Even when not in the scarlet robes of the Supreme Court there was something forbidding in his dress. He wore suits that were dark, with vests, and black boots with calfskin uppers, which he shined himself each morning down in his basement beside the coal stoker of his old furnace. His face was plank-like, crossed by rimless glasses and shaven to the quick.

To see him upon the bench was to be reminded of a chiffonier, made in the full flowering of the Victorian age. It was easy to believe that he also had ball-and-claw feet.

Behind the doors of this chiffonier there lay in the aromatic dust all sorts of impulses: to whoredom and tyranny and the cold adamantine luxury of pride; to warmth and the scent of lilac and the sweet words of poets, to God and to things too dark to be mentioned. He was, in short, very much like other men, but more prominent.

In the British House of Lords, or as a judge in Texas, he might have given free play to his eccentricities and by that means have adopted the protective colouration of normality. In the Canadian courts, which did not look kindly upon human impulse, he found it necessary to draw around him the cloak of that austere tradition of dignity. It had preserved many such a judge before him, and would probably serve for his lifetime.

About the only thing that broke through, as a rule, was his passion for nicotine. Sometimes when a case drew long he would reach inside the wide scarlet front of his robe, extract a cigar from a pocket, break off the end, place that end in his mouth with a movement like that of a man covering a yawn, and then chew it. He would chew it, slowly, and then swallow. Swallow all of it.

The Crown Counsel was a man of great ability. He was then about fifty or fifty-five and adorned with a Toronto Conservative moustache, a crisp new gown and an old purple Q.C.'s bag, which he dragged about after him in ostentatious carelessness, as if laying track for hounds. He was the owner of a colonial-style home set in forty acres of expensively watered lawn outside Quesnel. He had three race horses and a three-point-eight Jag and a wife who could still dye her hair pink and avoid censure. For his work, he drove a three-year-old Ford, standard. Ranchers mistrusted affluence, and he had many of their accounts. It was popularly though incorrectly believed that he had inherited three ranch estates from clients.

His first Assizes had been a joy. He knew the publicity value for a clever man, and he knew himself to be clever. Such was his success from that beginning that he continued to accept the chore of Crown Counsel once every three years. He abandoned more lucrative practice for this work at these intervals but did it, out of a sense of gratitude, or duty, or possibly superstition. Whether turning out a chess set on his basement lathe, or prosecuting a grubby rape case, he liked to do a thing well and he did not spare effort nor count his cost nor his profit in doing so.

He was somewhat irritated about the case immediately preceding Gabriel Jimmyboy's. It had been the most intriguing one of these Assizes, far more so than Gabriel's. A cowboy of the huge Burned Lake Ranch had been found lying in the sagebrush beside the Little Fort trail. He had been shot, strangled and beaten, but was still alive and continued so. Three of his fellow cowboys from the Burned Lake Ranch had been charged with attempting his murder.

Their defence had been simple. Their unfortunate friend, they all said, had had too much to drink. This made him remorseful. While all four men were driving home in the pickup truck on the Little Fort road, their friend had pulled the deer gun off the back of the seat and tried to kill himself, narrowly missing his brains.

Quickly sensing that all was not well, the four cowboys had got out of the truck and the three unshot ones had attempted to give first aid to the wounded man. He resisted them. They had to choke him and hit him a few times with a rock to make him relax sufficiently to receive first aid treatment. Having determined that he wasn't very badly hurt after all, they had all driven away in the pickup to seek more medical aid, leaving their companion resting in the sagebrush.

Somewhat to the surprise of the Crown, the victim corroborated all this. He had been drinking, he said, at the time, but the explanation sounded reasonable to him. The other cowboys were all his friends, he said, and he wished that the police would not get mixed up in things like this.

Acquittal had been prompt.

17. Percy Williams
at the Olympics

RAY GARDNER

This Canadian version of the David and Goliath story took place in Amsterdam at the 1928 Olympic Games. Ray Gardner, a Toronto writer and editor, wrote his lucid and dramatic account of the Percy Williams story for the November 24, 1956, issue of Maclean's *Magazine. (This selection is the second half of Mr. Gardner's longer article.) When Percy Williams achieved what was probably the most startling upset in the history of the Olympics, he was a slightly-built, completely unknown ex-high-school runner from Vancouver. Even present-day readers should have no trouble seeing why Percy Williams's victory over the bigger men he ran against served as a kind of national symbol for Canadians in 1928.*

Mr. Gardner's narration reproduces in its own structure the series of climaxes and anti-climaxes that constituted Percy Williams's athletic career. The selection also offers a particularly good example of an effective ending, in this case the use of an apt quotation to produce an anti-climax.

On Sunday, July 29, Percy Williams began his dash to glory. Eighty-seven sprinters were entered in the hundred metres. The overwhelming favorite was Frank Wykoff, an eighteen-year-old Californian schoolboy who four times had tied the Olympic record and had beaten Paddock[1] in a race billed as "the sprint of the century." Should Wykoff fail, there was Bob McAllister, the Flying Bowery Cop, and Claude Bracey, pride of Rice University. These three were specializing in the hundred-metre while other U.S. runners were saved for the two-hundred-metre.

Percy Williams won his first heat easily, in 11 seconds, but was forced to run his fastest race of the Games, 10.6 seconds, to win his second heat and enter the semifinals. His diary entry showed extreme modesty:

> July 29 – My ideals of the Olympic Games are all shot. I always imagined it was a game of heroes. Well, I'm in the semifinals myself so it can't be so hot.

[1]C. W. Paddock of the United States was the winner of the 100 metres at the 1920 Olympics.

At 2 p.m. on Monday, July 30, Bob Granger suffered a moment of supreme anguish when, for a split second, Williams was caught on his haunches at the start of the hundred-metre semifinal. He recovered brilliantly to finish four inches behind McAllister who had to equal the Olympic record to win. Second place qualified Williams for the final.

There were now two hours to kill before the final. Granger took Williams to the dressing room and gave him a book to read. As race time neared, Percy warmed up, and then Granger rubbed him down with the last precious piece of the cocoa butter he had brought from Canada.

"Keep calm, it's only another Sunday school race," he told the boy.

When they lined up for the hundred-metre final the young Canadian was dwarfed by the brawny Bob McAllister and Jack London, a two-hundred-pound British Negro. Frank Wykoff, George Lammers, of Germany, and Wilfred Legg, of South Africa, completed the field.

Thousands of Germans in the stands gave a mighty cheer for Lammers. The Canadians began to chant, "Williams, Canada! Williams, Canada!" and some of the crowd, perhaps taken by his size, joined in.

There were two false starts – first Legg broke, then Wykoff. Each time the crowd surged to its feet, then subsided again. The third start was perfect. Williams shot away with the gun, the rest on his heels. With thirty metres to go, Williams was still in front. Then London made a valiant effort to catch him, but missed by a yard. Lammers was third. Wykoff fourth, Legg fifth and McAllister sixth and last.

The stadium was in a riot. Granger, who later described the race as "ten seconds of breathless living," wept. P. J. Mulqueen, the Canadian Olympic chairman, rushed on the field and kissed the winner.

> July 30 – Well, well, well. So I'm supposed to be the World's 100 M Champion. (Crushed apples.) No more fun in running now.

Now began two days of grueling running in the two hundred metres. The favorite was the flaxen-haired California Comet, Charles Borah, who had won the United States trials in 21.6 seconds, equaling the Olympic record. To back him up, the United States had the veteran Paddock and Jackson V. Scholz, who had won the two hundred metres in the 1924 Games in the record time of 21.6. Germany had a strong contender in Helmut Koernig, an almost flawless runner.

Williams wasn't conceded a chance against these fresh, more experienced and, on the record, faster runners. His best time, 22 seconds, was two-fifths of a second off their pace. What no one could know was that Granger's tactics and Williams' "gear shift" – a unique ability to change running styles while in full flight – would single out Borah and Koernig, one at a time, and kill them off.

The secret of Williams' success – as Paddock, after Granger, was the first to perceive – was this ability to switch styles while running. Williams would take off with a driving start and keep driving until he had reached his maximum speed. Then he would shift into an easy, flowing style, a sort of overdrive. Near the finish, as his speed diminished, he would drive again, hitting the tape at top speed. "It was," Williams explains today, "like pedaling a bike downhill. There was no use trying to go faster, it would break my stride to try." (In 1929 Dr. Charles Best, of the University of Toronto, famous as co-discoverer with Sir Frederick Banting of insulin, conducted experiments on Williams. He found that in a seventy-yard dash the runner reached his maximum speed of 23.3 miles per hour at forty-five to fifty yards. This was the result of Williams' great driving start.)

On Tuesday, July 31, Williams romped through his first heat of the two hundred metres and was resting in his dressing room when Harry Warren burst in with the news that, by luck of the draw, Borah, Koernig and Williams, with three others, were drawn to run in the next heat.

"I can still remember my horror," says Warren. "It meant that one of these three great runners was to be eliminated even before the semifinals. Only the first two would qualify."

Granger gave Williams his instructions. "Don't try to win," he said. "Run to beat whoever is running second, Borah or Koernig." Then, to make the boy perspire without exertion, he smothered him under a pile of a dozen coats and blankets.

Koernig, the pride of Germany, flashed out in front from the start of the race, with Borah on his trail. At the halfway mark Williams was running third, four yards behind Borah. It was then that Williams, already traveling at top speed, tried to drive himself faster too soon. Momentarily he faltered, almost breaking his stride, and dropped farther behind. With sixty metres to go it appeared impossible for him to catch Borah. Now he shifted gears again – and this time moved smoothly into his drive, flashing past Borah in the last two yards. Driven by Borah and Williams, Koernig had equaled the Olympic mark of 21.6 in winning.

> July 31 – Miracles still happen. I'm in the semifinals. Eliminated Borah. One of the nicest fellows I have ever met. Ran two heats today. First one was easy. 2nd one against Borah and German champ.

Granger, who had watched every race in agony, was now beside himself. He spent the night in the corridor outside Williams' room. At intervals he slipped notes under the door to Williams' room-mate, Harry Warren. Percy had a habit of pulling the covers over his face as he slept – Warren was to pull them down. "He must have oxygen!" Granger wrote. In another note he asked, "Is he breathing easily?"

The afternoon of Wednesday, August 1, Williams won his semifinal race easily, with Paddock fourth. Only two years before Percy had shown his mother a picture of Paddock displayed in a Vancouver gas station and had told her, "There is the world's fastest human."

Now only one race stood between Percy Williams and a double Olympic championship. When they lined up for the final of the two hundred metres, Williams faced Koernig and Jacob Schuller, of Germany; John Fitzpatrick, a Canadian from Hamilton; Jackson Scholz, of the United States, the 1924 champion; and Walter Rangeley, of Great Britain.

Even before Amsterdam, Granger knew almost all there was to know about all the internationally known sprinters. Now, at Amsterdam, he had studied them in the flesh until, as Williams remarks today, "He even knew who their grandfathers were."

"Koernig is your man to beat," he told Williams. "He is a front runner – an inspirational runner – and if you come out of the curve even with him, or just ahead of him, you will kill his inspiration and win."

This strategy, and Williams' ability to carry it out, was to beat Koernig, who could actually run the distance faster than Percy could.

As they came out of the curve, Koernig and Williams were in the lead, running neck and neck. They ran that way until the last fifty metres. The crowd came to its feet as the Canadian ran on even terms with the great German. Thousands of Koernig's countrymen urged him on. Then Williams shifted gears, out of his flowing stride and into a blinding driving finish. For an instant the amazed Koernig seemed to hesitate. The skinny kid from Canada flashed by him and won by a yard over Rangeley, the Briton, who had come up fast to place second. Koernig finished third, in a dead heat with Scholz.

The crowd broke loose in the wildest demonstration that ever followed an Olympic victory. Granger, who had mentally run every stride with Williams, was limp. In his excitement, he had clenched his hands on a barbed-wire barrier and they were drenched with blood.

At the Holland Hotel, the cables arrived in a deluge – from Prime Minister Mackenzie King, from almost every Canadian provincial premier and most mayors. There were offers for Williams to run in New York, Berlin, Stockholm, Britain and Australia. Reporters surrounded him. "It doesn't feel any different being Olympic champion," he told them. "My lucky coin in the race was a good start." Then he had a supper of salad and mineral water and went to bed.

When Peerless Percy – as the papers called him – came home in September, he was met by his mother in Quebec and together they traveled across the land in triumph, their arrival in each city the headline news of the day. In Quebec Mayor Oscar Auger gave Percy a gold watch and said, "We want to prove that we are Canadians." Montreal's Mayor Camillien Houde told him, "You're a great kid, Percy. I say to you, stay Canadian." Hamilton gave him a golden key to the city. In Toronto thousands cheered Percy and his mother at the CNE. At Winnipeg, the CPR station was packed with people, and it was Percy Williams Day at the Polo Park race-track. At Calgary he had only a fifteen-minute stop but hundreds came to the depot to get just a glimpse of the champion.

In Vancouver, the streets for blocks around the CPR station were a solid mass of people that morning of September 14 when Percy and his mother finally reached home. Granger had traveled on ahead and was there to meet them. The moment Percy stepped off the train, the sun broke through dark rain clouds. ("Providence was kind," the Vancouver Sun observed.) A schoolboy band struck up See The Conquering Hero Comes.

Two thousand schoolchildren marched ahead of the big touring car that carried Percy, Bob Granger, Mayor Louis Taylor and Premier S. F. Tolmie past cheering crowds to Stanley Park. There twenty thousand gathered to see Percy presented with a car and Granger with a purse of five hundred dollars in gold. Premier Tolmie said, "Oh, what a homecoming! Never has there been such joy and pride."

For the next three years Canada watched and marveled as the World's Fastest Human kept on running and winning. A few scoffers, mostly U.S. sports writers, said he had been favored by the soft, slow track built on Amsterdam's marshlands. In February of 1929 he invaded the hard, fast, indoor tracks of the United States and took New York, Boston, Philadelphia, Newark and Detroit by storm as he reeled off a series of truly phenomenal victories over outstanding runners, most of whom specialized in indoor running. He set a new world's record of forty-five yards (4.9 seconds) and equaled three other world's records. In Detroit he beat Eddie Tolan, the famous Midnight Express, in a forty-yard dash – and thereby began one of running's most intense rivalries.

Twenty thousand people jammed Vancouver's Hastings Park on July 13, 1929, to see Williams win over Tolan by two inches in the hundred yards. A year later, in the same setting, ten thousand spectators groaned as he ran third to Tolan in the hundred metres. On August 9, 1930, in Toronto, Williams ran his fastest race, setting a new world's record of 10.3 seconds for the hundred metres. This time it was a genuine Charlie Paddock record, set in 1921, he had broken. His Toronto mark was half a second faster than his winning time at Amsterdam, and would have been good enough to win in any of the four Olympics held since 1928. In three Olympics since Amsterdam, the winning time has been 10.3, and in the fourth it was 10.4 seconds.

Now a classic duel between Williams and Tolan was anticipated for the

1932 Olympic Games, to be held in Los Angeles. But Percy had run his last really great race. The beginning of the end came on August 23, 1930, in the hundred-yard final of the first British Empire Games, at Hamilton. The day was cold and, after they had taken off their warm training suits, the finalists were kept standing in their flimsy track suits for almost ten minutes. It was the very situation Granger had always feared. Williams was flying almost certainly to a new world's record when, with thirty-five yards to go, he pulled a muscle in his left thigh. In agony, he kept running, staggering out of his lane at the tape. He won in the remarkable time of 9.9 seconds – and then crumpled to the track. His leg was never right again.

The end came – as fame had come – at the Olympic Games. He went to Los Angeles without Granger (they had quarreled over a petty matter) and certain he had only two good races left in him. He ran third in two hundred-metre heats and then, in the semifinal, ran fourth and out to Eddie Tolan. Tolan went on to become a double champion.

The late Lou Marsh, of the Toronto Star, wrote from Los Angeles, "Williams went down fighting gallantly, but the legs were gone."

After that Williams stepped deliberately out of the limelight and devoted himself to business and to golf.

Bob Granger also took his second shot at an Olympic double, in 1936 at Berlin. Again he placed his hopes in a twenty-year-old Vancouver boy, Howie McPhee, to win the hundred and two hundred metres. But Howie, a fast runner at other times, didn't last to the semifinals in either event.

Since then, little has been heard of Granger. Williams has lost touch with him and so have Granger's own brothers and sisters. He did bob up at the 1954 Empire Games in Vancouver – to tell the press they'd never see the likes of Percy Williams again – and then dropped from sight once more. For a while, after Amsterdam, Granger sold insurance, including a big annuity to boxer Jimmy McLarnin, but then moved on from job to job, taking them as they came. His family believes he may be working in a logging camp somewhere on Vancouver Island, but are not sure. He never married.

Today, at forty-eight, Percy Williams is a successful insurance agent with a passionate interest in golf, virtually none in track and field, and with so faded a memory of 1928 he could scarcely live in the past if he wanted to. He still looks younger than his years, as he did at Amsterdam. Long ago, in 1943, he drew out the last $3,000 of his trust fund.

A bachelor, he shares an apartment in Vancouver's west end with his mother, who still thrills to the memory of the day her son became the World's Fastest Human. Now and then Percy's day of glory is recalled – the last time when Vancouver began to build a stadium for the 1954 Empire Games and there was a campaign to have it named after him. Percy did turn the first sod but the name decided on was Empire Stadium. He didn't attend the Games but watched the Miracle Mile on television at his golf club.

Looking back over the years, Percy tries to remember how he reacted to sudden fame. "I was just like any kid of twenty," he says. "I was simply bewildered by it all. I didn't like running. Oh, I was so glad to get out of it all."

18. Success Story

EDITORS OF "TIME"

The cover story of Time *magazine for March 1, 1968, dealt with hockey super-star Bobby Hull of the Chicago Black Hawks. The following selection, which is the last half of the* Time *story, offers a quick biographical sketch of this small-town Ontario boy who is currently the highest-paid player in the National Hockey League.*

The biographical technique employed by Time's *writers is basically anecdotal. By means of a chronological series of selected episodes, the writers have told the story of Hull's life and suggested something about the kind of man he is. A careful examination of the diction employed in this selection, and the type of details that have been stressed, will reveal a good deal about the famous "Timestyle".*

It was, remembers the senior Robert Hull, 57, "a cold son-of-a-gun of a night" in Point Anne, Ont., when the doctor delivered his fifth child (of eleven) and announced: "The only difference between your son and you is that he doesn't eat so much." Bobby weighed 12 lbs. at birth. His father, a 240-lb. cement worker, could lift the front end of a car, and he was also a fair country hockey player – which is what folks do to keep warm in the long Ontario winters.

Situated 100 miles east of Toronto, Point Anne boasts two schools and three churches, but no bars, movie theater or shops. Now that MacDonald's general store has closed down for lack of business, people get their supplies at Belleville, five miles down the road. The population, according to Bobby's sister Judy, 20, is "about 1,000, if you count the dogs. And about 100 if you don't." The only industry is the cement plant. And the only dash of color in the grey landscape – since Bobby left – is a huge red, white and blue billboard that proudly proclaims: POINT ANNE, BIRTHPLACE OF BOBBY HULL, WORLD'S GREATEST HOCKEY PLAYER.

Come Home, Bobby. It was either that or the cement plant. All the Hulls learned to skate before they learned to read. Judy was such a hard-nosed hockey player that the boys around Point Anne once told her parents they wouldn't play with her any more because she was too rough. Dennis, 23, followed his older brother to Chicago, where he also plays left wing for the Black Hawks, and could some day make a name for himself. Bobby got his first pair of skates the Christmas he was four; by day's end, he was maneuvering on his own. "From then on," he recalls, "I went back every day and skated until I was exhausted. I would get up in the morning and put on the porridge pot, then go out to skate until breakfast was ready. I used to skate all morning and afternoon, and only come home for meals. After dinner, I always went out again, and Mum would have to send my sisters out to bring me home to bed."

One thing he remembers about that time was that he was constantly shoveling snow. "I was usually one of the first ones out there for a game of shinny," he says, "and it was up to the first arrivals to clear a skating area." By the time Bobby was eight, recalls Dr. Don Pringle, a childhood friend who now practices medicine in Montreal, "he had muscles rippling all over him," and Papa Hull was already spending hours on the ice, endlessly drilling his son on the technique of stick handling. "He was sometimes impatient," says Bobby, "but he liked to skate with me. 'Let's try it again, Robert,' he would say. 'Keep your head up. If the stick blade is angled properly, the puck will feel right on it.' "

From Bantam to Pro. In Canada, where hockey precocity is commonplace, Bobby Hull was a stick-out from the day he played his first Bantam League game, in Belleville, at the age of ten. There are seven levels of competition in Canada – Peewees, Bantams, Midgets, Juveniles, Junior B's, Junior A's and Professionals; Hull skipped the Peewees, Midgets and Juveniles. Officially. Actually, confides Pringle, who played against him in the Bantams, Bobby freelanced. When the Bantam game ended, he would tighten up his laces and join a Midget team in the next game. After that was over, he would skate back on the ice with the still older Juvenile League players. "He used to play hockey practically all Saturday morning," says Pringle. "Some mornings he'd score 25 goals in four different leagues."

That kind of performance was bound to attract the attention of pro scouts sooner or later. In Bobby's case, it was sooner – lots sooner. He was all of eleven when the Chicago Black Hawks' chief scout, Bob Wilson, saw him and decided to sew him up then and there. A quiet chat with Papa

Hull did it. Without telling Bobby until a year later, his father gave Chicago permission to draft him. In the curiously medieval world of Canadian hockey, Hull from that day on was indentured to the Black Hawks. They gave him three years to mature, and at 14 he was shipped off to Hespeler, Ont., 170 miles from home, to live with a strange family, go to a strange school and play hockey for a Junior B Chicago farm club. All for $5 a week. "I wrote him every day," says his mother, "but I didn't talk much about what was going on in Point Anne because I was afraid of making him homesick." One day Bobby wrote back: "Gee, Mom, keep all those letters coming with nothing in them."

Hull had his problems over the next four years. Chicago moved him from Hespeler to Galt to Woodstock to St. Catharines. He attended four high schools, was briefly expelled from one (for insubordination), and graduated from none. He had an appendectomy, and he had trouble in hockey: Rudy Pilous, Bobby's coach at St. Catharines, accused him of hogging the puck and suspended him for "indifferent play." What happened next comes straight out of Jack Armstrong. One September day in 1957, Hull spent the morning working out on the St. Catharines rink, and played a high-school football game in the afternoon. Back at his boardinghouse, in the middle of dinner, he got a phone call from Chicago scout Wilson. The Black Hawks were playing an exhibition game in St. Catharines that night against the New York Rangers, and Wilson wanted Bobby to suit up. Hanging up the phone, Hull finished his dinner. Then, with a full stomach and a full day of sports under his belt, Bobby went out on the ice and slammed in two goals against the Rangers. His parents were hastily summoned to St. Catharines, and that night, at 18, Bobby Hull became one of the youngest players ever to join the N.H.L.

Slide & Swing. Bobby's first year with the Black Hawks hardly hinted at the coups to come. Unused to the huge, animal-throated N.H.L. crowds, bounced around by older, wiser defensemen, he did not score his first big-league goal until the seventh game of the season, and then it was one that he would just as soon forget. "It was against Boston," recalls Bobby. "Somebody rapped me a good one, and down I went – right on top of the puck. All I did was slide into the net with the puck underneath me." From then on he scored from a more upright position. Black Hawks Coach Rudy Pilous shifted Bobby from center to left wing, where his tremendous left-handed shot could be put to better use, and by the end of the 1959-60 season, at the age of 21, he had his first scoring title, 39 goals, 42 assists, beating out Boston's veteran Bronco Horvath by a single point.

That was the year, too, when Bobby met his figure-skater wife, Joanne. Music, maestro, please. "It was at Christmas time. Joanne was performing in an ice show in Chicago. I showed up at the arena one day for practice, and there she was, swinging on the ice." Married two months later, the Hulls now have three children, all boys, all blond, all boisterous: Bob, 6; Blake, 5; and Brett, 3.

Hull's most vivid recollection of the 1960-61 season is the night Chicago beat Detroit 5-1 and won the Stanley Cup for the first time in 23 years – or, at least, the party afterward. "It was snowing so hard we couldn't get back to Chicago. We guzzled champagne in the locker room and on the bus ride to the airport, where they turned us away and we had to go back to the hotel in Detroit. The last thing I remember I was drinking beer out of somebody's hat and got sick as a dog." Hell-raising was S.O.P. for Hull in those days; on a wild train ride from Boston to Montreal, Bobby and Teammate Ron Murphy broke into a case of railroad flares, lit them and threw them into the other Black Hawks' roomettes. Several frantic hours and $599 worth of damage later, General Manager Tommy Ivan called a team meeting. "All right," demanded Ivan, "who did it?" "I decided somebody better say something," says Bobby, "so I piped up: 'I did, sir.' Ivan just said, 'That's all I wanted to know,' and walked away."

Ivan has long since forgotten that episode. "The incident that sticks most in my mind," he says, "is the '63 Stanley Cup playoffs against Detroit." It sticks in Hull's, too: every time he looks in a mirror he gets a reminder. In the first game against the Red Wings, Bobby scored two goals. In the second, charging the Red Wings' net, he was about to pass off to a teammate when Detroit's Bruce MacGregor spun around suddenly and caught Hull flush on the bridge of the nose with the heel of his stick. "People in the stands later said it sounded like a rifleshot," says Bobby. "It knocked me to my knees, but I was able to make it to the dressing room under my own power. When the doctor finally got there, I was bleeding all over the place. 'Son,' he said, 'I was on duty for the Zale-Graziano fight, but I've never seen a nose like that.' He didn't get through with me until after midnight."

Five days later, after the Red Wings had beaten the Hull-less Hawks in Detroit, Bobby was back on the ice. His nose was packed with medicated gauze, his eyes were swollen almost shut. He still played, and scored a goal, though Chicago lost. "Worse yet," says Bobby, "I got elbowed in the nose, so I had to go back to the doc next day when we returned to Chicago and get my nose set again." He played the next night, and scored another goal, but Detroit won again to take a 3-2 lead in the best-of-seven series. Finally came the sixth game, and with it, one of the most astonishing one-man shows in hockey history. At this point, Bobby turns laconic: "They scored, and I went out and got one. Then they got another, and I got another. And so on. They eventually wore us down and won 7-4." By then, packed nose, blood-filled eyes and all, Hull had assisted on one goal and scored three of his own – for a record-tying total of eight in the series.

Fit for the King. More than any of his other records, more than his skating speed or the velocity of his slap shot or his indifference to the way opponents knee and trip and hook him, that performance in Detroit explains why Hull's peers as well as his public regard him with something approaching awe. Yet respect, even adulation, are intangibles. Hockey has also given Hull the tangible trappings that befit its reigning king. Chicago is paying Bobby $40,000 this season, and if the second-place Black Hawks can overcome the Montreal Canadiens' eight-point lead in the East Division – or better yet, win the Stanley Cup – there will be some fancy bonus money as well. Next year, Hull says, he will demand $100,000, more than twice what any player has ever received before. But it still will not match his outside income. Endorsements (Ford cars and tractors, Jantzen sportswear, Supphose) and manufacturers' royalties (Bobby Hull sticks, pucks, T shirts) will net him at least $50,000 this year, and he has just signed a several-year "six-figure" contract with a Canadian firm to produce a whole new line of Bobby Hull hockey gear.

Plus, of course, the farm. "I'm no city boy," says Hull, "and never could be. As soon as the season is over, I want nothing but my farm." Yes, but which farm? Bobby owns a 150-acre spread near Millbrook, Ont., two more of 100 and 110 acres outside Demorestville, the 330-acre Hullvue Polled Hereford Farms near Picton, and a half interest in the 240-acre Golden Hawk Hereford Ranch near Demorestville. Around those various properties are scattered his 540 head of cattle, including a prize Polled Hereford bull named Hardean Woodrow Masterpiece – one of whose heifers sold at auction last year for $2,500. Hull does not really expect to get that much for any of the 57 head he will put on the block at his annual auction next August; he'll be satisfied if he clears $50,000 for the lot.

There are times when Bobby talks of retiring, of breeding the best Polled Hereford herd in the world. He probably will, some day. But not at 29, not when the winds turn chill, not when the pucks start flying and the artificial ice coats the pipes of arenas around the N.H.L. "Nobody loves hockey more that I do," he says. When the ice freezes, Bobby Hull is that kid from Point Anne, Ont., who got up in the dawn, put on the porridge pot, and skated until he was finally dragged home to bed.

19. Bicultural Angela

HUGH HOOD

Hugh Hood, who was born in 1928, is a professor of English at the University of Montreal. The son of an English father and a French mother, he knows at first hand something of the bicultural problems he describes in this story from his book Around the Mountain, *published in 1967, and sub-titled "Scenes from Montreal Life".*

Unlike the other narratives in this section, "Bicultural Angela" is a formal short story. The plot details have been carefully selected in order to develop the conflict *that lies at the heart of this narrative. But the skilled reader of fiction will realize that Mr. Hood's story has implications that extend beyond the personal difficulties faced by Angela during her Montreal romance.*

Not so long ago, in her mid-teens, growing up in Stoverville seventy miles from the Quebec border, Angela Mary Robinson heard her mother exclaim to a visitor from Montreal, "I do so much want to know what is happening to you people. So exciting, everything one hears about the new Quebec."

Angela had not heard her mother express this view before.

"Is Westmount burning?" said Mrs. Robinson playfully.

The visitor, an elegant bond salesman spending a weekend on somebody's houseboat, raised an eyebrow with a polite air of one who has heard the tune before. "Do you really want to know?" he said.

"I think it is my duty."

"Why not subscribe to *Le Devoir*? They cover the province so fully that they hardly talk about anything else. It would cost you twenty dollars a year, but it's worth much more."

Mrs. Robinson sighed. "Ah, but you see, I don't read a word of French."

Thinking this over afterwards, Angela decided that her mother's words implied several things: hypocrisy, frivolity, obstinate persistence in a dangerous prejudice. She was old enough to spot the tone in her mother's voice which meant that Mrs. Robinson was attempting to please by pretending an interest in an obscure, probably trivial, special subject.

Rejecting Queen's and the Conservatory, Angela went to Trinity College in the University of Toronto and wore pastel sweaters from Holt Renfrew, oatmeal-tweed skirts and a single strand of pearls through freshman and sophomore year. After that, involved with the production of a fugitive film and learning French voraciously, she switched to coarsely knit Italian sweaters in bright reds and yellows fitting loosely around the hips. She discarded skirts for slacks, often rather tight. She had a smart, navy-blue duffle coat. In her last year, she subscribed to the international edition of *Le Monde* and acquired a startling expertise connected with the General Agreement on Tariffs and Trade.

She read the film quarterlies, having been deeply influenced by Marshall McLuhan, and had a vague notion of doing a Master's degree on one of the media. By graduation, Angela Mary knew definitely that the one place to be, in Canada in the mid-sixties, was French Montreal, not Westmount, which she knew well from weekends, nor the McGill campus, but *le vrai Montréal,* as she considered it, of the Bonsecours market, old picturesque restored Montreal. She also had the idea that there was a lot of activity at *l'Office National du Film* and *Radio-Canada,* and she went to a lot of trouble to get herself a job in cBc-Montréal. Not much of a job. She was a trainee program organizer in FM, and hoped that she might have a chance to get into French-language programming if she worked very hard on her spoken French and cultivated obvious French types around the studios.

She took to spending a lot of time in various Montreal cafés and bars. When her duties took her as far south as the main building on Dorchester West, she would spend an hour after the completion of her errand at that little place just west of Mackay where you never knew whom you might run into. She watched the French girls, the way they did their hair, their make-up, and began to experiment with her looks, with metallic green eye-shadow, at first very discreetly applied. She bought some hairpieces and began to tease the acquired hair and her own into extremely bouffant situations. Whether in this she was fully *dans le vent* remains an open question. She discarded slacks for dresses like Petula Clark's with narrow fit and short skirt.

Angela was a very pretty and agreeable young woman and not stupid, and as she made great efforts in these directions she made friends, mostly men friends, in radio at first and later among TV people. She met boys who had film to sell, film by the mile, sometimes hijacked out of ONF stock, sometimes paid for by an indulgent parent in Outremont. After a while she found that she was seeing more French boys than English, which made her excited, content and prettier than ever.

Maplewood Avenue unveiled its charms to her. The street is in effect the dormitory of *l'Université de Montréal,* since there is little residence accommodation on the campus. West from the *Centre Social* as far as Cote des Neiges, the street is a long row of apartments housing professors, students and functionaries associated with university business. There is a certain amount of subterranean political activity carried on, usually in basement apartments rented by three or four students, providing each with low rent. These students are not rich. Many are poor, sometimes even hungry. They are older than the students Angela was used to and their interests are most various. They do not much like to speak English, and an English girl who speaks French is likely to seem an anomaly, perhaps to be taken up and examined with curious care, perhaps then to be put down.

She got a second-floor apartment on Maplewood just west of the campus and started to submit program ideas to her producer which took her into the university *ambiance*. First one of her programs got aired, then another; she learned how to make an acceptable tape under difficult conditions, huddled under a speaker's platform or in the cloakroom after a violent *conférence*.

I used to see her where I work, standing among the coffee and sandwich machines, talking rapid inaccurate French to students her own age, sometimes to a *chargé d'enseignement junior*, a writer or critic. She became rather well-known as a young woman who had made great strides, who might in the end manage to get all the way across. Then I heard that she was involved in the production of a half-hour film documentary for French TV, in which she was the star, interviewed in depth over several weeks in coffee houses, at work, *après-ski* and the rest of it. When it was finally telecast the half-hour was called "Miss Robinson", a Franglicism of the type which repels General de Gaulle, like *le barman, le weekend*, prevalent in certain Parisian circles, and creeping into Montreal society.

I had the feeling that this title may have concealed immediately under the surface a certain puritanical, if playful, contempt, typical of many of the younger French intellectuals in the city. Sometime later I learned that Miss Robinson had changed her given names to "Marie-Ange" pronounced with the strongly aspirated French "r" which is almost an "h". Apart from stressing it like a French word, giving each syllable equal emphasis in an un-English way, she couldn't do much about "Robinson".

The TV film had a certain impact when it appeared on *Canal Deux*. Full of nuance, half mocking and half encouraging, it managed to suggest much of the ambiguity and pathos in the situation of the transformed Marie-Ange. She used that name in the interviews. Whether she had attempted something impossible was left an open question in the viewer's mind. She photographed beautifully; perhaps part of the joke was this vivid presentation of her new beauty which owed very much to, might indeed be said to derive from, purely French manners.

Certainly her circle of men considered her a beauty. Stéphane Dérôme had been floating around film circles for a couple of years, working first in amateur film, then for a time for an independent producer, then as composer of the score for an expensive feature launched with much publicity which sank without trace. He took her up lovingly, on the waves of the "Miss Robinson" furore. She had become the mode.

In those days I was spending a lot of time out at the Montrose Record Center on Belanger, west of Montée Saint-Michel. As you come over from the center of town, east on Jean-Talon or Belanger, you'll be struck by the flatness and lack of charm of this neighbourhood. What is it, northern Rosemont or eastern City of Montreal? I've forgotten the boundary streets, if in fact I ever knew them. It's *calme plat, terne,* though you might be interested by the Italian neighbourhood between Papineau and D'Iberville, lots of *gelata* parlours and *sartorie*. On Papineau near Belanger, there are two dozen brand-new multiple dwellings, quadruplexes and octoplexes inhabited by Italians who have made a few bucks since they got here; they may own a store, or four dump-trucks, or a gardening business – the city is full of Italian gardeners – in which they employ relatives, more recent arrivals.

These enormous new places they're living in, along Papineau, are built exactly like others all over the island, but the Italian ones somehow or other have an unmistakeably Mediterranean air, very curious to discover in Montreal in the pale watery haze of early March, the snow melting, evaporating, obscuring the weak sun. It's the paint. They've all been painted in the most cheerful colours. Instead of brown brick and fake-modern light fixtures, you get yellow or white stucco or pink or electric blue, with plenty of enormous lamps in the wide windows.

This is certainly gay and distinctive, but when you are past the Italian strip, you're past the charm; the streets north and south no longer have names but numbers, First Avenue, Seventh Avenue, all the way out to the extreme east end, where Forty-fifth Avenue winds off into fields. In a city with a rue Mozart, rue Guizot, rue Dante, this dull system seems regrettable.

Around the Montrose Center the buildings are drab new housing dating from the mid-fifties, with little to distinguish one from the next. It's surprising to find the record store in such a location because, as I once told the owner, George Tabah, it's "the most exciting record store in town".

He thought this over while I went through the Nonesuch bin, featured that day at a very good price.

"I may use that in an ad," he said finally, "I like it. 'The most exciting record store in town'."

He never did use it though, whether because he didn't want to trust an amateur copywriter or because he advertises exclusively in *Le Devoir*. I think he places the ads by phone because they are oddly spelled, "Brethen" for Britten, or "Von Williams" for Vaughan Williams, surely the result of a garbled telephone report.

"The most exciting" for two reasons: because you can get a fine classical selection at the best prices in town, and because the store is the principal center for purchasers of discs by *les chansonniers* as well as a haunt of would-be or prospective *chansonniers*, live, in person, such as Stéphane Dérôme. In the display window underneath the perpetual announcement of a big sale VENTE DE DISQUES COLUMBIA BARCLAY FRANCAIS ET JAZZ, are ranked dozens of display album covers of the great singers of the province: "Le Nouveau Claude Leveillée", "Pauline Julien à la Comédie Cana-dienne", "Gilles Vigneault Chante". Once at the very back of the window, dusty and less shiny than the other gaily coloured albums, there was a copy of Stéphane's first record, "Stéphane Dérôme: Mon Cœur à Toi", over-shadowed by pyramids, circles, squares of "Monique Leyrac: Pleins Feux". There was a lot of Leyrac promotion on a streamer, *"Palmarès, concours international de la chanson"*, and so on.

Sometimes when I was idling away a chilly early spring afternoon talking to George about the complexities of record marketing, I would see Stéphane and Marie-Ange down at the end of the narrow aisle, holding up for inspection first one record then another. I could hear a continuous soft flow of critical comment from them.

"Not the real thing."

"Too much arrangement, do you think?"

"No, he is simply a poor poet. The music is not bad."

Marie-Ange took most of Stéphane's comments at face value, possibly because of his plan to become a *chansonnier* himself. You have to under-stand what this implies, and it's not simple. In French Canada, since the seventeenth century, there's been a great race of singers, a descending tradition, who compose their own songs – that's the most important thing. A Quebec *chansonnier* is *not* a collector and performer of folk songs, nor is he a popular entertainer; there is nothing primitive about his work. He has to be a poet, a good musician, a performer on some instrument. Sometimes, like Gilles Vigneault, he recites and acts things out. He must be a leader and encourager of his people. In Quebec now, there are three or four magnifi-cent singers of this kind, not more, and plenty of would-bes.

In France the term means something a bit less serious, like "singer-comedian-satirist", and here we move closer to the style of Aznavour, or Jacques Brel, who does what is really a night-club or theatre act. Brel sings, acts, writes, and in most respects resembles a Quebec *chansonnier* with the one great difference that he doesn't have the responsibility to protect and encourage the national tradition of a resentful minority. He has real gifts, but not the same social commitment. "Winter is my country", sings Gilles Vigneault, getting a strength that Jacques Brel can't quite manage: of course, there is a difference in their audiences. When Brel sings *"Ne me quitte pas*", his impersonation of an anguished lover can be recognized and appreciated anywhere in the world. But this is nevertheless a commercial love song.

In my book Stéphane Dérôme had the talent of a minor film composer or a commercial songwriter, not that of a poet, an actor or leader. An accomplished pianist with plenty of formal musical training, certainly good-looking and pleasant to talk to, able to get through an acceptable evening on a guitar, he reeked of Paroisse Saint-Germain and of Stanislas, not at all of small isolated Natashquan-type villages eight hundred miles east. He played dates in small restaurants, made a record, was praised by his friends, by Marie-Ange, by Victorine Boucher who had starred in that doomed feature film he'd composed.

This group flocked to the Montrose Record Center like the swallows in March, picking up disc after disc, buying many, discarding the unauthentic ones. They all seemed to know each other intimately, with the exception of Marie-Ange. She was always in the center of the group, forcing the pace of the chatter a little hysterically, flushed. "I knew that Stéphane was going to Quebec for the weekend, and that Victorine would likely be there, so I had to think twice about asking Jacques to find out if Stéphane planned to be back in town for the Leclerc concert, because I'd have to make up an extra bed so that François could stay over. I know that Victorine knows that I know that Stéphane was there because she was, but *ça, ça m'est égal*." At such times her eyes took on an earnest, hungry look. I began to watch the people with her, some of whom I knew, a contributor to *Cahiers* AGEUM, a boy preparing a volume for *Editions Hexagone*. They were kind to her, I thought, letting her run on as she pleased, rarely interrupting.

Her full flow of talk was assuming obsessive proportions, it seemed to me. Towards the end of March, I got a little extra money quite unexpectedly, which meant that for once I had enough money to gratify my need to buy records. I hustled out east, arriving at the Montrose about two o'clock, figuring on spending most of the afternoon talking to George and slowly and happily picking out forty dollars' worth of his bargains. I wasn't really happy to be interrupted in the middle of our conversation, which had developed through some long pauses over about an hour.

"Why don't you stock the Haydn Society reissues?"

Moments would pass slowly while he thought about this. He went next door and brought back a pear from the fruit store, which he began to eat slowly and with relish.

"Well?"

"Why won't you pay more than two-fifty for a record?"

"Can't afford it. Get me Haydn Society at two-fifty or under and I'll gradually take the whole line."

"Can't be done."

"They do it in New York."

We'd been over all this before, and we both started to laugh, and on the wave of our laughter Marie-Ange was carried in the door. She made straight for me and instantly began to talk as though we were the closest of friends, maybe even related, and as though in the middle of a sentence broken off seconds ago. Conversation with her was always exhausting for the first minutes, while you tried to figure out whom she was referring to and what was implied.

". . . Couldn't stand pets, any pets, so they had to go, as I couldn't consider moving, not right now with so much happening downstairs."

"Downstairs?"

"In our building, Victorine's apartment. She claims there has been a voyeur peeking in the bathroom windows, she's right in the basement you know, and thinks it may be dangerous. If you ask me, it's Gérard up to some trick or other."

"Voyeurism doesn't sound like Gérard. Satyriasis, more likely."

"I wish some of it would rub off on me," she said gloomily.

"Oh, come on."

"Then again it could be François, though he's still supposed to be in Quebec."

"It couldn't be Stéphane, I suppose?"

"I think it might, but then why go to all the trouble of peeking? He has full access to Victorine's apartment."

"Oh?"

She had been just on the boiling point, simmering as it were, and now boiled over. "Heaven knows I try," she said, "I do my best. *Je fais mon très petit possible, quoi?*"

"*Evidemment.*"

"What I have to put up with. I've been out with these guys every night in the week for months; it's affecting my skin. I've put them on the air. I want an AM show where I can do bilingual interviews and meet people and try to help. And then to be told that I can't really be part of the group because I can't understand their jokes, it's something else, really. *Pas gentille.*"

"It's very hard."

"What?"

"To catch the jokes. I speak a fair French myself and . . ."

"Pooh," she said, "pooh. A lot of it is smut, pure and simple, nothing but sex. Look at French theatre, intrigue, bare bosoms."

"I'm in favour of that."

"I can see you would be, but what woman can be bothered?" She glanced at George Tabah and moved to the back of the store; there was an unmistakeable air of strain and ill-health about her. When I followed her back, she lowered her voice. "There's something up that I don't know about, involving François and Gérard and Stéphane and Victorine, a plot of some kind, and I just can't keep up to what they're saying."

"Not politics, surely?"

"No, no, nothing like that. You can't see Stéphane risking it, can you? No revolutions for him." She had a Leo Ferré album in her hands and was examining his face with some bitterness.

"That's the stuff," she said, "Ferré, good and strong."

"I find him a little hard to take."

"You would."

This was simply generalized resentment – at least I hope it was – and I let it pass.

"I'm sorry," she said, "I'm not your responsibility, am I?"

That question always bothers me, and I didn't answer.

"I've been so miserable," she said.

George had left the store for a moment. He was standing outside with his back to the window, looking at the sky. The March light was extremely ambiguous, very pale, chilly looking, yet with a peculiar tone in some way evocative of the approach of finer weather. It was still plenty cold out, but another few weeks would see us out of it. The equinoctial gales, very troublesome in Montreal, had just begun, and the wind was gusting to fifty. And yet there was this almost imperceptible promise of fineness to come. The end of winter makes me feel better, encourages a certain buoyancy of feeling. Perhaps it had the reverse effect on Marie-Ange, and she was simply expressing physical discomfort induced by the weather. I said, "Tell me about it, if you like."

She gave a faint smile. "You don't want to hear."

"I'm not sure."

"I'll tell you something anyway. I love Stéphane."

I sometimes wonder whether there are any girls here and there burdening other men with the tale of their hopeless passion for me. The man who hears this story is bound to feel considerable distaste for the love-object, from feelings of unacknowledged rivalry perhaps; few men really care for the role of confidant. When she said this, I was conscious of a sharp pang of dislike for Stéphane. I felt like making a callous and flippant answer like, "Sorry about that, chief," but repressed the impulse. I said, "He's a very nice guy," thinking that, on the whole, he wasn't much.

Naturally Marie-Ange, far from stupid, sensed this, and putting down the Ferré disc she went out of the store more quickly, if anything, than she'd entered. You're a cold fish, I told myself. You might have been nicer. Must be the change in the weather.

When I heard about Victorine and Stéphane going off to Paris together, I kept my ears open and was able to collect a pretty full impression of the end of Marie-Ange's affair. Victorine, dark, small, fragile of ankle and wrist, adorable, had innocently announced that she would be in Paris for the principal event of the year, the opening at the Olympia of Claude Gauthier and Monique Leyrac. To such bait more considerable men than Stéphane Dérôme would have risen. They booked seats together on the appropriate Air Canada flight, Stéphane including his banjo and guitar and little else in his weight allowance.

He had a final meeting with Marie-Ange out at the Montrose, just checking over the new releases, I suppose. She turned to him with bewildered tears in her eyes, certainly incapable of understanding why she hadn't reached him.

"Ne me quitte pas!" she said.

"Brel," said Stéphane absently, and he turned away.

III. Shapers of History

The history of any nation is something more than new lands discovered and old battles lost and won. But in attempting to describe a nation's past, there is some justification for giving the explorers, the generals, and the statesmen more attention than is usually given to nameless members of the electorate, or to soldiers so private that even their names have been forgotten. For in the flow of events that is called history, there are occasions when the tide was turned, and there are individuals who are remembered because they played a major role in turning that tide. It would be unlikely that any two historians would make identical lists of the most important shapers – or tide-turners – in the Canadian past. But many of the figures discussed in this selection of comments on Canadian history would find their way onto the lists of most Canadian historians. In any case, some of the men dealt with here have been included for reasons that are external to their particular achievements. For one of the aims of this collection of historical readings is to represent different styles of historical writing, from the relaxed, colloquial manner of Ralph Allen, through the scholarly style of George F. G. Stanley, to the measured and dramatic prose of Donald Creighton. And in order to maintain some degree of historical balance, two of the figures represented here (Sir Wilfrid Laurier and Pierre Elliott Trudeau) have been invited to speak for themselves.

20. Louis XIV and New France

ALAN GOWANS

What follows is the opening section of an essay entitled "Architecture in New France" in which Alan Gowans, who is a professor of art at the University of Victoria, uses "architectural remains" to support his theory about why France failed in North America. "Architecture in New France" was originally published in the Canadian literary magazine The Tamarack Review.

Several points about effective writing are illustrated by this lucid piece of prose. It reveals, for example, how a writer can gain immediate interest by the use of a short, provocative opening sentence, and how he can sustain this interest through the effective use of rhetorical questions, as Mr. Gowans does in paragraphs one and three. And, on a somewhat more mechanical level, this selection illustrates how parenthetical statements can be used to bring into an essay related material that stands just outside the main flow of a paragraph's development.

By all the laws of probability, North America ought to speak French, not English, today. Seventeenth-century France was beyond comparison the strongest state in Europe; and New France was equally beyond comparison the most potentially powerful state in the New World. The founding of Louisbourg in 1714 at one end, and New Orleans in 1718 at the other, completed a chain of forts and settlements that dominated both main waterways into the continent; had this strategic arc of territory been filled in with anything like the population of the English colonies, they would have been neatly penned in by it against the Atlantic seaboard, and French mastery of most of North America would have been assured. But, of course, things did not work out that way. Within fifty years it was New France, not the English colonies, that had been wiped off the map in what seems retrospectively the unbelievably sudden, easy, and total defeat of a great power. What ever happened?

To analyse all the reasons for French failure in the New World would take many a book. But in general, I think, it could be all summed up in one word — absolutism. France was ruled, and New France was ruled, on a rigidly authoritarian principle; and this kind of government always defeats

142

itself. That is a platitude, of course. But then, like all platitudes, it happens to be true. And if the scanty architectural remains of New France have any lasting significance as cultural expression, it is surely in this – that they are above all a commentary on the theory, practice, and results of absolute government. We can begin the commentary best, perhaps, with a typical example of Huguenot building in the English colonies, like the Jean Hasbrouck house at New Paltz, New York.

How did such a typical north-of-France peasant house, with thick stone walls, two-to-one proportion of roof to wall, and general fortress-like appearance so unmistakably like contemporaries in the Montreal area of New France come to be built here in the Hudson Valley? Because New Paltz was a French settlement, founded in 1660 by a group of French Protestants coming to New York from a temporary refuge in the Palatinate (hence the name); Jean Hasbrouck, who built this house in 1712, was a native of Calais. And how did he and thousands like him come to settle here, give their talents and their future to the English colonies instead of New France? That, ultimately, was one result of the "absolute will and pleasure" of the King of France, Louis XIV.

Absolutism anywhere, at any time, in practice means government by whim. And government by whim not only makes successful long-term planning impossible, it makes disastrous mistakes inevitable. Human judgement being what it is, first thoughts are all too usually fallible; it is, then, no discredit to any man if the sparkling ideas he had at midnight look sick in the plain light of day. But when the man is an absolute ruler first thoughts rule his life. His midnight enthusiasms are law by morning; last night's whim may be felt for generations. Such a whim, for instance, was Louis Quatorze's decision to repeal the Edict of Nantes, and make French Protestants conform to his notions on religion. "To people Canada it would be necessary to depopulate France" – this had been the Sun King's excuse for the slow growth of his colony in 1667; yet this Revocation, combined with the previous decree of 1628 prohibiting Protestant settlement in New France (which also seems to have been largely a whim of Mazarin's), turned what had been a trickle of Huguenot immigration to the English colonies into a "great flood" of some 15,000 settlers before 1750 – at least as many Frenchmen as ever were induced to come to New France, and probably more. South Carolina (especially Charleston, where entire streets were built by Huguenots), Massachusetts (which received such families as the Reveres, Bowdoins, and Faneuils), and New York City (in 1688 a quarter of the population of New York City was Huguenot) benefited most from Louis's fatuous munificence; but every colony had its useful contingent of well-educated, hard-working settlers whose contributions to the prosperity of English America were literally invaluable.

143

Of course there are not many Huguenot buildings actually extant today – the New Paltz houses, the Demarest House in Hackensack, a few others here and there. But then, architectural remains for New France as a whole (outside Quebec) are notoriously scanty too. And while Huguenot remains are scanty largely because so many of the places they settled grew with their help into large and prosperous communities which (in what is unfortunately the usual American manner) tore down and built over their earliest architecture, French remains elsewhere are scanty for quite a different reason. New France had few buildings because it had so few people. And this is significant indeed.

France in the seventeenth century had every advantage over England in peopling colonies – better strategic position, more stable government (England, after all, had two revolutions and a civil war in this period), a population three times as large. There was only one reason why New France should not have been populated early and thickly – deliberate policy. While the one thing New France needed above all was people, the kings of France insisted on providing everything but. They subsidized troops of missionaries to make Christian settlers out of the Indians. They poured money into great fortresses to hold their territories. They provided legions (relatively speaking) of administrators and soldiers. But settlers they would not send. Almost every Frenchman who ever spent more than a few years in North America came to the conclusion that New France could not survive without steady and abundant immigration. But the kings of France never "heard" them. They listened instead to people who knew about Indians from philosophers' textbooks on the "noble savage" rather than those who had actually fought them and knew how many generations it would take to make "civilians" of them; they listened to court generals who managed their European armies and knew about occupying territories in Flanders or the Rhineland, rather than those who knew what wilderness conditions did to the morale of regular army troops far from home. And so the Indian schemes collapsed, and Louisbourg was taken by raw militia from New England fighting for their homeland; and so in the end a few thousand Frenchmen were left to face half a million English settlers in the final battles of the Seven Years' War; the result was inevitable.

But it had been inevitable from the beginning. For the absolute ruler can never, in the nature of things, have the kind of advice which he – again in the nature of things – more than any other kind of administrator must have. By definition he reserves all authority to himself; he delegates only responsibility (and blame, needless to say). He, of all people, therefore, most needs to know exactly what the factors in any given situation are, if he is to avoid making decisions on nonexistent grounds, or giving orders that cannot be carried out. But this is precisely the sort of information that he, being who he is, will never get – first, because there are always too many problems coming before him to concentrate properly on any one; but even more fundamentally, because he has no "loyal opposition" to give him the kind of advice and criticism he needs, regardless of how unpleasant it may be. Instead, he will be surrounded by a crowd of sycophants who tell him not what he ought to know, but what they think he wants to hear; who spend their energies not in discovering facts, or weighing considerations, but in guessing what the King – or President, or Chairman, or whoever it may be in this universal situation – is going to think about before he thinks it, so that they can flatter him with corroboration. These people are certainly not the sort to go off to a wild place like New France, or to tell the King what it really needs even in the unlikely event they do. The courtiers who surrounded the King of France in his Colony's crucial years were men who correctly guessed that his head was filled with illusions of glory, who adroitly praised him for sending men to battlefields all over Europe instead of peopling empty wastes of snow in New France. And because they had the King's ear, empty wastes of snow New France to all intents and purposes remained. Drive out from the old English colonies in any direction, and you will soon be passing through what was once the vast domain of the kings of France; in any direction but north, you would never know it. A ruined fort here and there; the odd restored French house; a few vaguely French blocks in New Orleans and nearby plantation houses with a "French flavour" – that is about all. It is what is not there that tells us most about the character of New France.

21. Montcalm and Wolfe at Quebec

DONALD CREIGHTON

Donald Creighton, who is professor of history at the University of Toronto, is considered by many critics to be the most effective stylist among contemporary writers of Canadian history. His best-known work is a two-volume biography of Sir John A. Macdonald: The Young Politician *(1952), and* The Old Chieftain *(1955). The following account of the events that took place on the Plains of Abraham on September 13, 1759, is from Professor Creighton's* The Story of Canada, *published in 1960.*

The effectiveness of Professor Creighton's style comes partly from his mastery of his subject, but equally from the clarity of his sentence structure. Each of his sentences is concise and exact; the general flow of his prose is varied and rhythmic.

In the spring of that fateful year, 1756, Louis Joseph, Marquis de Montcalm, arrived at Quebec. He was in all probability the greatest field general of the Seven Years' War; but in New France he faced a situation which was desperately, almost irremediably, serious. He had, in the seven splendid regiments of La Reine, Guienne, Béarn, La Sarre, Languedoc, Royal Roussillon, and Berry, a total of only a few thousand regulars; he could count upon an effective strength of perhaps eight or nine thousand Canadian militia. It was a pitifully small number with which to meet the far vaster potential resources of England and English America; and Montcalm knew – it was an inescapably gloomy fact in all his calculations – that the force at his disposal could not be regularly and certainly reinforced. The convoys still occasionally got through – the arrival of Montcalm himself and of the new battalions which came with him was sufficient proof of that; and even yet there were fortunate occasions when French warships managed to obtain a temporary mastery in Canadian waters. But these spacious moments of freedom were transitory, almost accidental. The British were slowly but relentlessly establishing their command of the Atlantic. It was only a question of time before they would attempt to bottle up the French fleets in their Atlantic ports, seal the St. Lawrence from all relief, and settle Quebec with a knock-out blow.

Inevitably, the one possible strategy for Montcalm was the strategy of defence. Almost certainly he could not win in North America; he could only play for time in the hope that the great military power of continental France would be strong enough to wrest a decision in Europe. He could play for time; but it was a desperate game in which, in the end, he would have to fall back upon the resources of New France; and New France, in this supreme crisis of its existence, displayed all its characteristic weaknesses and limitations to the full. As the months went by, as the state of war gradually became a virtual state of siege, the fur-trading colony relapsed into a condition of chronic distress. There were bad harvests, food shortages, constant inflation. There was something else – something far more lamentable – as well. Upon the misfortunes of economic and political weakness were piled the mistakes and crimes of blind ill-will and corrupt self-interest. Vaudreuil, the Canadian-born Governor, who was jealous of Montcalm and sensitively resentful of French prestige and patronage, paralysed the high command

146

with his constant interference. Bigot, the Intendant, battened upon the miserable colony with his light-hearted, swindling depredations. "What a country, what a country," Montcalm lamented, "where knaves grow rich and honest men are ruined."

Yet he struggled to defend it. There were, he knew only too well, three possible invasion routes. One, by the St. Lawrence, was from the sea; the second was the well-worn, obvious inland gateway by Lake Champlain and the Richelieu River; the third and last was the remote western approach through the headwaters of the Ohio and the Lower Lakes. The two routes from the interior were, of course, protected by forts; but Montcalm had no intention of waiting tamely for the enemy within these defences. For the first two years of the war, he successfully masked the essentially defensive nature of his strategy with vigorous offensive operations. In 1756, Oswego, the important British western base on the south side of Lake Ontario, was taken; and a year later Montcalm pushed resolutely down the Richelieu valley to capture Fort William Henry, the British stronghold at the head of Lake George.

It was only in 1758, the third year of the war, when the Anglo-Americans sought to thrust their way simultaneously and in force up the three approaches to the heart of New France, that Montcalm failed to preserve his system intact. At Fort Ticonderoga, it was true, he repulsed the inept Abercromby's frontal assault with coolly efficient slaughter. But, for sheer lack of manpower, the western outposts – Fort Oswego, Fort Duquesne, even Fort Frontenac – were all abandoned; and, what was infinitely worse, an overwhelming British land and naval force brought about the second and final capitulation of Louisbourg. The seaway to New France was open. Most of the western defences were down. In the spring of 1759 the Anglo-Americans mustered in overwhelming numbers for the renewal of their threefold attack; and General James Wolfe and Admiral Charles Saunders sailed up the St. Lawrence to Quebec.

Without hope of reinforcements, with a command which was torn by dissension and riddled by profiteers, Montcalm took his last stand on the rock which Champlain had chosen for his "habitation" a century and a half before. Quebec was not a scientifically constructed fortress like Louisbourg; it was at best a fortified town. The great cliffs about Cape Diamond gave the place superb natural protection; but further up the river, above Cap Rouge, the approaches were more open; and below the town nearly as far as the Montmorency River, the low Beauport flats invited attack. Montcalm, with his limited resources, could not be everywhere. He lost control of the whole south shore of the St. Lawrence. His defensive line – perhaps over-extended as it was – stretched the whole length of the Beauport shore, nearly six miles in all, between the rivers St. Charles and Montmorency.

Here he dug himself in systematically, and waited. He had not long to wait. On the last day of July, Wolfe launched an attack on the left of his position, where the low ground rose towards the Montmorency heights, and was beaten back with serious loss. It was Montcalm's fourth victory against the British. Oswego, William Henry, Ticonderoga, and now Montmorency – surely these were auspicious omens! The "old fox," as Wolfe called him, had never been beaten yet. If only he could hold out until the autumn! Autumn would mean the inevitable withdrawal of Saunders's fleet and the abandonment of the whole expedition. And slowly, painfully, autumn was drawing close. July had already gone. August was going. It was September!

And then a mysterious thing happened. Wolfe broke his camp on the north shore, immediately below Montmorency, and moved up the river on the south side. What was he doing? Where was he going to strike? Montcalm's intelligence was bad. The constant passage of ships and men up and down the river in front of Quebec was all part of an elaborate game of mystification in which the British navy and army zealously joined to deceive him. A break-through up river at some place such as Pointe aux Trembles was a distinct and dangerous possibility; but so also was a renewal of the attack on Beauport, under cover of the feint which these misleading activities above the town would supply. There were dangers everywhere. Even the great serene heights immediately above the town did not seem entirely secure.

It was perhaps possible for a man to clamber up one of the few breaks in the cliffs, such as the Anse au Foulon, to the Plains of Abraham above; but could an attack in any strength be mounted in this way? Was Wolfe, having drawn the French forces successfully to both wings, preparing, with incredible audacity, to make his main thrust in the centre, through the cove of the Anse au Foulon, up to the heights themselves? Montcalm began rapidly to strengthen his centre and right wing; and on September 5th he ordered the Guienne Regiment up to the high rolling plateau immediately above Quebec. One day later Vaudreuil sent it back to the Beauport lines. The Plains of Abraham were left virtually defenceless. Only the culpable Vergor, Bigot's friend, who had surrendered Beauséjour in 1755 without a shot, was stationed there with a small company of Canadian militia. And yet, four days later, on September 10th, a French officer stationed close to the Anse au Foulon, saw through his telescope a small group of British officers carefully surveying the heights about him from the opposite shore. Perhaps Montcalm and Vaudreuil underestimated the possibility of a successful ascent of the cliffs. Perhaps they disagreed about the urgency of guarding against it. They were, at any rate, bewildered by a multiplicity of dangers, and they made no further special efforts to defend the Plains of Abraham. The early autumn days slipped by. Tomorrow would be September 13th.

At about four in the morning of that day, a sentry at the French post of Point Sillery, a short distance above the Anse au Foulon, heard a curious sound from the river below.

"Qui vive?" he challenged.

"France." The reply was low but distinct.

"A quel régiment?" snapped the sentry.

"De la Reine."

The sentry hesitated. He was still curious. The voice was authoritative and confident – clearly an officer's voice. Yet there was something odd about it. Was it the accent or simply the low tone in which the words were uttered?

"Pourquoi est-ce que vous ne parlez pas plus haut?" he persisted.

The reply was impatient and brusquely commanding:

"Tais-toi! Nous serions entendus."

The sentry subsided in doubtful silence. He expected a convoy from up-stream, bearing badly needed provisions for Quebec, that very night. He might have feared a surprise attack by the British; but he could hardly have imagined that a Highland officer named Simon Fraser, who spoke excellent French, would have taken his place in the leading boat. Down below in the darkness there was silence. The British held their breath in painful expect-ancy. Then the boats moved softly on and a few minutes later they grounded on the shingle of the Anse au Foulon.

Wolfe was the first on shore. During much of the summer he had been seriously ill and depressed; but now, at the point of crisis, every ounce of his daring genius was flung into the execution of his "desperate plan." "I know perfectly well you cannot cure my complaint," he had told his surgeon only a little while before, "but patch me up so that I may be able to do my duty for the next few days and I shall be content." Now the crucial moment, for which he had tried to prepare himself, was at hand. Swiftly, silently he led the way to the spot he had chosen for the first ascent.

"I don't think," he said anxiously to his leading soldiers, "we can by any possible means get up here, but however we must use our best endeavour."

Only a few minutes later, most of de Vergor's miserable guard was over-powered in its sleep. Vaudreuil slept soundly. They all slept; and it was not until after six o'clock that Montcalm, riding up from the Beauport lines, learnt the full enormity of what had happened. Hurriedly he collected his men. Almost the whole of the army's left wing, by Vaudreuil's express in-structions, remained inactive in the Beauport entrenchments; and the five regiments which assembled that morning a little west of the town were a sadly mixed company which had been reinforced, not with regulars from France – for none had reached the St. Lawrence – but with drafts of Cana-dians. The rolling plain ahead of them was not the forested road leading to Fort Duquesne nor the heights above the Montmorency River. It was almost a parade ground. And everything might depend upon the disciplined fighting cohesion which Montcalm's force so tragically lacked. He hesitated. And yet, he realized, it might be fatal to delay. Delay would enable the enemy to entrench, to bring up cannon, and consolidate his position. If Montcalm attacked now, he might catch the British off balance. He might, at one stroke, convert the complete surprise into an overwhelming disaster.

It was ten o'clock. The rain, which had been falling earlier, now slackened, and the sun broke magnificently through the clouds. Montcalm signalled the advance, and the whole array of white- and blue-clad soldiers surged forward. The troops started with a shout of confidence; but soon the long lines began ominously to lose both their symmetry and their resolution. The Canadians fired, dropped to the ground to reload, or scurried to cover on either side of the battlefield. The French regulars, unnerved by the increasing disorderliness of their formation, halted, fired, moved forward again uncertainly and repeated their ragged fusillade. And then, at the forty paces Wolfe had specified, the two long lines of redcoats broke their unnerving silence with a crashing volley. The French charge was stopped dead. The French lines began to waver. Wolfe, in his moment of triumph, was shot and dying. Montcalm was mortally wounded while he tried in vain to rally his men. There was no rallying them. They broke, turned, and fled. And Montcalm's black horse walked his dying master slowly back into the city through the St. Louis gate.

22. Lord Durham and His Report

EDGAR McINNIS

This brief summary of the political unrest in Upper and Lower Canada following the Rebellions of 1837 is taken from The North American Nations, *published in 1963. Its author, Edgar McInnis, is a professor of history at York University in Toronto.*

This essay illustrates a structural pattern that makes use of enumeration. This variation on what has previously been referred to as "Basic Essay Structure" consists of an introduction (paragraphs 1 and 2), then a topic statement pointing out that three aspects of the subject will be considered (paragraph 3). Each of the next three paragraphs (4, 5 and 6) is devoted to one of the divisions indicated in the topic sentence. The essay ends with a conclusion in paragraph 7. Although a structure such as this can become mechanical, it can also be used – as this selection illustrates – as an effective means of presenting material that divides itself logically into two, three, or four parallel divisions.

The rebellion of 1837 jolted the British ministry into fresh efforts to find remedies for colonial discontents. Perhaps, as Lord Melbourne reflected, the Canadas would be no great loss, but their separation would be a blow to British prestige and would be politically fatal to the government of which he was Prime Minister. His opponents had to be disarmed by forestalling any Tory accusations that the ministry was about to surrender the empire, while assuring the Radicals that it had no intention of restoring its rule by repression. It was to satisfy these conditions that Melbourne persuaded Lord Durham, an advanced liberal who had taken an active part in the struggle over the Reform Act of 1832, to go out to North America as Governor General and special commissioner for the purpose of reporting on conditions and suggesting remedies.

The Durham Report was one of the great landmarks in the development of Canadian self-government and the evolution of the British Commonwealth. Its basis was a firm rejection of the pessimistic view that colonies must inevitably separate from the mother country once they came of age. It asserted a robust faith in the extension of British institutions as the means of maintaining the ties between the colonies and the motherland. Durham grasped from the outset that the key to the problem lay not only in local conditions but also, and to a greater extent, in the relations between the colonies and the British government; and the solution that he advocated was capable of being applied not only to the Canadas, but to other parts of the empire as they in their turn became ready for self-government. It was because of his report that British North America was enabled to make its great and original contribution to imperial development and to pioneer in the process that led from the old concept of Empire to the modern Commonwealth.

The report dealt with a number of practical aspects of the situation in the Canadas – the absence of municipal government in Lower Canada, the problem of public finance, the unsatisfactory features of the land system, and the need to encourage immigration. But these points, important as they were, were secondary to the three outstanding recommendations that made the report so unique and significant.

The first point concerned the union of the two Canadas. Durham believed strongly that the racial antagonism between French and English lay at the root of all internal difficulties, and that this could only be overcome if the French were absorbed into a predominantly British community. In a phrase that gave bitter offence, he described the French Canadians as "a people with no history and no literature", lacking any separate future of their own in a province whose national character must inevitably be that of the British race. A union of the two provinces would make it possible to overcome French obstruction of immigration and the building of canals, thus opening the way for an expansion of population that would reduce the French to a hopeless minority and reconcile them to becoming English in outlook as well as allegiance.

Central to this whole prospect was the granting of responsible government. Here was an idea that had already been put forward by a number of the colonial reformers, and none had been more vigorous and unswerving in its advocacy than Robert Baldwin. Unlike Mackenzie and the radicals, with their advocacy of the elective system for the executive and a leaning toward American republicanism, Baldwin stood firmly for the maintenance of the British connection and the extension of the full benefits of British institutions. He saw clearly that the conflict between legislature and executive would be solved by adopting the British cabinet system, under which the ministry held office only as long as it commanded the confidence of a majority in the legislature. Baldwin had failed to get a hearing for his views at the Colonial Office, but he conveyed them urgently to Lord Durham, and they were views with which Durham was in hearty agreement. "It is difficult to understand," Durham wrote, "how any English statesman could have imagined that representative and irresponsible government could be successfully combined." He vigorously rejected the argument that self-government would lead to the loss of the colonies. The Canadian people were worthy of trust, and their loyalty would be strengthened by the grant of British liberties. The British government, he insisted, must "submit to the necessary consequence of representative institutions; and if it has to carry on the government in unison with a representative body, it must consent to carry it on by means of those in whom that representative body has confidence".

What this clearly implied was that the colonists must be left free to manage their own affairs with a minimum of interference on the part of the British government. Durham's third recommendation was therefore the definite separation of local from imperial matters. Britain should still keep control over areas that affected her own interests or those of the empire as a whole, but these were relatively few. The most important were the colonial constitutions, foreign relations, imperial and foreign trade, and the disposal of public lands. If these were reserved for the government at Westminster, everything else could be left for the colonies to deal with, and the end of vexatious interference by the home government in local affairs would remove one of the chief sources of friction and strengthen rather than weaken the bonds of loyalty.

The report revealed a completely new approach to imperial problems. It brought to the fore the concept that the true path of imperial development lay not in the effort to keep the colonies subordinate, but in allowing the progressive development of their freedom in a free association with the mother country. Its immediate effects, however, were limited. No clear separation was made between imperial and colonial affairs. The union of the Canadas was achieved in 1841, but the French were neither submerged nor absorbed. On the contrary, they drew together with fresh determination to maintain their distinctive culture and institutions. Durham's criticisms turned out to be a challenge to which the French responded with vigorous resistance and which in the end contributed to the survival of the racial division which Durham so confidently expected to disappear. As for responsible government, that was something to which the British government was still resolutely opposed, and the issue was finally decided only after nearly a decade of further political conflicts.

23. On the Death of Sir John A. Macdonald

SIR WILFRID LAURIER

Sir John A. Macdonald, who was Canada's first prime minister and by all accounts this nation's most famous personage, died on June 6, 1891. Macdonald served as prime minister from 1867 until the time of his death, except for the years 1872 to 1878, when the Conservatives were banished to the opposition benches as a result of the "Pacific Scandal". The following selection is part of a eulogy delivered in Parliament on June 8, 1891, by Sir Wilfrid Laurier, the leader of the Liberal opposition, who himself became prime minister in 1896. The selection will indicate why Laurier is considered to be one of Canada's greatest orators, both in French and English. This selection provides an example of the high rhetorical style. Notice the use Laurier makes of elevated diction, metaphor, and balanced and climactic sentences in order to gain his effects. Also worth considering is whether this speech does or does not present a balanced view of Macdonald.

I fully appreciate the intensity of the grief which fills the souls of all those who were the friends and followers of Sir John Macdonald, at the loss of the great leader whose whole life has been so closely identified with their party; a party upon which he has thrown such brilliancy and lustre. We on this side of the House who were his opponents, who did not believe in his policy, nor in his methods of government; we take our full share of their grief – for the loss which they deplore to-day is far and away beyond and above the ordinary compass of party range. It is in every respect a great national loss, for he who is no more was, in many respects, Canada's most illustrious son, and in every sense Canada's foremost citizen and statesman. At the period of life to which Sir John Macdonald had arrived, death, whenever it comes, cannot be said to come unexpected.

Some few months ago, during the turmoil of the late election, when the country was made aware that on a certain day the physical strength of the veteran Premier had not been equal to his courage, and that his intense labour for the time being had prostrated his singularly wiry frame, every-body, with the exception, perhaps, of his buoyant self, was painfully anxious lest perhaps the angel of death had touched him with his wing. When, a few days ago in the heat of an angry discussion the news spread in this House, that of a sudden his condition had become alarming, the surging waves of angry discussion were at once hushed, and every one, friend and foe, realized that this time for a certainty the angel of death had appeared and had crossed the threshold of his home. Thus we were not taken by sur-prise, and although we were prepared for the sad event, yet it is almost im-possible to convince the unwilling mind, that it is true, that Sir John Mac-donald is no more, that the chair which we now see vacant shall remain forever vacant; that the face so familiar in this Parliament for the last forty years shall be seen no more, and that the voice so well known shall be heard no more, whether in solemn debate or in pleasant and mirthful tones. In fact, the place of Sir John Macdonald in this country was so large and so absorbing, that it is almost impossible to conceive that the political life of this country, the fate of this country, can continue without him. His loss overwhelms us.

For my part, I say with all truth, his loss overwhelms me, and it also overwhelms this Parliament, as if indeed one of the institutions of the land had given way. Sir John Macdonald now belongs to the ages, and it can be said with certainty, that the career which has just been closed is one of the most remarkable careers of this century. It would be premature at this time to attempt to fix or anticipate what will be the final judgment of history upon him; but there were in his career and in his life, features so prominent and so conspicuous that already they shine with a glow which time cannot alter, which even now appear before the eye such as they will appear to the end in history. I think it can be asserted that for the supreme art of governing men, Sir John Macdonald was gifted as few men in any land or in any age were gifted; gifted with the most high of all qualities, qualities which would have made him famous wherever exercised and which would have shone all the more conspicuously the larger the theatre. The fact that he could congregate together elements the most heterogeneous and blend them into one compact party, and to the end of his life keep them steadily under his hand, is perhaps altogether unprecedented. The fact that during all those years he retained unimpaired not only the confidence, but the devotion – the ardent devotion and affection of his party, is evidence that beside those higher qualities of statesmanship to which we were the daily witnesses, he was also endowed with those inner, subtile, undefinable graces of soul which win and keep the hearts of men. As to his statesmanship, it is written in the history of Canada. It may be said without any exaggeration whatever, that the life of Sir John Macdonald, from the date he entered Parliament, is the history of Canada, for he was connected and associated with all the events, all the facts which brought Canada from the position Canada then occupied – the position of two small provinces, having nothing in common but a common allegiance, united by a bond of paper, and united by nothing else – to the present state of development which Canada has reached.

Although my political views compel me to say that, in my judgment, his actions were not always the best that could have been taken in the interest of Canada, although my conscience compels me to say that of late he has imputed to his opponents motives as to which I must say in my heart he has misconceived, yet I am only too glad here to sink these differences, and to remember only the great services he has performed for our country – to remember that his actions always displayed great originality of views, unbounded fertility of resources, a high level of intellectual conceptions, and, above all, a far-reaching vision beyond the event of the day, and still higher, permeating the whole, a broad patriotism – a devotion to Canada's welfare, Canada's advancement, and Canada's glory. The life of a statesman is always an arduous one, and very often it is an ungrateful one. More often than otherwise his actions do not mature until he is in his grave. Not so, however, in the case of Sir John Macdonald. His career has been a singularly fortunate one. His reverses were few and of short duration. He was fond of power, and, in my judgment, if I may say so, that may be the turning point of the judgment of history. He was fond of power, and he never made any secret of it. Many times we have heard him avow it on the floor of this

Parliament, and his ambition in this respect was gratified as, perhaps, no other man's ambition ever was.

In my judgment, even the career of William Pitt can hardly compare with that of Sir John Macdonald in this respect; for although William Pitt, moving in a higher sphere, had to deal with problems greater than our problems, yet I doubt if in the intricate management of a party William Pitt had to contend with difficulties equal to those that Sir John Macdonald had to contend with. In his death, too, he seems to have been singularly happy. Twenty years ago I was told by one who at that time was a close personal and political friend of Sir John Macdonald, that in the intimacy of his domestic circle he was fond of repeating that his end would be as the end of Lord Chatham – that he would be carried away from the floor of the Parliament to die. How true that vision into the future was we now know, for we saw him to the last, with enfeebled health and declining strength, struggling on the floor of Parliament until the hand of fate pinned him to his bed to die. And thus to die with his armour on was probably his ambition.

---

24. Louis Riel and the Prairie Uprisings

GEORGE F. G. STANLEY

*As the following selection states clearly, Louis Riel is one of the most controversial figures in Canadian history. This examination of some of the causes and effects involved in the Riel Rebellions is by George F. G. Stanley, Dean of Arts at the Royal Military College in Kingston and an acknowledged expert on Riel and his times. Professor Stanley is the author of a full-length book on Riel (*Louis Riel, *published in 1963), although the following account is not from this book, but from a pamphlet entitled* Louis Riel: Patriot or Rebel? *published in 1956 by the Canadian Historical Association. The selection that follows consists of the first eight and the last six paragraphs of this pamphlet, with a brief summary bridging the omitted section.*

The style employed by this particular writer of history is a formal one. What specific qualities of the prose help to create its scholarly tone? Con-

sider especially the sentence structure, the diction, and the type of allusions that Professor Stanley employs.

Few characters in Canadian history have aroused such depth and bitterness of feeling as that of the métis chieftain, Louis "David" Riel. The mere mention of his name bares those latent religious and racial animosities which seem to lie so close to the surface of Canadian politics. Despite the fact that he identified himself, not with the French Canadians of Quebec, but with the mixed-blood population of the western plains, Louis Riel became, for a few years, the symbol of the national aspirations of French Canada and the storm-centre of political Orangeism. French-speaking Canadians elevated him to the pedestal of martyrdom; English-speaking Canadians damned him as a rebel. In Riel the people of Quebec professed to see another Papineau, a heroic patriot defending on the far away prairies the cause of Canadians living in the valley of the St. Lawrence; the people of Ontario saw in him only the dastard murderer of an Ontario Protestant. Even today the racial controversies which emerged from Riel's actions in Manitoba in 1869-70, and the political turmoils stirred up by his trial and execution in Saskatchewan fifteen years later, make it difficult to assess fairly the contribution of this strange and rather pathetic creature, whose remains now lie but a few steps from those of his grandparents, in the peaceful cathedral yard of St. Boniface.

In essence the troubles associated with the name of Louis Riel were the manifestation, not of the traditional rivalries of French Catholic Quebec and English Protestant Ontario, but of the traditional problems of cultural conflict, of the clash between primitive and civilized peoples. In all parts of the world, in South Africa, New Zealand and North America, the penetration of white settlement into territories inhabited by native peoples has led to friction and war; Canadian expansion into the North-West led to a similar result. Both in Manitoba and in Saskatchewan the métis had their own primitive society and their own primitive economy. They hunted the buffalo, they trafficked in furs, they freighted goods for the Hudson's Bay Company, and they indifferently cultivated their long narrow farms along the banks of the rivers. Few of them were equipped by education or experience to compete with the whites, or to share with them the political responsibilities of citizenship. When faced with the invasion of civilization they drew together; they did not want to be civilized; they wanted only to survive. Their fears and bewilderment drove them into resistance which, when reduced to armed conflict, held small chance of success.

Fundamentally there was little difference between the métis and the Indian problems. Even less than the mixed-bloods were the native Indians prepared to take a place in the highly competitive civilization of the white men. To the Indian and métis alike, civilization meant the destruction of their culture, with assimilation or extinction as their ultimate fate. The Riel risings were not, as the politicians said and believed, a war between French and English, but between plough and prairie. But these facts were hidden from the Canadian public by the timidity and prejudices of politicians; and the visionary defender of an obsolete cultural epoch in Western Canadian history became the martyr of a race.

The dates of the two risings associated with the name of Louis Riel are not without significance. The first, 1869-70, coincided with the passing of the Hudson's Bay Company as the governing power of the North-West. The second, 1885, coincided with the completion of the Canadian Pacific Railway, an event which definitely marked the end of the old order in the North-West. With the suppression of the last effort on the part of Canada's primitive peoples to withstand the inexorable march of civilization, and the execution of Riel, the domination of the white man was forever assured. Henceforth the history of Western Canada was to be that of the white man, not that of the red man or of the half-breed.

Simple as are the conflicts of 1869 and 1885 when viewed as episodes in the history of the cultural frontier, they have always been complicated by the enigmatic personality of their leader. A man with a real popular appeal and considerable organizing ability, Riel was able to give unity and corporate courage to his followers. In him the self-assertive tendencies of the métis were liberated; to him they owed that self-confidence which they had never previously possessed and were never to possess again. Whether Riel was mad will ever remain a matter of debate. Medical opinion inclines to the view that his grandiose visions, his obsessional neurosis, his intense egotism, his intolerance of opposition, were all symptoms of a paranoid condition. It must be remembered that primitive aggressiveness and hostility lurk deep in the minds of all of us. Unless these tendencies can get adequate sublimation they reveal themselves in strong self-assertion, ruthless desire for power, delusions of persecution, irrational fixations and megalomania. That Louis Riel fits into this pattern there seems little real doubt. Perhaps the psychologist has the final answer to the problem of Riel's personality when he suggests that a repressed primitive aggressiveness explains, in part at least, Riel's behaviour in 1869 and in 1885.

The half-breeds of the Hudson's Bay Company Territories were a remarkable people. Children of the fur traders and the Indian women of the plains, they combined many of the best qualities of both races. Physically they excited the admiration of visitors. They were as much at home on the prairie as any Indian tribesmen and in their elaborate organization for the buffalo hunt they had a self-made military organization as efficient for its own purpose as the Boer Commando. Despite their semi-nomadic life and their mixed blood they were not savages. They were religious and reasonably honest; and in the golden days of the Red River Settlement serious crime was unknown. The authority of the Hudson's Bay Company was almost entirely moral; and when left to themselves the métis got on well with the Indians, with each other and with their rulers.

The serpent in this Eden was progress. For a long time the menace came from the south. American settlement proceeded faster than Canadian, and while there was still an empty wilderness between Fort Garry and Western Ontario there were fast growing settlements in the United States. Developments south of the frontier made it difficult if not impossible to enforce the fur monopoly; and developments south of the frontier meant the end of the buffalo and the demoralization of the Indians.

The newly created federation of Canada, fearful – and with ample justification – of American expansion northwards and of the intrigues of Senator Alexander Ramsey and the Minnesota party, finally concluded an agreement with the Hudson's Bay Company for the transfer of the Company's territories to Canada. To Canada and to the Canadians the acquisition of the North-West was a logical and necessary corollary to confederation; but to the people of Red River it meant their transfer to a "foreign" government whose interests were very different from their own. Evidence of these differences was soon afforded by the arrival in Red River of a party of Canadian surveyors who proceeded to lay out the land in a symmetrical pattern, taking little or no heed of the irregularities of the métis holdings, and precursing, in any event, close settlement, the destruction of the buffalo and the end of the wandering life of the prairie. The sons of Isaac were advancing on the lands of the sons of Ishmael. A clash was inevitable.

[Louis Riel was born in St. Boniface in 1844. He received the bulk of his formal education during eight years spent at a seminary in Montreal. In 1868 he returned to the Red River community and took over as leader of an insurrection against the government of Canada that was developing there. His career reached its peak on February 9, 1870, when a provisional government was established in Fort Garry with Riel as its president. In the negotiations that followed, many of the demands made by this provisional government were acceded to by Ottawa, and in May of 1870 Manitoba became part of Canada. But unfortunately for Riel he had, in March of the same year, made what would prove to be the most serious mistake of his career. This was the execution of Thomas Scott, a Canadian who had been involved in activities offensive to Riel's government. A storm of indignation over Scott's death rose in Ottawa, and when a force of militia was sent to Fort Garry Riel was forced to flee, despite the valuable contribution he had made in helping to establish Manitoba as a province and save the western plains for Canada.

As a result of these events in Manitoba, John A. Macdonald's government became involved in a political dilemma, with Quebec demanding that Riel be granted amnesty, and Ontario demanding that he be charged with Scott's murder. But neither action was taken, and Riel remained in exile, even after his métis followers had elected him to parliament in 1873. Brooding over the injustices that he felt he had endured, Riel suffered a nervous breakdown, and was confined to an asylum between the years 1876 and 1878. When he left the asylum, he settled in Montana, became an American citizen, married a métis woman, and became a teacher at a Jesuit mission school. It was from these circumstances that he was called in 1884 to lead a second protest movement against the government of Canada. Finding legislative methods of reform too slow, Riel once again proclaimed a provisional government, and armed rebellion soon followed as métis and Indian peoples combined to resist the federal forces. The uprisings were at first successful, but in 1885 the federal government was in a much stronger position for taking decisive action than it had been in 1870. An armed force of eight thousand men was rushed west on the newly completed railroad, and after a series of skirmishes the federal troops put down the rebels. Riel gave himself up on May 15, 1885.]

On July 6th, 1885, a formal charge of treason was laid against Louis Riel, then in gaol at Regina. This was the beginning of that trial which was to have such drastic consequences, not only for Riel himself, but for the whole of Canada. The jury was entirely Anglo-Saxon and Protestant, the defendant French and, by training at least, Catholic. Here were the old familiar elements of discord. And into the little courtroom stalked the ghost of Tom Scott, whose memory his Orange brethren had never permitted to rest. As the howl for vengeance grew louder in Orange Ontario so too did the cry for clemency in Catholic Quebec. A madman, a heretic, a métis he might be, to the people of Quebec Louis Riel was nevertheless a French Canadian, a victim of Anglo-Saxon persecution. Even while shots were still being fired at Canadian soldiers on the plains, Quebeckers had expressed admiration for Riel's heroic battle for the rights of his people, and when he surrendered they sprang to his defence and provided him with eminent counsel.

The argument adopted by the defence lawyers was that Riel was insane. It was pointed out that he had twice been in asylums, that he had committed the folly of attacking the church, that he had planned the establishment of a Canadian Pope and spent valuable time during the actual rising changing the names of the days of the week. But Riel would not accept this defence. He repudiated the plea of insanity. "I cannot abandon my dignity!" he cried. "Here I have to defend myself against the accusation of high treason, or I have to consent to the animal life of an asylum. I don't care much about animal life if I am not allowed to carry with it the moral existence of an intellectual being . . ." Twice he addressed the court in long rambling speeches; but the jury was only bored, and after one hour and twenty minutes' deliberation they declared him guilty. Henry Jackson, despite similar denials of insanity and an expressed desire to share the fate of his leader, was acquitted within a few minutes. To an English-speaking jury the English-speaking Jackson must obviously have been insane to have taken part in the rebellion. There was much truth in the statement made by one of the jurors fifty years later: "We tried Riel for treason, and he was hanged for the murder of Scott."

As the date set for Riel's execution approached feelings throughout Canada became more and more intense. Efforts to save the métis leader were redoubled in Quebec; efforts to ensure his death never slackened in Ontario. The Prime Minister temporized. He was uncertain what course to follow. The execution was postponed, and then put off again while a medical commission examined the question of Riel's sanity. But the terms of reference of the commission limited it to a determination of Riel's capacity to distinguish right from wrong and did not allow an investigation of his delusions; and when the report of the commission was published it was published in a truncated form. Throughout the autumn months petitions and letters from all parts of the world poured into Ottawa. Sir John had not a jot of sympathy for Riel, but he had to balance the political consequences of death or reprieve. There was danger of political disaster if Riel were hanged, but perhaps Sir John could trust to the loyalty of his French Canadian colleagues, Hector Langevin, Adolphe Caron and Adolphe Chapleau, and to the support of a Catholic hierarchy offended at Riel's apostasy. There might be still greater danger of political disaster if Riel were not hanged with every Orangeman in Ontario baying for his death. So Riel was hanged. On November 16th, once more a son of the church, the métis, Louis Riel, mounted the gibbet of Regina. The madman became a martyr.

It is hard to escape the conclusion that Riel's execution, to some extent at least, was determined by political expediency, that, in the final analysis, it represented the careful assessment by the Canadian government of the relative voting strengths and political loyalties of the two racial groups in Canada. If this were so then, for the moment, Macdonald's choice was not unsound. Admittedly the "nationalists" in Quebec, led by Honoré Mercier, succeeded in 1886 in overthrowing the provincial Conservative government in an election fought largely on the Riel issue; but in the federal election of 1887 Macdonald, with the support of his French Canadian ministers, still retained a sufficient number of Quebec seats to keep in power.

Yet he had lost ground. And even if he did not recognize it, the election results were an ominous warning of the fate which awaited the Conservative party in Quebec. In the long run the trial and execution of Louis Riel and the racial bitterness which it engendered led to a profound revolution in Canadian politics. As a result of the crisis of 1885 the most conservative province in Canada swung over to the Liberal party, a change in political allegiance which was cemented by the selection of a French Canadian, Wilfrid Laurier, as leader of that party. This shift in the political weight in Quebec, not as the result of any fundamental change in political outlook, but under the stress of a racial emotion, brought about a new orientation in Liberal policy. The old radical tradition of Clear Grittism and Rougeism was swamped by a basic rural conservatism; and for over seventy years the paradox endured of the backbone of the Liberal party being provided by rural Quebec.

Louis Riel was not a great man; he was not even what Carlyle would call a near great. Nevertheless he became, in death, one of the decisive figures of our history. By historical accident rather than by design he became the symbol of divisions as old as the Franco-British struggle for the control of northern North America. It is this historical accident which has obscured the fundamental character of the two risings which bear Riel's name; for the Riel "rebellions" were not what the politicians argued and what the people believed, a continuation on the banks of the Red and the Saskatchewan of the traditional hostilities of old Canada. They were, instead, the typical, even inevitable results of the advance of the frontier, the last organized attempts on the part of Canada's primitive peoples to withstand what, for want of a better word, may be termed progress, and to preserve their culture and their identity against the encroachments of civilization. To present-day Canadians Riel appears, no longer as the wilful "rebel" or "murderer" of Thomas Scott, but as a sad, pathetic, unstable man, who led his followers in a suicidal crusade and whose brief glory rests upon a distortion of history. To the métis, the people whom he loved, he will always be, mad or sane, the voice of an inarticulate race and the prophet of a doomed cause.

25. Clifford Sifton's Medicine Show

RALPH ALLEN

One of the most colourful chapters in Canada's history is concerned with the opening up of the western provinces just prior to the turn of the century. Ralph Allen captured something of the excitement of this time in an article that first appeared in the June 25, 1955, issue of Maclean's Magazine. *Mr. Allen (1913-66) was one of Canada's most successful journalists during the first half of this century. For several years he was managing editor of Maclean's, and at the time of his death held the same position on the Toronto Star. He was also the author of several novels, the best-known of which is* Peace River Country, *published in 1958.*

This account of Clifford Sifton's "Medicine Show" provides a sharp stylistic contrast with the preceding selection by Professor Stanley, especially in the level of diction employed. What other aspects of Mr. Allen's writing make it different in tone from the essay on Louis Riel?

From the start, the story of the two provinces that were carved out of the Northwest Territories fifty years ago has been a story of the unexpected and the unknown. It must remain so for at least another fifty years. For Saskatchewan and Alberta represent a union whose fruit is unpredictable almost by definition – the union of a very old land with a very young people. Some of the land, the northern rocks of the Canadian Shield, is as old as any land in the world. The prairies are older than the Nile, older than the hills of Jerusalem, older than Galilee and the valley of the Jordan. And the people are just as spectacularly young. Among voluntary settlers and descendants of settlers, they are second in their newness to their home only to the modern Jews of Israel, and the Jews knew Israel centuries before they returned to it.

It took the old land many millions of years to hew out its rocks and mountains, to bury its twenty-ton lizards and flying dragons, to sift and grind its soil, to hide its lakes of inflammable ooze and its underground hills of coal and metal. It took the young people who came there a maximum of decades and a minimum of weeks to size up the land and guess how best to live with it. In reality they knew very little of what to expect from the climate, or what the soil would stand, or what lay secreted beneath the soil.

It was no accident that they were naïve and ill informed. As the transcontinental railway pushed through the plains in the early 1880s it pushed through empty country. The whole prairie from Winnipeg west had only sixty thousand white inhabitants when the decade began. Halfway through the Eighties the Dominion government had had fewer than twenty thousand takers for the free homesteads it had begun offering more than ten years earlier, and more than half of these had already abandoned their farms and gone back to Ontario or the U.S. The CPR had no traffic for its railway and no buyers for its twenty-five million acres of land along the right of way. By the mid-Nineties the expected wave of settlement still had shown no sign of coming. Clearly, unless something quick and drastic were done the rails would turn to rust and with them the dream of a Canadian nation stretching from coast to coast.

The needed and drastic thing was done, by a quick and drastic man named Clifford Sifton. Sifton was federal Minister of the Interior. His was the chief responsibility for trying to fill a void a third as large as Europe. During the years between 1896 and 1905 Sifton and the CPR, with some help from the Hudson's Bay Company, the Grand Trunk Pacific and a few private colonization companies, staged the largest, noisiest and most successful medicine show in history. It covered two continents and was conducted in a dozen languages. Its message was simple and direct: whatever ails you, come to western Canada! In his role as chief barker, Sifton published millions of pamphlets extolling the free land of the Northwest Territories, and offering it gratis to anyone who would come and get it. In impressive rounded phrases worthy of a multilingual W. C. Fields, his literature cajoled the Swedes in Swedish, harangued the Germans in German, beguiled the French in French, coaxed the Hollanders in Dutch, wheedled the Norse in Norwegian.

The CPR supported him by sending out equally persuasive pamphlets in Welsh, Gaelic, Danish and Finnish, as well as the more common Western languages. At one time Sifton had twenty-one advertising agencies working for him. He and the CPR brought free-loading American editors to the prairies by the trainload. Successful western farmers from Britain and the U.S. were sent back home, as guests of the Dominion government, to carry the gospel to their old neighbors. Sifton sold huge tracts of Canadian government land at give-away prices to private colonization companies, then paid them a bounty out of the Dominion treasury for every settler they could produce – five dollars for the head of a family, two dollars each for women and children.

For every worthy human aspiration, and for some that weren't so worthy, the new paradise offered the virtual certainty of fulfillment. *Poor?* Where else could you acquire a hundred and sixty acres of land for a ten-dollar registration fee? Where else would a railroad take you halfway across a continent for six dollars? *Opposed by conscience to military service?* What other nation would offer conscientious objectors a guarantee against conscription? *In a hurry?* This from a pamphlet that bore Sifton's name: "The shrewd and sturdy settler who plants a little capital and cultivates it can, with due diligence, in a few years, produce a competency." *Lazy?* J. Obed Smith, one of Sifton's departmental assistants, assured the prospective immigrant: "He can make his crop in less than four months."

Sifton and his associate spellbinders answered possible hecklers in advance. *Schools inadequate, sir?* "Educationists," a Sifton circular announced solemnly in 1903, "assert the school system of the Northwest Territories is equal, if not superior, to that of any other country." *Communications unsatisfactory, sir?* "Excellent railway facilities, admirable postal arrangements." *Greater opportunities, my dear sir, in the United States?* As a minister of the crown, Sifton doubtless felt he could not personally denigrate a friendly nation. The CPR handled the question with a deft effusion of crocodile tears: "The decadent condition of many American farms is no doubt due to the prevalence of the tenant system."

One CPR circular, aimed directly at attracting immigrants from the U.S.A., borrowed the satisfied-user technique so popular with pill manufacturers. Typical headings above the testimonials read: "Would not Return to Indiana"; "Dakota Farmer Succeeded Without Capital"; "Prefers the Weyburn District to the States"; "Easily Earns Holiday Trips to Ohio."

The cold prairie winters and the hot dry prairie summers were never a serious embarrassment to Sifton, who contented himself with calling them "splendid." To have said anything less would have been, according to the relaxed idiom of the times, to have tampered with the truth. Even as late as 1910 by which time a good deal more evidence about western weather was on the record, not all of it favorable, a Grand Trunk pamphlet trumpeted: "The time has probably passed when the impression can exist that western Canada has a forbidding climate. Such fabrications have been put forth freely in the past by designing persons, but the greatest factors in advertising the delightful features of the climate, which quite submerge the few slight drawbacks, are the people already settled there, prosperous and happy. The summers are ideal in every respect with sufficient rainfall properly distributed, and when winter sets in with its bracing dry atmosphere and clear days, there is nothing to dread, but much to enjoy in this season of meeting friends and indulging in the sports and pastimes of the season."

The siren song was heard halfway around the world. Those earthy mystics, the Doukhobors, heard it in Russia and in a single month seven thousand of them streamed off the gangplanks at Saint John and boarded the colonist cars for Winnipeg and the central plains of Saskatchewan. Heartsick Ukrainians, without land and without a country, heard it under the flag of Austria, under the flag of the Imperial Czar, even under the flag of Brazil. They were soon to be western Canada's second largest racial group, second only to the Anglo-Saxons. Cockneys heard it in the crowded mews of Hackney. Members of the minor gentry heard it on the minor estates of Surrey and invited their younger sons into the study for a serious talk about the future. Ontario farm boys heard it as their time grew near for leaving home. So did ranchers from Texas, Oklahoma and Montana, cramped by fences.

Once the people started coming, Sifton did his best to retrieve his promises. At the railway terminals and along the staging routes, the Dominion government opened ninety immigration halls and staging camps, where bunks, cookstoves, surveyors' maps, advice and interpreters were available free of charge. By 1901 Saskatchewan's population was more than ninety thousand and Alberta's more than seventy thousand and in the next ten years these figures were quintupled. The dream of a nation had been redeemed.

The cost of its redemption and its reaffirmation in the half century since 1905 bore no relation to the estimates on the immigration folders. The ancient land proved alternately hospitable and cranky, kind and savage, benign and spiteful. Thousands of the settlers were wholly ignorant of agriculture. Even the relatively experienced Europeans knew little about farming large acreages; to them the basic tools were the grub hoe, the scythe, the hand flail and winnow and the wooden plow. Erosion and soil drifting were as foreign to the settlers' thoughts as nuclear energy. Drought, hail and autumn frost were unheard of – at least in the sunny folklore of the Department of the Interior. Grasshoppers, rust and weeds did not begin to appear north of the border until well after the turn of the century.

Thus the pioneers were ripe for ambush. Their mistakes were frequent, and ranged from the tragic to the bizarre. So did the vindictiveness of nature and the land. Of the first four white people to die in Saskatoon, two froze to death in blizzards, one drowned in the Saskatchewan River and the other died of exhaustion after fighting a prairie fire. In Alberta in 1906-7 the Chinook failed. The owners of the big ranches had no hay for their herds, for they had come to depend on the soft winter wind to uncover the uncut grass. Cattle and horses starved or froze by the tens of thousands. The Bar-U Ranch alone lost twelve thousand head. In 1903, a year of blizzards and bright sunshine, hundreds of horses went snow-blind and lost their lives by tumbling over precipices or blundering into gullies. A physician attached to the famous Barr colony, a mass pilgrimage of English families to Saskatchewan in 1903, complained that he spent most of his time patching up self-inflicted axe wounds.

The individual settlers' ideas of how to equip themselves for life on the frontier were often imaginative but odd. Not long ago Ray Coates, who arrived from England in 1903, recalled with amusement that he had come armed with dumbbells, boxing gloves and other muscle-building devices. At least one somewhat earlier arrival is known to have brought a case of Gold Cure, a contemporary remedy for alcoholism. Georgina Binnie-Clark, a spinster lady of quality, arrived in the Qu'Appelle Valley in 1905 with an expensive and ornate bathtub. She discovered that to fill it she would have to haul water three hundred yards, a pail at a time, from a well barely capable of supplying enough drinking water. So she sold the tub to another English lady, who discovered that *she* would have to haul water two miles to fill it. It ended up as a storage bin for seed. Mrs. Robert Wilson, of Bienfait, Sask., recently recalled a disaster that may have been unique: a horse once fell through the roof of her family home, a sod hut which her father had built on a hillside.

Their loyal children and their sentimental grandchildren have tried to enforce the tradition that the pioneers endured their troubles, large and small, with unfailing cheerfulness and courage. The theory is only partly supported by the written history of the period and by a cross-check with almost any of the thousands of men and women who lived through it and are still here to tell about it. Not long ago, I talked to a retired Leduc farmer named Luke Smith, born Lucan Smzt in Poland. Smith arrived in Halifax nearly sixty years ago. His pocket was picked aboard the ship and he docked without a penny. He borrowed two dollars from the fellow immigrant who was later to be his father-in-law and with that and his railway ticket he got to Edmonton. He went to work as a railway section hand at a dollar a day and after four years had saved enough money to make the down payment on a quarter section of land.

It took years to clear the land but he sustained himself by selling willow posts and firewood. By 1946 he had every right to call himself a success. He had raised and seen to the education of five children and he had a good farm with good crops, good cattle and good buildings. A man called in one day and offered him five dollars, plus a per-barrel oil royalty, for his mineral rights. Smith took it like a shot. ("I drilled twenty times for water and got nothing. So who's going to find *oil*? I was so glad about the five dollars I took it to town and bought a bottle of whisky.") A few months later the Leduc discovery well came in and Smith's next-door neighbor sold his mineral rights for $200,000. If Smith had any regrets on this score, they were not serious enough to remember; his per-barrel oil royalties still run as high as $3,000 a month and Luke and his vigorous, smiling wife give all but $200 of this to their children and grandchildren.

Just before Franklin Arbuckle and I left the cottage to which Luke and Mrs. Smith have retired, I asked a fairly routine question: Were you as happy in the early days as you are now? I half expected a routine answer about the joys and satisfactions of hardship and struggle honorably endured. Luke Smith and his wife have richly earned the right to clothe their memories in sentiment. But Luke was silent for several seconds, his strong, serene face deep in thought. Then he looked up gravely toward the kitchen doorway where Mrs. Smith stood with a dishcloth and the last of the supper dishes. The look they exchanged clearly said: *This question must be answered truly, but is it best that the man answer it, or the woman?* At last it was Mrs. Smith who answered. "He cried lots of times," she said with quiet dignity. "They all did."

In one way or another nearly everyone who was farming in Saskatchewan or Alberta fifty years ago says the same thing. In the last few years the provincial archives office of Saskatchewan has been asking original settlers to put their experiences on paper in order to flesh out the sparse printed records of the time. To the question, "How did you learn farming?", Frank Baines, of Saltcoats, replied succinctly: "By trial and error, with large portions of the latter." R. E. Ludlow recalled: "Nobody had nothing, and we all used it." Mrs. May Davis, who came to Canada from England in 1883, drew a haunting picture of the finality with which so many people committed all their earthly hopes into what for many of them was a literal void. "I can most particularly remember one poor sick-looking woman who was coming to Canada to join her husband, who had left England some months before. She had seven little boys with her, the youngest a baby at her breast. At our last sight of her she was on the wharf at Halifax, seated on a box of her 'effects,' waiting for her husband to come and claim them all. Did he come, I wonder – oh, but surely! – and where did they go and what became of them all? Perhaps by now one of those poor shabby little fellows has his name on the roster of Canada's famous men. Who can say? This is a land of opportunity and it is all a long, long time ago."

26. The First Fourteen

CHRISTOPHER ONDAATJE
and
ROBERT CATHERWOOD

The following essay is the summarizing chapter of a book entitled The
Prime Ministers of Canada, 1867-1967, *by two Toronto writers, Christopher
Ondaatje and Robert Catherwood. In one way at least, Mr. Ondaatje is
unique among Canadian historians: he was a member of Canada's eight-
man bob-sled team that won a gold medal in the Winter Olympics of 1964.*

*As well as touching on many of the main political events during the first
hundred years of Confederation, this essay develops a thesis about the role
of the prime minister in Canadian political life, particularly (as the clinch-
ing sentence makes clear) how the record of each prime minister is to a
large degree dependent on "the unpredictable tides of history". This thesis,
along with several other ideas related to the prime-ministership, is developed
by numerous specific details and illustrations. The essay provides an example of how the writer of history can use factual details as a basis for
making broad generalizations.*

The fourteen men[1] who led this country through its first hundred years had
little in common but the eminence of their office and the magnitude of
their task. Yet each has made his special imprint on Canada's history and
each has, during his years in power, changed the very nature of the Prime
Ministry. The kind of man he is determines the kind of Prime Minister he
becomes, and somehow reshapes the office forever after. Sometimes, when
he makes an historic decision or a single gargantuan error of judgment, his
influence is conspicuous. More often it emerges almost imperceptibly in the
rhythms of the nation's daily business. Gradually it alters the dimensions of
the office itself.

Though some Prime Ministers have been inept or unpopular, the power
of the office has steadily increased since 1867. As Canada has grown from
an infant nation of 3,000,000 to a middle-aged, middle-ranked citizen of

[1]Sir John A. Macdonald, Alexander Mackenzie, Sir John Abbott, Sir John
Thompson, Sir Mackenzie Bowell, Sir Charles Tupper, Sir Wilfrid Laurier,
Sir Robert Borden, Arthur Meighen, W. L. Mackenzie King, R. B. Bennett,
Louis St. Laurent, John Deifenbaker, Lester B. Pearson.

the world, the authority of her highest statesman has grown too. When Canada was born, around the conference tables of Charlottetown and Quebec, Macdonald's strength and stature made him appear pre-eminent among a number of able and imaginative leaders. The reins were in his hands; the decisions of the men who worked with him were often reflections of his individual vision. Today the business of government, which once seemed immediate and almost personal, has proliferated into an enormously complicated network of administration. Yet it is still the Prime Minister who holds the nation's purse, dominates Parliament, chooses the men who run the country and is ultimately responsible for their actions. Despite the growing responsibilities of the provinces, the Prime Minister is still easily the most powerful man in the country.

The measure of each Prime Minister's success lies not in the extent of his power but in what he was able to do with it. What each man accomplished depended partly on his native ability, but even more on the political facts of life in this strange northern country. His contribution emerged from the interplay between his particular talents and the social and economic forces at work in Canada in his era.

Though emphasis shifts from generation to generation, the overriding issues of Canadian government have scarcely changed over the past century. Economic independence, federal unity, provincial rights, racial and religious harmony and the encouragement of production and trade were the concerns of our earliest Prime Ministers and remain paramount today. Any man who hopes to run Canada must be capable of maintaining a series of incredibly delicate balances. He is pledged to international co-operation, and at the same time to resisting commercial and military pressure from the United States. He must be able to weigh his sympathetic response to the French spirit against his practical judgment of what is possible. He has to continue Canada's well-established social welfare measures without discouraging free enterprise. He must recognize the demands of provincial premiers without allowing them to erode federal authority. And, while he pursues all these righteous objectives, he can never forget that as a practising politician he has harnessed his career to his party and his public. Though the oratory of Macdonald and Laurier has been superseded by the television images of Diefenbaker and Pearson, a leader's success at the polls depends as much on his legend as on his actual record.

For many Canadians there is something distasteful about unconcealed ambition. We still cherish the idea that the office seeks the man, and those who take power foster the myth with pious expressions of bowing to the pressures of supporters and the call of duty. Seven of the fourteen men who became Prime Minister – Mackenzie, Abbott, Thompson, Laurier, Borden, St. Laurent and Pearson – originally had to be persuaded to accept leadership, yet in the end none of them refused the country's highest office.

Willing or not, none of the fourteen had an easy time as party leader or Prime Minister. For some the job was indeed a "splendid misery", as Thomas Jefferson called the Presidency of the United States. As well as attacks from other parties, some had to contend with the rivalry of their colleagues. Mackenzie and Bowell were rejected by their own parties. Even Laurier, the peerless leader and master of "sunny ways", eventually broke with the difficult Sir Clifford Sifton and the impossible Henri Bourassa. The pressures of office have proved severe enough for every leader without having to ward off his own supporters. Macdonald twice tried to quit; Laurier often longed for a quieter life; and King was always threatening resignation, probably never seriously, even for such petty reasons as being disturbed on a Sunday by a party worker.

The problems our early leaders faced seem strikingly familiar today. Then, as now, Confederation was no easy task. Macdonald's dream of a great nation called Canada, stretching from Atlantic to Pacific, proud and self-sufficient, uniting French and English in a new experiment in human co-operation, has dominated this country's politics to the present day. But, in Macdonald's time as in our own, a vocal body of Canadians insisted that economic union with the United States was the only route for citizens who wanted a high standard of living. French-English unity, then as now, was an aspiration not an accomplishment, and the façade was ready to shatter at the slightest test from Orangeman or separatist. Indeed, throughout the first thirty years of Canadian history, Canadians were highly pessimistic about their country's future and often doubtful of the advantages of Con-federation. In 1887, while Newfoundland was considering entry into the Dominion, the *Manitoba Free Press* commented, "If the people of New-foundland know when they are well off, they will give the Dominion a wide berth. There are few provinces, if any, in it today that would not rejoice to be out of it, and that would not forever stay out if they were."

What Macdonald brought to Confederation was the determination to make it work. He *was* Canada, and if the young nation had a surplus of pessimists, he would be the eternal optimist who overawed them. His accomplishment was to give meaning to the Canadian dream and hold together the tender threads of nationhood until they acquired a strength of their own. And, by the year 1880, other men were starting out in life on paths that would ultimately follow his own. In a small New Brunswick town, Richard Bennett was a schoolboy of ten, while in two Ontario villages, Arthur Meighen and Mackenzie King were just starting school. Robert Borden was now a promising Halifax lawyer of twenty-six, and Wilfrid Laurier was already an accomplished parliamentarian.

Throughout those early years of Confederation, Canadians were on the move. If the pessimists, annexationists and racial extremists were doing all the talking, other Canadians were getting about the job of building a country. In Toronto, just two years after Confederation, Timothy Eaton set up a shop that grew into one of the biggest retail empires on the continent. In the 1880s several of the giants of Canadian industry were first incorporated, including Imperial Oil, the Bell Telephone Company and the Canadian Pacific Railway Company. Aided by Macdonald's protectionist National Policy of 1878, Canadian business was starting to grow, though the Dominion's chief exports at that time were lumber, cheese and fish.

While Disraeli and Gladstone guided Great Britain, and a cluster of America's least-known politicians led that country, Macdonald dominated Canadian politics. In 1870, just three years after Confederation, he realized the essential link in his grand design. For only $1,500,000 he acquired the western territories of the Hudson's Bay Company and the Northwest Territories, an area of land, five times the size of the existing Dominion, which included most of what is today Northern Ontario and Quebec, as well as the great prairie region. That year a new province, Manitoba, was created, to be followed by British Columbia in 1871 and Prince Edward Island in 1873.

In those days, most Canadians lived in the country, as farmers, shopkeepers, blacksmiths or school teachers. In the 1871 census only 400,000 Canadians, out of 3,700,000, lived in cities, and in fact only twenty communities had populations of more than 5,000. Montreal was easily Canada's largest city, with 107,000 inhabitants, while Quebec City was second with 60,000 and Toronto third with 57,000.

If Macdonald left a monument to Canadians it was the C.P.R. Rarely has so much been at stake in the building of a railway. Physically, the construction of the C.P.R. must rank as one of the marvels of that age, anywhere in the world. Through dense bush and uncompromising rock across Northern Ontario, skirting perilously close to the bluff edges of Lake Superior, through the land of a thousand lakes past Kenora, the thousand-mile stretch of the prairies, and then the search for a pass through the Rockies, the tortuous climb through the mountains, and down through the marshy Pacific coastland to Vancouver. It also tested the political ingenuity of Macdonald. But built it was, and opened in 1885, just in time to thwart the rebellion of Louis Riel.

In the interregnum after Macdonald's death, only the unfortunate Sir John Thompson seemed capable of wearing the old chieftain's mantle, but Canada continued to grow in population and enterprise. In 1896 the discovery of gold in the Klondike sparked North America's last great gold rush. That same year, Wilfrid Laurier took control of a country already bustling with trade. Eastern manufacturers flourished while Sifton's vigorous immigration policy attracted European settlers to the west, and by 1911 Canada's population had risen to 7,200,000. With the new century came new methods of transportation. In Nova Scotia in 1909, J. A. D. McCurdy in his Silver Dart was the first Canadian to fly, and in 1911 the Ford Motor Company of Canada was established. In government, Laurier set up two new departments that also reflected the changing times: labour and external affairs. Canada's first Minister of Labour was Laurier's successor Mackenzie King.

The great achievement of Robert Borden, who defeated Laurier over reciprocity, was to secure for Canada a place in international affairs and, in the process, prepare a way for the Commonwealth and the 1931 Statute of Westminster. His premiership was dominated by the first World War, when 750,000 Canadians joined the armed services. Among the raw recruits who sailed for Europe were John Diefenbaker from Saskatchewan and Lester Pearson from Toronto.

Borden's successor, Arthur Meighen, had already earned the enmity of powerful Montreal financial interests by guiding through Parliament the legislation establishing the Canadian National Railway. Unequalled in debate, he had been the workhorse of the Conservatives. He took office in the turbulent period following a deadly flu epidemic, the Winnipeg general strike, the rapid rise of the Progressive movement in the west and other protest movements across Canada. In the election of 1921 he finished third behind Liberals and Progressives.

Under Mackenzie King, the Twenties in Canada were years of political stalemate and apparent prosperity, but the economy was in trouble and in 1929 the Great Depression hit, with all its cruel suddenness. For once King's sense of timing failed him and he allowed himself to be backed into a corner, opposing federal aid for the fast-rising number of unemployed. He was defeated by the decisive and confident R. B. Bennett, still one of the least understood Prime Ministers. Caricatured as ultra-conservative, he was in some respects a radical thinker of his day. His solution to the Depression was massive public spending, the Keynesian approach that the United States would adopt only two years later. He strengthened Canadian banking with the Bank of Canada, bolstered western farmers with the Wheat Board, established forerunners of Air Canada and the Canadian Broadcasting Corporation and worked vigorously but vainly for U.S. support of the St. Lawrence Seaway.

The Depression proved invulnerable to the boldest measures, and radicalism and protest were widespread. Social Crediter William Aberhart became Premier of Alberta, while in Regina a new socialist party, the Co-operative Commonwealth Federation, was formed. In Quebec, Maurice Duplessis was on the rise. Canada returned to King, but even a King who had now adopted Keynes was unable to speed economic recovery. Soon the country faced another world war, and King faced a new conscription crisis.

In 1948, as Alberta oil and Ontario uranium led Canada into its greatest economic expansion, Louis St. Laurent quietly succeeded King and administered the country as a giant corporation, with C. D. Howe as his executive vice-president. During his premiership, Canada joined NATO, took part in the Korean War and built the St. Lawrence Seaway, the Trans-Canada Highway and started on the much-debated pipeline. By 1956, the population had reached 16,100,000.

As a western radical, John Diefenbaker brought a new viewpoint to Ottawa. As a Canadian with Dutch ancestors, he represented the coming of age of the New Canadian. His greatest asset was his concern with individual rights, with the contribution of races other than French and English, and with the plight of the prairies, the Maritimes and Quebec and Ontario farm areas, the regions not sharing in national prosperity.

The first aim of Lester Pearson, Diefenbaker's antithesis in almost every respect, was the amelioration of Quebec's sense of estrangement. His main achievements, such as a Canadian flag and incentives for bilingualism, were intended to strengthen Canada in a different way.

In the end, what each Prime Minister manages to accomplish is partly determined by the accidents of history. In a country like Canada, where compromise is woven into the fabric of national existence, the most impressive leader is often the man forced by circumstances to move in a direction opposite to his own natural bent. Thus Macdonald, once reluctant to consider Confederation, became at last its triumphant advocate. When Laurier defied the Roman Catholic hierarchy over the Manitoba schools question, he won the support of English Canada without losing Quebec. Borden, too mild and rational to cherish dreams of martial glory, made his greatest contribution under pressure from a world war, when he insisted that Canada must have an independent voice in the war cabinet and at the peace conference. King, grey and cautious, and Bennett, with his capitalist instincts, initiated policies of welfare and state control that have been built into the platforms of every major party since their day. Diefenbaker, a proclaimed Anglophile, made his most impressive contribution to world affairs when, at the Commonwealth Prime Ministers' Conference in 1961, he defied Great Britain by censuring the racial policies of South Africa.

The premiership will never be easy. How should any man govern such a collection of illusions and harsh realities? Who can spin policies to embrace our fretful factions, strung along the border like snowballs on a fence, ready to slide into the American melting pot when the economic heat rises? What able person would be fool enough to risk his reputation on the chance outcome of an election?

The answer is, of course, that many people will want to be Prime Minister, and most of those who succeed will make a reasonable job of guiding Canada along a familiar path. With luck, a few may have the wit and audacity to rival the greatest men of our first century. All we can safely guess is that the size of the task will go on growing with the country. But in the future as in the past, the record of each Prime Minister will depend to a large extent on the unpredictable tides of history.

27. Checks and Balances

PIERRE ELLIOTT TRUDEAU

The meteoric political career of Canada's fifteenth prime minister is already well known. The essential facts are that he first entered Parliament in 1965, became minister of justice in 1967, and prime minister in 1968. What is perhaps not so well known is that Mr. Trudeau had for many years prior to his entry into federal politics been a prolific and aggressive writer, usually on national affairs as they affect Quebec. The selection that follows is part of the foreword written for a collection of nine of his essays published in 1968 under the title Federalism and the French Canadians. *The selection that follows is part*

The type of writing found in Mr. Trudeau's essay is essentially abstract. As a result, the reader must approach it with a determination to understand the numerous ideas introduced and follow the step-by-step development of the arguments presented.

The only constant factor to be found in my thinking over the years has been opposition to accepted opinions. Had I applied this principle to the stock market, I might have made a fortune. I chose to apply it to politics, and it led me to power – a result I had not really desired, or even expected.

In high school, when the only politics I was taught was history, I had already made up my mind to swim against the tide. But what was then an ill-defined reflex against intellectual regimentation became a conscious choice as soon as I went to university.

In 1944, and particularly in 1948, society in Quebec fell under the domination of the Union Nationale. I fought this régime until its downfall

175

in 1960. During the entire period, while nearly everyone connected with the Left was urging Ottawa to redress the situation in Quebec, I remained a fierce supporter of provincial autonomy.

By 1962, however, the Lesage government and public opinion in Quebec had magnified provincial autonomy into an absolute, and were attempting to reduce federal power to nothing; and so, to defend federalism, I entered politics in 1965.

I did so as a member of the federal Liberal Party, which I had often condemned while it was at the height of its power. Then the Party had lost its majority and was not to regain it for some time; but in spite of everything it advocated an open federal system, and that was what attracted me to it.

In joining the Liberals, I turned my back on the socialist party for which I had campaigned at a time when Quebec considered socialism to be treason and heresy; but I had no regrets because by then – in 1965 – most of its Quebec followers were in fact exchanging socialism for nationalism. They did this in the hope of finding a foothold in Quebec, but as a result they merely drew closer to the rising *bourgeoisie*. The latter was beginning to use Marxist terminology to justify its preaching of *national* socialism.

The fifteen years that followed the war saw the height of clerical power in Quebec. I was then "anti-clericalist" and advocated, among other things, the separation of Church and State. This is how I came to advocate the establishment of a Ministry of Education at a time when those who were later to establish it did not even dare mention the word.

My reputation as a radical was, however, based mainly upon the fact that I defended the importance of the provincial state as an instrument for collective action and progress. That was what was considered radical, before 1960! Since then the idea has gone such a long way – unfortunately in the wrong direction – that I have had to start denouncing ethnocentric and *bourgeois* abuses.

The *Quebec* State was becoming the *French-Canadian* State, and was sacrificing true social and economic progress to policies designed merely to promote *bourgeois* prestige. Worse still, people began to believe that the *Quebec* State (which people in our province persist in writing with a small "s") could give French Canadians more than they collectively possessed. So, for example, professional associations put pressure on the State to allow their members to be the highest paid in the country: nothing less could possibly satisfy the honour of Quebec! In this way, doctors, nurses, policemen, university professors, teachers, engineers, technicians, civil servants, and everyone involved in some way with public service, managed to wrest from the Quebec government salaries that were among the highest in the land. As these salaries were paid from tax revenues, and as taxes were levied in a province that was economically *below* average, the result was that the State's role in the new Quebec consisted of transferring to the rising middle classes funds taken from the mass of workers. I could not agree with that.

From 1952 to 1960 I worked for labour unions, both as a lawyer and as an economist. At that period they represented a movement for social liberation struggling against entrenched power. I began to feel uneasy about them when an excessive number of their leaders started to promote nationalism, thus joining forces with the secure, rising middle classes.

Still, in the years between 1952 and 1960, I was several times forbidden to teach in the universities, supposedly because of my anti-clerical and communist leanings. But I was invited to do so, with almost indecent haste, when power had passed to the other camp. In universities I found a rather sterile atmosphere: the terminology of the Left was now serving to conceal a single preoccupation: the separatist counter-revolution. . . .

I have never been able to accept any discipline except that which I imposed upon myself – and there was a time when I used to impose it often. For, in the art of living, as in that of loving, or of governing – it is all the same – I found it unacceptable that others should claim to know better than I what was good for me. Consequently, I found tyranny completely intolerable.

In Canada, and this includes Quebec, we have never known tyranny except in its figurative forms, for example the tyranny of public opinion. I am, however, far from considering that particular form the least terrible. For public opinion seeks to impose its domination over everything. Its aim is to reduce all action, all thought, and all feeling to a common denominator. It forbids independence and kills inventiveness; condemns those who ignore it and banishes those who oppose it. (Anyone who thinks I am exaggerating may count the number of times I have been called a "traitor" in recent years by the nationalist pundits of Quebec.)

I early realized that ideological systems are the true enemies of freedom. On the political front, accepted opinions are not only inhibiting to the mind, they contain the very source of error. When a political ideology is universally accepted by the élite, when the people who "define situations" embrace and venerate it, this means that it is high time free men were fighting it. For political freedom finds its essential strength in a sense of balance and proportion. As soon as any one tendency becomes too strong, it constitutes a menace.

The oldest problem of political philosophy, although it is not the only one, is to justify authority without destroying the independence of human beings in the process. How can an individual be reconciled with a society? The need for privacy with the need to live in groups? Love for freedom with need for order? . . . The most useful conclusion philosophy has come to is

177

that one must keep an equal distance from both alternatives. Too much authority, or too little, and that is the end of freedom. For oppression also arises from lack of order, from the tyranny of the masses: it is then called the Reign of Terror.

In this sense it is possible to say that there are no absolute truths in politics. The best ideologies, having arisen at specific times to combat given abuses, become the worst if they survive the needs which gave them birth. Throughout history all great reformers were sooner or later betrayed by the excessive fidelity of their disciples. When a reform starts to be universally popular, it is more than likely that it has already become reactionary, and free men must then oppose it.

There is thus the danger that mass media – to the extent that they claim to reflect public opinion – constitute a vehicle for error, if not indeed an instrument of oppression. For my part, I have never been able to read newspapers without a sense of uneasiness, especially newspapers of opinion. They follow their customers and are therefore always lagging behind reality.

Since the function of political science is to seek and define the conditions of progress in advanced societies, this discipline naturally favours institutions that guarantee freedom without destroying order. This is the reason for their great interest in parliamentary and federal systems. The former, because they make the various organs of power independent of each other and give a prominent role to the opposition. The latter, because they divide the exercise of sovereignty between the various levels of government, and give none of them full powers over the citizen. Strangely enough, the classic analyses of these two systems are found in French thinkers: Montesquieu observing the British parliamentary system, and de Tocqueville describing American democracy. (In view of the fact that it was the Canadian constitution that united the qualities of these two systems for the first time in history, it is rather paradoxical that French-Canadian "thinkers" should have such difficulty in perceiving its merits.)

The theory of checks and balances, so acutely analysed by these two writers, has always had my full support. It translates into practical terms the concept of equilibrium that is inseparable from freedom in the realm of ideas. It incorporates a corrective for abuses and excesses into the very functioning of political institutions.

My political action, or my theory – insomuch as I can be said to have one – can be expressed very simply: create counter-weights. As I have explained, it was because of the federal government's weakness that I allowed myself to be catapulted into it.

IV. Changing Patterns in Canadian Life

As historian Arthur Lower has pointed out, social history is concerned with the effect that man's environment has upon him. It follows from this that any collection of readings concerned with how people live, or have lived, will be extremely broad in its range and will be obliged to deal with a wide variety of things: the houses people build, the food they eat, the transportation available to them, and the kind and quality of the metaphysical and human values they cherish. In one sense, nearly everything that is written provides material for the social historian, since all writing in some degree reflects the world in which it was written. However, there are some works that are especially useful because they deal *directly* with the substance of social history. Excerpts from works of this kind have been brought together here, not in the vain hope that these mere ten will be able to delineate the entire social history of Canada, but rather in the expectation that they will suggest to the reader some of the major changes that have taken place during the last two hundred years when Canada was emerging from a relatively simple rural society into the complex, urban, and industrialized way of life that prevails today. Four of the selections included here (those of Marcel Trudel, Frederick Lewis Allen, Arthur Lower, and John Porter) are expositions. These authors comment directly on the societies that they deal with. But the other six are narrations, and here the reader must attempt to find within the events described the implied comments on social history.

28. Life in New France

MARCEL TRUDEL

This description of certain aspects of life during the earliest period of Canadian settlement is taken from a book entitled Canada, Unity in Diversity, *written by a quartet of Canadian scholars and published in 1967. The author of this material on French Canada is Marcel Trudel, a professor of history at the University of Ottawa.*

The writing in this selection can be described as the didactic style. What are some of the distinguishing qualities of this style? Consider especially the length and pattern of the sentences, and the use made of transitional devices as a means of attaining clarity of expression.

An attempt was made to pattern the society of New France after a European monarchy. Once the settlement had become permanent, however, this society rapidly lost its European characteristics and became American. The hierarchical strata remained rigidly apparent, but it often disguised the social confusion that prevailed in New France and, in fact, all the European colonies. The confusion stemmed from the impossibility of transplanting the mental orientations and traditional class privileges of the old country to the new land. The immigrants of the French Regime did not represent the whole of French society. The new immigrant found, in face of the great lack of men, that he was exposed to a greater variety of social functions. This could only happen, at this time, in a colony.

A great levelling process was at work in the colonies. The nobility was virtually without privileges, hard working and responsible for the same social duties as everybody else; thus it was readily lost in the group of common people. The commoners, on the other hand, were not condemned from birth to remain so, as was the situation in Europe. Commoners easily rose to high ranks in the colony. The motivating force and final criterion was the individual's personal dynamism and success. By the end of the French Regime, most seigneurs had issued from the common people. Proficient commoners such as Charles Le Moyne and Cavelier de La Salle rapidly reached the nobility. A young man, Pierre Boucher, who had begun as a domestic servant, became judge, seigneur, governor and nobleman. All were equal in this adventure.

If this society of New France was disparate in the elements that composed it, it was also disparate in its national origins. Although the proportions have yet to be determined, the national group was an integrated composite of many European nationalities and, more important, of Amerinds. The emergent American Frenchman, infused with a wide range of blood-lines and under the influence of the new environment, was characterized by his independence, instability, amazing endurance, taste for risk and hazard, faculty of adapting to new conditions and a habit of spending immediately what he had so painfully earned.

It is often said that even by 1760 the American Frenchman had come to consider himself as a different entity from the continental Frenchman. It was, in effect, the entire society that had become conscious of no longer being European.

A specific framework was needed in this new country to promote immigration, assure the immigrants protection, and prevent the disordered distribution of land. This framework was also needed to make the large landowners establish the most inhabitants possible on their land.

As a result, the seigneurial system was formed. In this, a tract of land of varying size was granted to an entrepreneur, or a seigneur, for the purpose of settling it. The reciprocal rights and duties were determined in advance and were closely supervised by the State in their execution.

The methodical application of a permanent seigneurial system occurred only in the Saint Lawrence Valley of Canada, and here France adopted a system of division that complied with the natural geographical features of the land. The river divided the country from the southwest to the northeast, and, therefore, served as frontage for the seigneuries to be established on both shores. In order that the greatest number of seigneuries might have access to the river, the holdings were narrow; but they were extended great distances inland without causing inconvenience. Lastly, in this unique patterning, all the seigneuries were extended away from the river in the same direction. This was done in an attempt to establish geometrically regular divisions in the new country. Two parallel lines were drawn at right angles to the frontage of the seigneuries on the northeast axis of the river, with the result that the tracts of land were formed into a series of long, narrow rectangles which ran in a northwest-southeast direction. Several geographical features like the larger islands, the Ottawa and Richelieu Rivers, and Lake Champlain imposed irregularities in these patterns.

The seigneuries were divided geometrically within their own boundaries as well. Similar to the major divisions, the seigneuries were sectioned off parallel to the borders of the property. These strips were also long and narrow for the purpose of allowing access to the river to the greatest number of habitants. Canada seemed to be divided into an infinite number of thin strips of land running northwest to southeast.

From the hierarchical point of view, the most important subdivision in the typical seigneurie was the personal domain of the seigneur. For example, the seigneur of Port-Joly owned a seigneurie of 168 *arpents*[1] frontage by two leagues deep, and within this held personal control over a tract of twelve arpents by two leagues. The size of these holdings varied from one seigneurie to another.

The remaining land was ceded by the seigneur. The building land was granted for the purpose of erecting the church and presbytery and the commune was granted for use as grazing land for the habitants' stock. The tracts ceded to the habitants had a shape analogous to the seigneurie as a whole, and usually measured three arpents frontage by two leagues deep. They were arranged in rows, the tracts in the first row being adjacent to the river. Finally, there was the land not yet ceded.

Usually there was no village (not to be mistaken for a parish) in a seigneurie. To allow the habitants to occupy as much land as possible, the State forbade the construction of buildings on areas less than one arpent and a half by thirty.

---

29. Building Bee in the 1830s

CATHERINE PARR TRAILL

At the beginning of the nineteenth century, most of Ontario was still pioneer country where the rough life of the settler offered few intellectual refinements. Despite this fact, several highly literate accounts of these times were written by pioneers. The two accounts that have remained particularly interesting are those by Susanna Moodie (1803-85), who wrote Roughing It in the Bush, *and her sister, Catherine Parr Traill (1802-99), who wrote* The Backwoods of Canada. *It is from this latter work that the following selection has been taken. Mrs. Traill's book consisted of a collection of letters, ostensibly written to her mother in England, but really designed to supply would-be immigrants to Canada with information and advice about*

[1]Arpent – a linear measure in use locally in Canada, being the length of the side of a square arpent, or approximately 65 yards.

*life in the Ontario bush. These letters were published in book form in
1836. Mrs. Traill, Mrs. Moodie, and their brother, Samuel Strickland (the
S—— of the narrative), settled on homesteads not far from the present-
day city of Peterborough.*

*Two things are curious about Mrs. Traill's writing. First is the contrast
between the roughness of the events described and the elegant tone and
diction of her description. Second is the revealing structural pattern that is
found in so many of her paragraphs. Notice how often she begins by describing some misfortune or lodging some complaint, then ends with an
attempt to see the brighter side of the way things are working out.*

But it is time that I should give you some account of our log-house, into
which we moved a few days before Christmas. Many unlooked-for delays
having hindered its completion before that time, I began to think it would
never be habitable.

The first misfortune that happened was the loss of a fine yoke of oxen
that were purchased to draw in the house-logs, that is, the logs for raising
the walls of the house. Not regarding the bush as pleasant as their former
master's cleared pastures, or perhaps foreseeing some hard work to come,
early one morning they took into their heads to ford the lake at the head of
the rapids, and march off, leaving no trace of their route excepting their
footing at the water's edge. After many days spent in vain search for them,
the work was at a stand, and for one month they were gone, and we began
to give up all expectation of hearing any news of them. At last we learned
they were some twenty miles off, in a distant township, having made their
way through bush and swamp, creek and lake, back to their former owner,
with an instinct that supplied to them the want of roads and compass.

Oxen have been known to traverse a tract of wild country to a distance
of thirty or forty miles going in a direct line for their former haunts by
unknown paths, where memory could not avail them. In the dog we consider
it is scent as well as memory that guides him to his far-off home – but how
is this conduct of the oxen to be accounted for? They returned home through
the mazes of interminable forest, where man, with all his reason and
knowledge, would have been bewildered and lost.

It was the latter end of October before even the walls of our house were
up. To effect this we called "a bee". Sixteen of our neighbours cheerfully
obeyed our summons; and though the day was far from favourable, so
faithfully did our hive perform their tasks, that by night the outer walls were
raised.

The work went merrily on with the help of plenty of Canadian nectar
(whiskey), the honey that our *bees* are solaced with. Some huge joints of salt
pork, a peck of potatoes, with a rice-pudding, and a loaf as big as an

enormous Cheshire cheese, formed the feast that was to regale them during the raising. This was spread out in the shanty, in a *very rural style*. In short, we laughed, and called it a *picnic in the backwoods*; and rude as was the fare, I can assure you, great was the satisfaction expressed by all the guests of every degree, our "bee" being considered as very well conducted. In spite of the difference of rank among those that assisted at the bee, the greatest possible harmony prevailed, and the party separated well pleased with the day's work and entertainment.

The following day I went to survey the newly raised edifice, but was sorely puzzled, as it presented very little appearance of a house. It was merely an oblong square of logs raised one above the other, with open spaces between every row of logs. The spaces for the doors and windows were not then sawn out, and the rafters were not up. In short, it looked a very queer sort of a place, and I returned home a little disappointed, and wondering that my husband should be so well pleased with the progress that had been made. A day or two after this I again visited it. The *sleepers* were laid to support the floors, and the places for the doors and windows cut out of the solid timbers, so that it had not quite so much the look of a bird-cage as before.

After the roof was shingled, we were again at a stand, as no boards could be procured nearer than Peterborough, a long day's journey through horrible roads. At that time no saw-mill was in progress; now there is a fine one building within a little distance of us. Our flooring-boards were all to be sawn by hand, and it was some time before any one could be found to perform this necessary work, and that at high wages – six-and-sixpence per day. Well, the boards were at length down, but of course of unseasoned timber: this was unavoidable; so as they could not be planed we were obliged to put up with their rough, unsightly appearance, for no better were to be had. I began to recall to mind the observation of the old gentleman with whom we travelled from Cobourg to Rice Lake. We console ourselves with the prospect that by next summer the boards will all be seasoned, and then the house is to be turned topsy-turvy by having the floors all relaid, jointed, and smoothed.

The next misfortune that happened was that the mixture of clay and lime that was to plaster the inside and outside of the house between the chinks of the logs was one night frozen to stone. Just as the work was about half completed, the frost suddenly setting in, put a stop to our proceeding for some time, as the frozen plaster yielded neither to fire nor to hot water, the latter freezing before it had any effect on the mass, and rather making bad worse. Then the workman that was hewing the inside walls to smooth them wounded himself with the broad axe, and was unable to resume his work for some time. . . .

Every man in this country is his own glazier; this you will laugh at: but if he does not wish to see and feel the discomfort of broken panes, he must learn to put them in his windows with his own hands. Workmen are not easily to be had in the backwoods when you want them, and it would be preposterous to hire a man at high wages to make two days' journey to and from the nearest town to mend your windows. Boxes of glass of several different sizes are to be bought at a very cheap rate in the stores. My husband employed himself by glazing the windows of the house preparatory to their being put in. . . .

But while I have been recounting these remarks, I have wandered far from my original subject, and left my poor log-house quite in an unfinished state. At last I was told it was in a habitable condition, and I was soon engaged in all the bustle and fatigue attendant on removing our household goods. We received all the assistance we required from S——, who is ever ready and willing to help us. He laughed, and called it a "*moving* bee"; I said it was a "fixing bee"; and my husband said it was a "settling bee." I know we were unsettled enough till it was over. What a den of desolation is a small house, or any house under such circumstances. The idea of chaos must have been taken from a removal or a settling to rights, for I suppose the ancients had their *flitting*, as the Scotch call it, as well as the moderns.

Various were the valuable articles of crockeryware that perished in their short but rough journey through the woods. Peace to their manes. I had a good helper in my Irish maid, who soon roused up famous fires and set the house in order.

We have now got quite comfortably settled, and I shall give you a description of our little dwelling. The part finished is only a portion of the original plan; the rest must be added next spring, or fall, as circumstances may suit.

A nice small sitting-room with a store closet, a kitchen, pantry, and bed-chamber form the ground floor; there is a good upper floor that will make three sleeping-rooms.

"What a nut-shell!" I think I hear you exclaim. So it is at present; but we purpose adding a handsome frame front as soon as we can get boards from the mill, which will give us another parlour, long hall, and good spare bed-room. The windows and glass door of our present sitting-room command pleasant lake-views to the west and south. When the house is completed we shall have a verandah in front and at the south side, which forms an agreeable addition in the summer, being used as a sort of outer room, in which we can dine, and have the advantage of cool air, protected from the glare of the sunbeams. The Canadians call these verandahs "stoups." Few houses, either log or frame, are without them. The pillars look extremely pretty, wreathed with the luxuriant hop-vine, mixed with the scarlet creeper and "*morning glory,*" (the American name for the most splendid of major convolvuluses.) These stoups are really a considerable ornament, as they conceal in a great measure the rough logs, and break the barn-like form of the buildings.

Our parlour is warmed by a handsome Franklin stove with brass gallery and fender. Our furniture consists of a brass-railed sofa, which serves upon occasion for a bed; Canadian painted chairs; a stained pine table; green and white muslin curtains; and a handsome Indian mat which covers the floor. One side of the room is filled up with our books. Some large maps and a few good prints nearly conceal the rough walls, and form the decoration of our little dwelling. Our bed-chamber is furnished with equal simplicity. We do not, however, lack comfort in our humble home; and though it is not exactly such as we could wish, it is as good as, under existing circumstances, we could expect to obtain.

---

30. A Public Event, 1847

"PATRICK SLATER"

Although this selection is from a work of fiction entitled The Yellow Briar, *there is historical evidence to support the accuracy of this account of a public hanging during the early years of Victorian Toronto. The* Yellow Briar, *which purports to be the actual reminiscences of a retired farm labourer named Patrick Slater, was actually written by a Toronto lawyer named John Mitchell, who was not born until thirty-five years after the events described here. But, despite the hoax, Mitchell's "novel" does present a reasonably accurate account of some aspects of life in Canada before Victorian respectability set in. The* Yellow Briar *was first published in 1933; John Mitchell died in 1951.*

The narrative technique employed by the author is rather loose, especially in what is generally termed the "point of view". What inconsistencies in the point of view are discernible in this selection?

One June day, we were down to the foot of Berkeley Street to see a double hanging; and that surely was one glorious, well-filled day. There was a high stone wall clear around the prison which stood close to the bay-shore; and the Fair Grounds lay open to the west. Two men, Turney and Hamilton, were to be hanged on a Tuesday morning. To give the public a tidy view of the drops, both before and after taking, a double gallows had been built facing the Fair Grounds and high on top of the prison wall.

Before the early-risers were abroad, hundreds of heavy farm carts and lumbering wains came creaking into town with their loads of merry, holiday-making country folk from far and near. Along the muddy roads came also bands of stalky farm lads, faring stoutly on foot, with stick in hand and bag on back, stepping down thirty miles or so to see the doings. Two men were to be killed by the law in the morning as an example to the public; and the schools throughout the district were closed that the children might benefit by so valuable a lesson in morals and good living. That day the taverns of Toronto did a stirring business.

"Your soul to the devil!" said young Jack to me. "Let us hooray down and see the necks stretched."

The hangings had been set for ten o'clock in the morning; but an hour ahead of time there was a good-natured throng of thousands jostling one another before the grim prison walls. It was the sort of crowd one sees nowadays at a big country fall fair. Neighbours were greeting neighbours, and joshing over local affairs. Men carried their liquor well in those days; and, of course, mothers had brought the young children in their arms. What else could the poor dears do?

A stir among the men on the prison walls told us the death procession was coming. A hush of awed expectancy fell upon the great throng. And this gaping crowd, stirred with thoughts of human slaughter, was standing in the most humane and tolerant colony Europe ever established beyond the seas! New England had been developed by the labour of convicts transported to be sold as serfs on an auction-block. We are often told of the *Mayflower* landing the Pilgrim Fathers on the Plymouth Rock. Oh yes! But we hear little of the fact that for a century every other merchant ship touching a New England port landed a cargo of convicts on the Pilgrim Fathers. The outposts of those colonies were pushed westward by rough frontiersmen who murdered as they went on frolics of their own. The southern colonies were developed by slave labour, and the full wages of that slavery have not yet been paid. One of the first laws passed in Upper Canada, in 1793, provided for the abolition of slavery; and, in dealing with another human, there has never been a time or place in Canada, save in her wretched prisons, that any man could with impunity make his will a law to itself.

You ask what brought thousands of people together to see such a terrible sight as a double hanging; and I answer you that fifty thousand of the likes

189

of you would turn out any morning to view a well-bungled hanging today. A murderer is a celebrity; and people run open-mouthed to see a celebrity, to hear him speak and see him decorated – or hanged – as the case may be. Every crowd hungers for excitement and is looking for a thrill. Every mob is by nature cruel and blood-thirsty. With all his clothing and culture, man remains a savage, a fact that becomes obvious when a few of them run together.

The breath going out of thousands of throats made a low murmur as the murderer, William Turney, in his grave clothes and pinioned, came into public view and stoutly mounted the stairs of the scaffold platform. A priest walked beside him. Behind them strode a hangman, who was closely masked.

It was a matter of good form – and decently expected in those days – that a murderer make a speech and exhort the public. A lusty cheer went up as William Turney stepped smartly forward to make his speech from the gallows. His was an Irish brogue; and his voice was loud and clear.

"Die – like – a – man!" shouted loud-voiced Michael, the smuggler.

Turney had been working the fall before as a journeyman tailor at Markham Village. He dropped into a local store one dark night to get a jug of whisky to take to an apple-paring bee. As the clerk, McPhillips, was bending over the liquor-barrel, Turney stove the man's skull in with a hammer, and then rifled the till. He turned off the spigot, blew out the candles, closed the wooden shutters, and quietly went home to bed. The dead body was not found till the morning after. No one had seen Turney abroad the night before. He came under suspicion the next day because he rode to Toronto on a borrowed horse, and bought himself for cash money a pair of boots and a leather jacket. But that, you'll agree, was not hanging evidence.

Turney, however, needed money for his defence; and while lying in gaol at Toronto he got a letter smuggled out to his wife. The poor simple woman was no scholar; and she asked a neighbour to read it for her. The letter told her the sack of money was hidden under a loose board in the floor of their back-house at Markham Village. He bade her get the money and give it to the lawyer-man. So the damaging evidence leaked out. How much wiser to have let the solicitor's clerk visit the privy!

On the scaffold, Turney made a rousing speech. He shouted to us that he had been a British soldier in his day, and was not afeared of death. Turney thanked us all kindly for the compliment of coming to his hanging. It was sorry he was for killing the poor man, McPhillips, who had never hurted him and had treated him as a friend. The crime, he told us, had not been planned, but was done on the spur of the moment. The devil had tempted him, and he fell. He had run home that dark night in a terrible fear. The wind in the trees sounded in his ears like the groans of poor tortured souls in hell. Hanging, he told us, was what he deserved. Let it be a lesson to us all.

Turney's feelings then got the better of him. He broke down and wailed loudly, praying that God would prove a guardian to his poor wife and fatherless child. The crowd did not like the tears. The high-pitched cries of women jeering at the miserable creature mixed with the heavy voices of men urging him to keep his spirits up.

"Doo – ye – loo-ike – a – maa-hun!" boomed Michael, the leather-lunged.

In the pause, Turney got a fresh holt on his discourse. He went on to tell us he had been a terrible character in his day. He had started serving the devil by robbing his mother of a shilling; and, in after years, while plundering a castle, he had helped wipe out an entire family in Spain. He explained that a full account of his high crimes was in the printer's hands. He beseeched everyone to buy a copy for the benefit of his poor wife and child. In the hope of getting a few shillings for them, Turney stepped back to his death with these great lies ringing in our ears.

At the foot of the scaffold stairs, the other felon requested the Protestant minister who walked beside him to kneel and have a session in prayer. The murderer seemed in no hurry to be up to finish his journey. The clergyman tried the stairs carefully, stepping up and down to prove them solid and sound. But it is hard to convince a man against his will. The hangman waited a tidy space, and then spit on his fist. He took the victim by the scuff of his neck and the waist-band and hoisted him up the stairs, the clergyman lending a helping hand. The crowd jeered loudly; but, once up in open public view, the felon's courage revived. Hamilton came forward with stiff, jerky little steps; and, in a high-pitched voice, he admonished us all to avoid taverns, particularly on the Sabbath.

Then the serious business began. The executioners hurried around, strapping the legs of their victims and adjusting the caps and halters. The culprits assumed a kneeling position over the traps and prayed to God for mercy.

A loud murmur went up from the thousands of throats – "Aw!" – as the bolts were shot. The two bodies tumbled down to dangle on the ropes and pitch about. It took Turney quite a while to choke to death. The other body seemed to drop limp.

This business of hanging folk should be intensely interesting to every Canadian of old-country British stock. The blood strain of every one of us leads back to the hangman's noose. Many a man was smuggled out of Ireland to save his neck from stretching for the stealing of a sheep.

And public hanging had something to justify it. In the olden days, human life was of little more account than it is today; and hoisting bodies in the air, and leaving them to rot on gibbets, was thought to be a rough-and-ready warning to evil-doers. What a pity public hangings were ever done away with! Had they continued a few years longer, the horrible practice of hanging men would have passed away under the pressure of public opinion.

---

31. A Victorian Gentleman

MARY-ETTA MACPHERSON

Not long after Canada entered Confederation, a young Irish immigrant opened a dry-goods store in Toronto. By the end of the century, the T. Eaton Company had developed into Canada's largest merchandising empire. In a book entitled Shopkeepers to a Nation, *freelance Toronto writer Mary-Etta Macpherson has told the story of the Eaton empire, and described its founder. The following is an excerpt from this book. Timothy Eaton lived from 1834 to 1907;* Shopkeepers to a Nation *was published in 1963.*

The events described in this selection are relatively simple, but they imply many things. What characteristics of Victorian society are epitomized by Timothy Eaton?

What sort of man was Timothy Eaton, who in twenty to thirty years could create a mercantile empire with nothing but his own work and inner convictions? A full portrait at this distance is hardly possible, yet there are illuminating glimpses still worth seeking out from past records and family memories. He believed profoundly in personal integrity in business, and his restless search for quality was directed even more toward men's minds and characters than to the merchandise they would sell. Almost all his relatives were invited at one time or another to join his organization. Many accepted, but if they failed to measure up he dismissed them as summarily as he would a lazy parcel boy. There was an awesome crisis – still somewhat of a mystery – which he resolved with the overnight firing of three trusted directors, one of them his sister Eliza Jane's grandson.

Timothy was a man of few words, and they were delivered in a crisp, quick way. He had early learned, and admitted, that this trait unsuited him for face-to-face dealings with shoppers at the counter. He had a fondness for slogans and mottoes, one of them being "the greatest good for the greatest number," which he found applicable to both customers and employees. He could quote the Bible effectively for any type of occasion. His remarks at an annual meeting of directors concluded with, "Go to the ant, thou sluggard, consider her ways and be wise"; business, he declared, would improve if each man present would take the earliest opportunity to study "what goes on at an ant hill."

For years he had written his own advertising; when pressure of expansion necessitated turning this duty over to a department, he passed on the following note in his own vigorous, sprawling handwriting (a scrap of paper reverently guarded by managers there for many years): "Tell your story to public – what you have and what you propose to sell. Promise them not only bargains but that every article will be found just what it is guaranteed to be. Whether you sell a first rate or a 3rd rate article, the customer will get what they bargain for.... Use no deception in the smallest degree – nothing you cannot defend before God and Man."

In all the ways essential to mercantile success Timothy Eaton was a total modern, even a revolutionist; yet he had little use for much of the paraphernalia that would soon become indispensable to twentieth-century business: memos, wordy reports, downtown clubs, head tables, personal publicity. Most of his philanthropy was done in secret, often on the spur of the moment. One day in the middle of a long, severe winter he dropped in at the store's employment office to see the manager. "There must be quite a few of our people away, sick and in need," he said. "I want you to use this to help them," he went on, handing over a cheque for three thousand dollars, drawn on his private account. "When it's all gone, let me know." Out of such informal incidents and the concern that prompted them was to grow the welfare service with its branches of nursing and medical help, sick-visiting and emergency financial aid where required.

Away from the store Timothy Eaton's chief interests were church and home. In the 1890's he ensconced his family in one of the city's grandest new residences, a rambling mansion at the northwest corner of Spadina Road and Lowther Avenue, a new district to the north-west of central Toronto. (The building is now the national headquarters of the IODE, a gift to this women's organization from an Eaton daughter, Josephine.) In its family heyday the house was much admired for its size; it was almost as big as Government House on King Street, ample with corridors, staircases, fireplaces, palm-filled conservatories, reception rooms hung with *pointe de Venise* lace curtains, and furnished with French gilt chairs and rich ornaments in countless numbers on display in glass cabinets and on every available inch of flat surface.

At home, Timothy was always "Father," and for years his name for his wife was simply "Mother."

Any guest who might happen to be staying with the Eatons over the weekend would inevitably find themselves at morning service with the family in the regular pew at nearby Trinity Methodist, the church which Timothy and a few other gentlemen, including his nephew John Crabbe, a senior executive with the Toronto *Star*, had recently founded on Bloor Street in the developing area "uptown."

A careful mother could send her daughter to the Eaton home with perfect confidence: it was one of the few great mansions where cards, dancing, and any drink stronger than tea were totally banned. But Margaret Eaton's hospitality was famous. At Sunday dinner, as butler and maid hovered about behind the guests, the hostess would call out merrily, "Eat hearty and give the house a good name." Sometimes at the end of the meal, guests would be amazed to see a small bowl of cold mashed potatoes and a jug of buttermilk placed before the host, who would proceed to pour the latter over the former and eat the mixture with great relish. This was one of his favourite Irish combinations but, rather than interrupt his wife's meticulously planned menu, he waited till after dessert for his special dish.

Timothy loved to sit at the head of a long tableful of people, especially if they were The Family. He made it a point to remember the names of all the Eatons, even down to the latest third-generation newcomer. He was their patriarch, their tribal chieftain. Some within the connection resisted his supremacy, some turned away, and their sons and daughters were to grow up unacquainted with their Toronto cousins. But not one among them was so foolish, so blind, or so bitter as to deny that the fatherless boy from Clogher had indeed "done well."

---

32. The Coming of the Model T

HARRY J. BOYLE

A popular literary pastime for many contemporary Canadians of a certain age is writing nostalgic memoirs about their boyhood back in those turn-of-the-century days when life was rural and uncomplicated and home was a farm. One of the most successful of such works is Harry J. Boyle's Mostly in Clover, *the book from which the following selection has been taken. Mr. Boyle, who for many years was a Toronto executive of the* CBC, *published his reminiscences of rural Ontario in 1961. The Model T first appeared on the market in 1909.*

This brief narrative can be looked at in several different ways. For example, it can be seen as symbolizing the spirit of what are often termed the "yeoman" days of agriculture, that period which stands between the pioneer-homestead era and the advent of the highly mechanized farm. A second approach might be to consider the type of characterization that Mr. Boyle has made use of here. To what extent are his characters stereotypes that appear again and again in the folklore of North American family life?

All things change, even in the country. The biggest change came with the advent of the Model T. Many words have been spilled in praise of the Model T. Some are earned and others are just plain sentimental. The years have glossed over some of the cantankerous qualities of the tinny monster. It's strange, that after a very few years, a person can even forget the "kick" of the crank that sent him spinning when the "Lizzy" was feeling on the temperamental side.

There was one time, however, when no car could compare with the Model T. That was during the spring season when our roads froze over at night and melted to a gooey morass during the day. I've seen a man get stuck with a horse and buggy, but my father was always able to get around in the "puddle jumper."

How thrilling it was when that brass-nosed car arrived at the house! There was a "sassy" quality about the flowing F on the radiator beginning the word Ford. The brass shone. The body was jet black and the side curtains with their mica windows were piled neatly on the back seat. The headlamps burned carbon with gas that came in some mysterious fashion from water and a chemical compound.

Albert Gibson, the cream-separator man turned car-dealer, brought the car into our front yard on a Saturday morning. Mother came out wiping her hands on her apron and even Grandfather, who had a prejudice against anything that challenged horses, ventured off the back veranda. Father, trying to appear casual, but really brimming over with excitement, made the announcement.

"Take a good look, folks. It's ours!"

With the selfishness of a small boy I immediately thought of how, for a change, we could scare *other* people's horses on the way to church or the village. Albert tried to coax Mother to get into the car. She refused and made a retreat to the house. The car salesman looked defeated but Father grinned.

"Don't worry. She'll be back."

Then he leaned over and whispered, "She wants to change her clothes."

A ride in a jet couldn't have compared with that first ride in the car. Mother, Grandfather and I were in the back seat, while Father rode up front with Albert. We scooted out and wheeled onto the road, fairly sailing down the hill. We coasted across the creek bridge and built up a fair speed for the grade.

"See the way she takes the hill?"

Mother was hanging on to the back of the front seat with one hand, clutching her hat with the other and looking frightened.

"We're going awfully fast, aren't we?"

Albert was elated.

"Oh no, ma'am. There's no danger. No blow-outs on this job."

There couldn't be blow-outs; we had solid rubber tires. At that time I didn't notice the bumps.

Father spent the afternoon with Albert in the big pasture field. The stock spent the afternoon in the swale, alarmed and confused by the whole thing. The cows gave a good deal less milk that night. Grandfather said it was because of the gasoline fumes. Mother said they were nervous.

She insisted that we take the horse and buggy to church the next day. My father was angry when his brother, who had been driving a car for a year, asked him if he had tied ours up before coming to church. That afternoon when Grandfather and Mother were having their usual Sunday rest, Father took off in the car. He made the roadway and got past the creek bridge but it stalled on the far grade and he ended up in the ditch.

Father was not a man to admit defeat. He mastered the driving and even learned the art of cranking, in spite of having almost put his shoulder out of joint when the spark was down too far. There was one thing he wouldn't admit. Those hard rubber tires gave one a bone-shaking ride. Mother began to pack the eggs for selling in oats in baskets so they wouldn't break on the way to the village.

There was something daring and graceful about the way that car could be steered to avoid the pot-holes and the places where the frost had pushed out corduroy in some of the roads through the long swamp. Grandfather said it reminded him of the way the daddy-long-legs navigated the creek water.

196

33. A Girl with Ambition

MORLEY CALLAGHAN

Novelist and short-story writer Morley Callaghan has been writing fiction with a Canadian setting since the mid 1920s when he was a law student in Toronto. The following is Mr. Callaghan's first published story. It is typical of his spare and ironic style and of his interest in characters living on the fringe of success. Among Mr. Callaghan's best-known novels are Such Is My Beloved *(1934),* More Joy in Heaven *(1937), and* The Loved and the Lost *(1951).*

One possible approach to this story is to examine its plot structure in terms of the various choices that are open (or seem to be open) to Mary Ross, the story's central character. The point that Mr. Callaghan makes is closely connected with why she rejects (or is unable to choose) the alternatives that she thinks are open to her.

After leaving public school when she was sixteen Mary Ross worked for two weeks with a cheap chorus at the old La Plaza, quitting when her stepmother heard the girls were a lot of toughs. Mary was a neat clean girl with short fair curls and blue eyes, looking more than her age because she had very good legs, and knew it. She got another job as cashier in the shoe department of Eaton's Store, after a row with her father and a slap on the ear from her stepmother.

She was marking time in the store, of course, but it was good fun telling the girls about imaginary offers from big companies. The older salesgirls sniffed and said her hair was bleached. The salesmen liked fooling around her cage, telling jokes, but she refused to go out with them; she didn't believe in running around with fellows working in the same department. Mary paid her mother six dollars a week for board and always tried to keep fifty cents out. Mrs. Ross managed to get the fifty cents, insisting every time that Mary would come to a bad end.

Mary met Harry Brown when he was pushing a truck on the second floor of the store, returning goods to the department. Every day he came over from the mail-order building, stopping longer than necessary in the shoe department, watching Mary in the cash cage out of the corner of his eye while he fidgeted in his brown wicker truck. Mary found out that he went to high school and worked in the store for the summer holidays. He hardly spoke to her, but once when passing, he slipped a letter written on wrapping paper under the cage wire. It was such a nice letter that she wrote a long one the next morning and dropped it in his truck when he passed. She liked him because he looked neat and had a serious face and wrote a fine letter with big words that was hard to read.

In the morning and early afternoons they exchanged wise glances that held a secret. She imagined herself talking very earnestly, all about getting on. It was good having someone to talk to like that because the neighbours on her street were always teasing her about going on the stage. If she went to the corner butcher to get a pound of round steak cut thin, he saucily asked how was the village queen and the actorine. The lady next door, who had a loud voice and was on bad terms with Mrs. Ross, often called her a hussy, saying she should be spanked for staying out so late at night, waking decent people when she came in.

Mary liked to think that Harry Brown knew nothing of her home or street, for she looked up to him because he was going to be a lawyer. Harry admired her ambition but was a little shy. He thought she knew too much for him.

In the letters she called herself his sweetheart but never suggested they meet after work. Her manner implied it was unimportant that she was working in the store. Harry, impressed, liked to tell his friends about her, showing off the letters, wanting them to see that a girl who had a lot of experience was in love with him. "She's got some funny ways but I'll bet no one gets near her," he often said.

They were together the first time the night she asked him to meet her downtown at 10:30 p.m. He was at the corner early and didn't ask where she had been earlier in the evening. She was ten minutes late. Linking arms they walked east along Queen Street. He was self-conscious. She was trying to be very practical, though pleased to have on her new blue suit with the short stylish coat.

Opposite the Cathedral at the corner of Church Street, she said: "I don't want you to think I'm like the people you sometimes see me with, will you now?"

"Gee no, I think you away ahead of the girls you eat with at noon hour."

"And look, I know a lot of boys, but that don't mean nothing. See?"

"Of course, you don't need to fool around with tough guys, Mary. It won't get you anywhere," he said.

"I can't help knowing them, can I?"

"I guess not."

"But I want you to know that they haven't got anything on me," she said, squeezing his arm.

"Why do you bother with them?" he said, as if he knew the fellows she was talking about.

"I go to parties, Harry. You got to do that if you're going to get along. A girl needs a lot of experience."

They walked up Parliament and turned east, talking confidentially as if many things had to be explained before they could be satisfied with each other. They came to a row of huge sewer pipes along the curb for a hundred yards to the Don River Bridge. The city was repairing the drainage. Red lights were about fifty feet apart on the pipes. Mary got up on the pipes and walked along, supporting herself with a hand on Harry's shoulder, while they talked in a silly way, laughing. A night-watchman came along and yelled at Mary, asking if she wanted to knock the lights over.

"Oh, have an apple," Mary yelled back at him.

"You better get down," Harry said, very dignified.

"Aw, let him chase me," she said. "I'll bet he's got a wooden leg," but she jumped down and held on to his arm.

For a time they stood on the bridge, looking beyond the row of short poplars lining the hill in the good district on the other side of the park. Mary asked Harry if he didn't live over there, wanting to know if they could see his house from the bridge. They watched the lights on a street-car moving slowly up the hill. She felt that he was going to kiss her. He was looking down at the slow-moving water wondering if she would like it if he quoted some poetry.

"I think you are swell," he said finally.

"I'll let you walk home with me," she said.

"Gee, I wish you didn't want to be an actress," he said.

They retraced their steps until a few blocks from her home. They stood near the police station in the shadow of the fire hall. He coaxed so she let him walk just one block more. In the light from the corner butcher store keeping open, they talked for a few minutes. He started to kiss her. "Oh, the butcher will see us," she said, but didn't care, for Harry was very respectable-looking and she wanted to be kissed. Harry wondered why she wouldn't let him go to the door with her. She left him and walked ahead, turning to see if he was watching her. It was necessary she walk a hundred yards before Harry went away. She turned and walked back home, one of a row of eight dirty frame houses jammed under one long caving roof.

She talked a while with her father, but was really liking the way Harry had kissed her, and talked to her, and the very respectable way he had treated her, all evening. She hoped he wouldn't meet any boys who would say bad things about her.

She might have been happy if Harry had worked on in the store. It was the end of August and his summer holidays were over. The last time he pushed his wicker truck over to the cash cage, she said he was to remember she would always be a sincere friend and would write often. They could have seen each other for he wasn't leaving the city, but they took it for granted they wouldn't.

Every week she wrote to him about offers and rehearsals that would have made a meeting awkward. She liked to think of him not because of being in love but because he seemed so respectable. Thinking of how he liked her made her feel a little better than the girls she knew.

When she quit work to spend a few weeks up at Georgian Bay with a girl friend, Hilda Heustis, who managed to have a good time without working, she forgot about Harry. Hilda had a party in a cottage on the beach and they came home the night after. It was cold and it rained all night. One of Hilda's friends, a fat man with a limp, had chased her around the house and down to the beach, shouting and swearing, and into the bush, limping and groaning. She got back to the house all right. He was drunk. A man in pajamas from the cottage to the right came and thumped on the door, shouting that they were a pack of strumpets, hussies and rotters and if they didn't clear out he would have the police on them before they could say Tom Thumb. He was shivering and looked very wet. Hilda, a little scared, said they ought to clear out next day.

Mary returned to Toronto and her stepmother was waiting, very angry because Mary had left her job. They had a big row. Mary left home, slamming the door. She went two blocks north to live with Hilda.

It was hard to get a job and the landlady was nasty. She tried to get work in a soldiers' company touring the province with a kind of musical comedy called "Mademoiselle from Courcelette", but the manager, a nice young fellow with tired eyes, said she had the looks but he wanted a dancer. After that Mary and Hilda every night practised a step dance, waiting for the show to return.

Mary's father one night came over to the boarding-house and coaxed her to come back home because she was really all he had in the world, and he didn't want her to turn out to be a good-for-nothing. He rubbed his brown face in her hair. She noticed for the first time that he was getting old and was afraid he was going to cry. She promised to live at home if her stepmother would mind her own business.

Now and then she wrote to Harry just to keep him thinking of her. His letters were sincere and free from slang. Often he wrote, "What is the use of trying to get on the stage?" She told herself he would be astonished if she were successful, would look up to her. She would show him.

Winter came and she had many inexpensive good times. The gang at the east-end roller-rink knew her and she occasionally got in free. There she met Wilfred Barnes, the son of a grocer four blocks east of the fire hall, who had a good business. Wilfred had a nice manner but she never thought of him in the way she thought of Harry. He got fresh with little encouragement. Sunday afternoons she used to meet him at the rink in Riverdale Park where a bunch of the fellows had a little fun. Several times she saw Harry and a boy friend walking through the park, and leaving her crowd, she would talk to him for a few minutes. He was shy and she was a little ashamed of her crowd that whistled and yelled while she was talking. These chance meetings got to mean a good deal, helping her to think a lot about Harry during the first part of the week.

In the early spring "Mademoiselle from Courcelette" returned to Toronto. Mary hurried to the man that had been nice to her and demonstrated the dance she had practised all winter. He said she was a good kid and should do well, offering her a try-out at thirty dollars a week. Even her stepmother was pleased because it was a respectable company that a girl didn't need to be ashamed of. Mary celebrated by going to a party with Wilfred and playing strip poker until four a.m. She was getting to like being with Wilfred.

When it was clear she was going on the road with the company, she phoned Harry and asked him to meet her at the roller-rink.

She was late. Harry was trying to roller-skate with another fellow, fair-haired, long-legged, wearing large glasses. They had never roller-skated before but were trying to appear unconcerned and dignified. They looked very funny because everyone else on the floor was free and easy, willing to start a fight. Mary got her skates on but the old music box stopped and the electric sign under it flashed "Reverse". The music started again. The skaters turned and went the opposite way. Harry and his friend skated off the floor because they couldn't cut corners with the left foot. Mary followed them to a bench near the soft-drink stand.

"What's your hurry, Harry?" she yelled.

He turned quickly, his skates slipping, and would have fallen, but his friend held his arm.

"Look here, Mary, this is the damnedest place," he said.

His friend said roguishly, "Hello, I know you because Harry has told me a lot about you."

"Oh, well, it's not much of a place but I know the gang," she said.

"I guess we don't have to stay here," Harry said.

"I'm not fussy. Let's go for a walk, the three of us," she said.

Harry was glad his friend was noticing her classy blue coat with the wide sleeves and her light brown fur. Taking off his skates he tore loose a leather layer on the sole of his shoe.

They left the rink and arm-in-arm the three walked up the street. Mary was eager to tell about "Mademoiselle from Courcelette". The two boys were impressed and enthusiastic.

"In some ways I don't like to think of you being on the stage, but I'll bet a dollar you get ahead," said Harry.

"Oh, baby, I'll knock them dead in the hick towns."

"How do you think she'll do, Chuck?" said Harry.

The boy with glasses could hardly say anything, he was so impressed. "Gee whiz," he said.

Mary talked seriously. She had her hand in Harry's coat pocket and kept tapping his fingers. Harry gaily beat time as they walked, flapping the loose shoe leather on the sidewalk. They felt that they should stay together after being away for a long time. When she said that it would be foolish to think she would cut up like some girls in the business did, Harry left it to Chuck if a fellow couldn't tell a mile away that she was a real good kid.

The lighted clock in the tower of the fire hall could be seen when they turned a bend in the street. Then they could make out the hands on the clock. Mary, leaving them, said she had had a swell time, she didn't know just why. Harry jerked her into the shadow of the side door of the police station and kissed her, squeezing her tight. Chuck leaned back against the wall, wondering what to do. An automobile horn hooted. Mary, laughing happily, showed the boys her contract and they shook their heads earnestly. They heard footfalls around the corner. "Give Chuck a kiss," said Harry suddenly, generously. The boy with the glasses was so pleased he could hardly kiss her. A policeman appeared at the corner and said, "All right, Mary, your mother wants you. Beat it."

Mary said, "How's your father?" After promising to write Harry she ran up the street.

The boys, pleased with themselves, walked home. "You want to hang on to her," Chuck said.

"I wonder why she is always nice to me just when she is going away," Harry said.

"Would you want her for a girl?"

"I don't know. Wouldn't she be a knock-out at the school dance? The old ladies would throw a fit."

Mary didn't write to Harry and didn't see him for a long time. After two weeks she was fired from the company. She wasn't a good dancer.

Many people had a good laugh and Mary stopped talking about her ambitions for a while. And though usually careful and fairly strict, she slipped into easy careless ways with Wilfred Barnes. She never thought of him as she thought of Harry, but he won her and became important to her. Harry was like something she used to pray for when a little girl and never really expected to get.

It was awkward when Wilfred got into trouble for tampering with the postal pillars that stood on the street corners. He had discovered a way of getting all the pennies people put in the slots for stamps. The police found a big pile of coppers hidden in his father's stable. The judge sent him to jail for only two months because his parents were very respectable people. He promised to marry Mary when he came out.

One afternoon in the late summer they were married by a Presbyterian minister. Mrs. Barnes made it clear that she didn't think much of the bride. Mr. Barnes said Wilfred would have to go on working in the store. They took three rooms in a big rooming-house on Berkeley Street.

Mary cried a little when she wrote to tell Harry she was married. She had always been too independent to cry in that way. She would be his sincere friend and still intended to be successful on the stage, she said. Harry wrote that he was surprised that she had married a fellow just out of jail even though he seemed to come from respectable people.

In the dancing-pavilion at Scarboro beach, a month later, she talked to Harry for the last time. The meeting was unexpected and she was with three frowsy girls from a circus that was in the east end for a week. Mary had on a long blue knitted cape that the stores were selling cheaply. Harry turned up his nose at the three girls but talked cheerfully to Mary. They danced together. She said that her husband didn't mind her taking another try at the stage and he wondered if he should say that he had been to the circus. Giggling and watching him closely, she said she was working for the week in the circus, for the experience. He gave her to understand that always she would do whatever pleased her, and shouldn't try for a thing that wasn't natural to her. He wasn't enthusiastic when she offered to phone him, just curious about what she might do.

Late in the fall a small part in a local company at the La Plaza for a week was offered to her. She took the job because she detested staying around the house. She wanted Harry to see her really on the stage so she phoned and asked if he could come to the La Plaza on Tuesday night. Good-humouredly, he offered to take her dancing afterward. It was funny, he said laughing, that she should be starting all over again at the La Plaza.

But Harry, sitting solemnly in the theatre, watching the ugly girls in tights on the stage, couldn't pick her out. He wondered what on earth was the matter when he waited at the stage door and she didn't appear. Disgusted, he went home and didn't bother about her because he had a nice girl of his own. She never wrote to tell him what was the matter.

But one warm afternoon in November, Mary took it into her head to sit on the front seat of the rig with Wilfred, delivering groceries. They went east through many streets until they were in the beach district. Wilfred was telling jokes and she was laughing out loud. Once he stopped his wagon, grabbed his basket and went running along a side entrance, yelling "Grocer." Mary sat on the wagon seat. Three young fellows and a woman were sitting up on a veranda opposite the wagon. She saw Harry looking at her and vaguely wondered how he got there. She didn't want him to see that she was going to have a baby. Leaning on the veranda rail, he saw that her slimness had passed into the shapelessness of her pregnancy and he knew why she had been kept off the stage that night at the La Plaza. She sat erect and strangely dignified on the seat of the grocery wagon. They didn't speak. She made up her mind to be hard up for someone to talk to before she bothered him again, as if without going any further she wasn't as good as he was. She smiled sweetly at Wilfred when he came running out of the alley and jumped on the seat, shouting "Gidup" to the horse. They drove on to a customer farther down the street.

34. Freedom in the 1920s

FREDERICK LEWIS ALLEN

Only Yesterday, *the book from which the following comment on the Jazz or Aspirin Age has been taken, is sub-titled "An Informal History of the Nineteen Twenties". Published in 1931, it presents an immediate and detailed account of the decade it describes, and even though Mr. Allen was focusing on the American scene, much of what he said was also true of Canada. One way the contemporary reader might approach the revolution in manners and morals that is described in the following selection is to see it as the somewhat pale beginning of a trend that has continued into the equally revolutionary 1960s. Frederick Lewis Allen, who died in 1954, was the author of two other books of social history:* Since Yesterday, *covering the period 1929 to 1939 and published in 1940; and* The Big Change, *dealing with the years 1900 to 1950 and published in 1952.*

This excerpt from Only Yesterday *illustrates a fundamental fact about composition: good writing is specific. Mr. Allen's success as a recorder of social change is largely due to his ability to support his generalizations with concrete evidence.*

One indication of the revolution in manners which her headlong pursuit of freedom brought about was her rapid acceptance of the cigarette. Within a very few years millions of American women of all ages followed the lead of the flappers of 1920 and took up smoking. Custom still generally frowned upon their doing it on the street or in the office, and in the evangelical hinterlands the old taboo died hard; but in restaurants, at dinner parties and dances, in theater lobbies, and in a hundred other places they made the air blue. Here again the trend in advertising measured the trend in public opinion. At the beginning of the decade advertisers realized that it would have been suicidal to portray a woman smoking; within a few years, however, they ventured pictures of pretty girls imploring men to blow some of the smoke their way; and by the end of the decade billboards boldly displayed a smart-looking woman cigarette in hand, and in some of the magazines, despite floods of protests from rural readers, tobacco manufacturers were announcing that "now women may enjoy a companionable smoke with their husbands and brothers." In the ten years between 1918 and 1928 the total production of cigarettes in the United States *more than doubled.* Part of this increase was doubtless due to the death of the one-time masculine prejudice against the cigarette as unmanly, for it was accompanied by somewhat of a decrease in the production of cigars and smoking tobacco, as well as – mercifully – of chewing tobacco. Part of it was attributable to the fact that the convenience of the cigarette made the masculine smoker consume more tobacco than in the days when he preferred a cigar or a pipe. But the increase could never have been so large had it not been for the women who now strewed the dinner table with their ashes, snatched a puff between the acts, invaded the masculine sanctity of the club car, and forced department stores to place ornamental ash-trays between the chairs in their women's shoe departments. A formidable barrier between the sexes had broken down. The custom of separating them after formal dinners, for example, still lingered, but as an empty rite. Hosts who laid in a stock of cigars for their male guests often found them untouched; the men in the dining-room were smoking the very same brands of cigarettes that the ladies consumed in the living-room.

Of far greater social significance, however, was the fact that men and women were drinking together. Among well-to-do people the serving of cocktails before dinner became almost socially obligatory. Mixed parties swarmed up to the curtained grills of speak-easies and uttered the mystic password, and girls along with men stood at the speak-easy bar with one foot on the old brass rail. The late afternoon cocktail party became a new American institution. When dances were held in hotels, the curious and rather unsavory custom grew up of hiring hotel rooms where reliable drinks could be served in suitable privacy; guests of both sexes lounged on the beds and tossed off mixtures of high potency. As houses and apartments became smaller, the country club became the social center of the small city, the suburb, and the summer resort; and to its pretentious clubhouse, every Saturday night, drove men and women (after a round of cocktails at somebody's house) for the weekly dinner dance. Bottles of White Rock and of ginger ale decked the tables, out of capacious masculine hip pockets came flasks of gin (once the despised and rejected of bartenders, now the most popular of all liquors), and women who a few years before would have gasped at the thought that they would ever be "under the influence of alcohol" found themselves matching the men drink for drink and enjoying the uproarious release. The next day gossip would report that the reason Mrs. So-and-so disappeared from the party at eleven was because she had had too many cocktails and had been led to the dressing-room to be sick, or that somebody would have to meet the club's levy for breakage, or that Mrs. Such-and-such really oughtn't to drink so much because three cocktails made her throw bread about the table. A passing scandal would be created by a dance at which substantial married men amused themselves by tripping up waiters, or young people bent on petting parties drove right out on the golf-links and made wheel-tracks on the eighteenth green.

Such incidents were of course exceptional and in many communities they never occurred. It was altogether probable, though the professional wets denied it, that prohibition succeeded in reducing the total amount of drinking in the country as a whole and of reducing it decidedly among the workingmen of the industrial districts. The majority of experienced college administrators agreed – rather to the annoyance of some of their undergraduates – that there was less drinking among men students than there had been before prohibition and that drinking among girl students, at least while they were in residence, hardly offered a formidable problem. Yet the fact remained that among the prosperous classes which set the standards of national social behavior, alcohol flowed more freely than ever before and lubricated an unprecedented informality – to say the least – of manners.

It lubricated, too, a new outspokenness between men and women. Thanks to the spread of scientific skepticism and especially to Sigmund Freud, the dogmas of the conservative moralists were losing force and the dogma that salvation lay in facing the facts of sex was gaining. An upheaval in values was taking place. Modesty, reticence, and chivalry were going out of style; women no longer wanted to be "ladylike" or could appeal to their daughters to be "wholesome"; it was too widely suspected that the old-fashioned lady had been a sham and that the "wholesome" girl was merely inhibiting a nasty mind and would come to no good end. "Victorian" and "Puritan" were becoming terms of opprobrium: up-to-date people thought of Victorians as old ladies with bustles and inhibitions, and of Puritans as bluenosed, ranting spoilsports. It was better to be modern, – everybody wanted to be modern, – and sophisticated, and smart, to smash the conventions and to be devastatingly frank. And with a cocktail glass in one's hand it was easy at least to be frank.

"Listen with a detached ear to a modern conversation," wrote Mary Agnes Hamilton in 1927, "and you will be struck, first, by the restriction of the vocabulary, and second, by the high proportion in that vocabulary of words such as, in the older jargon, 'no lady could use.' " With the taste for strong liquors went a taste for strong language. To one's lovely dinner partner, the inevitable antithesis for "grand" and "swell" had become "lousy." An unexpected "damn" or "hell" uttered on the New York stage was no longer a signal for the sudden sharp laughter of shocked surprise; such words were becoming the commonplace of everyday talk. The bar-room anecdote of the decade before now went the rounds of aristocratic bridge tables. Everyone wanted to be unshockable; it was delightful to be considered a little shocking; and so the competition in boldness of talk went on until for a time, as Mrs. Hamilton put it, a conversation in polite circles was like a room decorated entirely in scarlet – the result was over-emphasis, stridency, and eventual boredom.

---

35. New Arrivals in Horizon

SINCLAIR ROSS

What follows is the opening chapter of one of Canadian literature's most respected novels, As For Me and My House, *published in 1941. Although not a prolific writer, Mr. Ross is the author of several excellent short stories and one other novel,* The Well, *published in 1958. In his writing Mr. Ross has been concerned with life on the Canadian prairies, especially during the depression and dustbowl years. The author of* As For Me and My House *was born near Prince Albert, Saskatchewan, in 1908. For many years he was an employee of the Royal Bank of Canada, at first in several small prairie towns, and later in Montreal. He is currently living in Athens, Greece.*

This excerpt from As For Me and My House *illustrates the principle that the major themes and tensions of a novel are usually introduced in the opening chapter. Even before reading the entire novel, the attentive reader of this opening chapter should be able to recognize what the central con-*

*flicts are going to be. And he should be able to recognize the ideas that have
been introduced symbolically.*

Philip has thrown himself across the bed and fallen asleep, his clothes on
still, one of his long legs dangling to the floor.

It's been a hard day on him, putting up stovepipes and opening crates,
for the fourth time getting our old linoleum down. He hasn't the hands for
it. I could use the pliers and hammer twice as well myself, with none of his
mutterings or smashed-up fingers either, but in the parsonage, on calling
days, it simply isn't done. In return for their thousand dollars a year they
expect a genteel kind of piety, a well-bred Christianity that will serve as an
example to the little sons and daughters of the town. It was twelve years
ago, in our first town, that I learned my lesson, one day when they caught
me in the woodshed making kindling of a packing box. "Surely this isn't
necessary, Mrs. Bentley – your position in the community – and Mr. Bentley such a big, able-bodied man ——"

So today I let him be the man about the house, and sat on a trunk among
the litter serenely making curtains over for the double windows in the
living-room. For we did have visitors today, even though it was only yesterday we arrived. Just casual calls to bid us welcome, size us up, and see how
much we own. There was a portly Mrs. Wenderby who fingered my poor
old curtains and said she had better ones in her rag bag I could have; and
there was a gray-haired, sparrow-eyed Miss Twill who looked the piano up
and down reprovingly, and all but said, "If they were really Christians now
they'd sell such vanities and put the money in the mission-box."

She introduced herself as the choir leader, and in expiation of the piano
the least I could do was consent to play the organ for her. All the musicians
in the town, it seems, are a backsliding lot, who want strange new hymns
that nobody knows at an ungodly pace that nobody can keep up with. In
Miss Twill's choir they sing the old hymns, slowly.

It was about tomorrow's hymns that she came, and Philip, his nerves all
ragged, and a smear of soot across his face, didn't make a particularly good
impression.

"Any ones you like, Miss Twill," he tried to be pleasant. "I'm sure you'll
make a better choice than I could anyway." But with her lips thin she re-
proved him, "Other ministers we've had have considered the musical part
of the service rather important. Of course, if it doesn't matter to you
whether the hymns are in keeping with the text or not ——"

"You'll understand tomorrow when you hear his sermon," I slipped in
quickly. "It's a special sermon – he always preaches it on his first Sunday.
Any good old-fashioned gospel hymns will do. I think, though, he would
like *The Church's One Foundation* to start off with."

So we got rid of her at last, and steeled ourselves for the next one. Poor Philip – for almost twelve years now he's been preaching in these little prairie towns, but he still hasn't learned the proper technique for it. He still handicaps himself with a guilty feeling that he ought to mean everything he says. He hasn't learned yet to be bland.

He looks old and worn-out tonight; and as I stood over him a little while ago his face brought home to me how he shrinks from another town, how tired he is, and heartsick of it all. I ran my fingers through his hair, then stooped and kissed him. Lightly, for that is of all things what I mustn't do, let him ever suspect me of being sorry. He's a very adult, self-sufficient man, who can't bear to be fussed or worried over; and sometimes, broodless old woman that I am, I get impatient being just his wife, and start in trying to mother him too.

His sermon for tomorrow is spread out on the little table by the bed, the text that he always uses for his first Sunday, *As For Me and My House We Will Serve the Lord*. It's a stalwart, four-square, Christian sermon. It nails his colors to the mast. It declares to the town his creed, lets them know what they may expect. The Word of God as revealed in Holy Writ – Christ Crucified – salvation through His Grace – those are the things that Philip stands for.

And as usual he's been drawing again. I turned over the top sheet, and sure enough on the back of it there was a little Main Street sketched. It's like all the rest, a single row of smug, false-fronted stores, a loiterer or two, in the distance the prairie again. And like all the rest there's something about it that hurts. False fronts ought to be laughed at, never understood or pitied. They're such outlandish things, the front of a store built up to look like a second storey. They ought always to be seen that way, pretentious, ridiculous, never as Philip sees them, stricken with a look of self-awareness and futility.

That's Philip, though, what I must recognize and acknowledge as the artist in him. Sermon and drawing together, they're a kind of symbol, a summing up. The small-town preacher and the artist – what he is and what he nearly was – the failure, the compromise, the going-on – it's all there – the discrepancy between the man and the little niche that holds him.

And that hurt too, made me slip away furtively and stand a minute looking at the dull bare walls, my shoulders drawn up round my ears to resist their cold damp stillness. And huddling there I wished for a son again, a son that I might give back a little of what I've taken from him, that I might at least believe I haven't altogether wasted him, only postponed to another generation his fulfillment. A foolish, sentimental wish that I ought to have outgrown years ago – that drove me outside at last, to stand on the doorstep shivering, my lips locked, a spatter of rain in my face.

It's an immense night out there, wheeling and windy. The lights on the street and in the houses are helpless against the black wetness, little unilluminating glints that might be painted on it. The town seems huddled together, cowering on a high, tiny perch, afraid to move lest it topple into the wind. Close to the parsonage is the church, black even against the darkness, towering ominously up through the night and merging with it. There's a soft steady swish of rain on the roof, and a gurgle of eave troughs running over. Above, in the high cold night, the wind goes swinging past, indifferent, liplessly mournful. It frightens me, makes me feel lost, dropped on this little perch of town and abandoned. I wish Philip would waken.

It's the disordered house and the bare walls that depress me. I keep looking at the leak in the ceiling, and the dark wet patch as it gradually seeps its way towards the wall. There's never been a leak before, Mrs. Finley told me this afternoon, reproach in her voice that set me fiddling with my apron like a little girl. "Only last week we papered this room for you" – she's President of the Ladies Aid, entrusted with the supervision of the parsonage – "Only last week, and it's worse now than before we touched it. I don't know when we'll be able to do the ceiling over for you. Couldn't your husband get up on the roof and put a few new shingles on?"

She met us at the train yesterday, officially, and took us home with her for dinner. There's one at least in every town, austere, beyond reproach, a little grim with the responsibilities of self-assumed leadership – inevitable as broken sidewalks and rickety false fronts. She's an alert, thin-voiced, thin-featured little woman, up to her eyes in the task of managing the town and making it over in her own image. I'm afraid it may mean some changes for Philip and me too, for there's a crusading steel in her eye to warn she brooks no halfway measures. The deportment and mien of her own family bear witness to a potter's hand that never falters. Her husband, for instance, is an appropriately meek little man, but you can't help feeling what an achievement is his meekness. It's like a tight wire cage drawn over him, and words and gestures, indicative of a more expansive past, keep squeezing through it the same way that parts of the portly Mrs. Wenderby this afternoon kept squeezing through the back and sides of Philip's study armchair. And her twelve-year-old twins, George and Stanley, when they recited grace in unison their voices tolled with such sonority that Philip in his scripture reading after dinner sounded like a droney auctioneer. Philip at the table, I noticed, kept watching them, his eyes critical and moody. He likes boys – often, I think, plans the bringing-up and education of *his* boy. A fine, well-tempered lad by now, strung just a little on the fine side, responsive to too many overtones. For I know Philip, and he has a way of building in his own image, too.

It was a good dinner though, and after breakfast on the train, of milk and arrowroot we found it hard to keep our parson manners uppermost. They're difficult things at the dinner table anyway, eating with a heartiness that compliments your hostess, at the same time with a reluctance that attests your absorption in the things of the spirit. Often we have lapses. Our fare at home is usually on the plain side, and the formal dinner of a Main Street hostess is invariably good. Good to an almost sacrificial degree. A kind of rite, at which we preside as priest and priestess – an offering, not for us, but through us, to the exacting small-town gods Propriety and Parity.

Mrs. Finley, for instance: she must have spent hours preparing for us, cleaning her house, polishing her cut glass and silver – and if I know any-thing at all about Main Street economics she'll spend as many more hours polishing her wits for ways and means to make ends meet till next allowance day. Yet as President of the Ladies Aid, and first lady of the congregation, she had to do the right thing by us – that was Propriety; and as Main Street hostess she had to do it so well that no other hostess might ever invite us to her home and do it better – that was Parity.

But just the same they're a worthy family, and Philip and I shall be deferential to them. Feeble as it is, we have a little technique. Philip will sometimes have them help pick out the hymns, and I'll ask Mrs. Finley about arranging the furniture in our living-room; and in two or three weeks, when we're settled, our first social duty will be to return their dinner. Ours, of course, a simple, unpretentious meal, for of such must be the household of a minister of God.

36. The Great God Car

A. R. M. LOWER

The fullest social history of Canada that has yet been attempted is Arthur Lower's Canadians in the Making, *published in 1958. It is from this book that the following comment on North America's most distinctive invention has been taken. Professor Lower, who recently published his autobiography, entitled* My First Seventy-Five Years, *writes history in a pungent and per-sonal style, a style that is in large measure achieved by his lively choice of words.*

The unifying structural element in this selection is the analogy *that runs through it. Is the comparison that Professor Lower makes a pejorative one? Is this or is it not a balanced account of the great god car?*

That inventive society known in Canada as "the country to the south," could make a new goddess as quickly as it made a new car. But in making new cars, it made a new god. For the god, no better name could be found than simply – CAR!

In one of the annual reports of a great motor-car company during the mid-century years, there might be seen pictured the dignified and elegant ritual which surrounds the birth and renewal of this god – his Easter! The artist who depicts the scene has drawn a great crowd of people, of every conceivable social type, gathered about altars on which current images of the god CAR are displayed. In the upper left of his picture, there is a vast symphonic band of music, possibly a heavenly choir, its every violin bow at the ordained, precise angle. In the centre, richly but decorously dressed ladies grace a stage, beside which fountains play and from whose wings ballet dancers make appropriate obeisance. At the back of the stage, on a higher level than ladies and audience, surrounded by a nimbus of light clouds, at the point reserved in temples for the principal altar of the god, CAR is pictured midway between heaven and earth. "Lo, He comes, in clouds descending," the rapturous beholders seem to cry, as they greet the great god in his form of "The New Model for the Coming Year".

CAR's worship detracted even from that of Aphrodite herself (though the two were not without their intimate relationships). "Cars outshine the stars," says a popular magazine, picturing a daughter of the goddess reclining languidly, though with a second-best look, against one of the elegant new images of the god. All ranks and classes burned incense to CAR – save a few sour intellectuals who thought to avoid the industrial revolution he symbolized by ignoring it. "Yesterday I bought a Cadillac, and realized a lifelong ambition," says one of the gentlemen reported in that anthropological study of a wealthy Toronto suburb, *Crestwood Heights*. CAR's devotees increased with the years. And no wonder. A patient, obedient god who takes you where you want to go, faster than any magic carpet. A comfortable, well-upholstered god. A god whose priests well knew how to gain new worshippers by playing on the qualities of vulgarity and ostentation. And above all, the god of power, who multiplied man's ego manifold. Yet a ruthless god, sometimes, too, who could turn on his idolater and rend him.

CAR brought in his company a whole host of lesser godlets (most of them born of Electra), which their worshippers called "modern conveniences" or more simply "progress" – the labour-saving devices that stood in every housewife's kitchen, and the long series of instruments of communication such as the radio, television, and the rest. What this vast upheaval would mean before it reached its logical conclusion – and what is its logical conclusion? – who was to say? We all worshipped CAR and his fellows, that is, the innumerable by-products of science, power and human ingenuity, and some of us thought we saw these gods admitting us to a cheerful, effortless heaven. Slowly it dawned on the less simple that there was not much satisfaction in that type of "progress" which eventuates in hydrogen bombs. And so we come again, by another route, to the disillusionments of the day, to that look of dread in human faces that was not there before.

Meanwhile, CAR and his associates changed our society out of recognition. They scattered our homesteads far beyond the cities, so that many of us became once more, after a fashion, country dwellers. Others, yielding to the logic of CAR, married themselves to him for better and for worse, moving their habitation from place to place under the hauling power that he provided. CAR threatened to turn us all into nomads, and his wheels, like Juggernaut, levelled every physical and psychical obstacle they met. They invaded every urban open space and threatened to destroy every blade of urban grass. They knocked down houses. They called imperiously for straight, wide roads to be carved out of our diminishing fertile fields. They tore up our precious peach orchards and ordained that factories for making new parts of CAR should be erected in their place.

More than that, CAR forced on men, far more effectively than French Revolutionary slogans could ever do, the worship of another great god, Equality (though not of Fraternity), for once surrounded by his metal-and-glass turret, every man became equal to every other man, just as every metal-and-glass turret, despite the efforts of their advertisers to the contrary, was approximately equal in value and in efficiency to every other metal-and-glass turret. But it was not a new brotherhood that our god created for us, for once inside his fortress, a man became a world in himself, proudly independent, to whom the objects shaped like his own were threats which approached and passed, forgotten as quickly as avoided. They might contain millionaires or paupers, good men or rogues: to each other as they whirled by they were just shapes.

Were there no good words to be used of CAR? Of course there were, many. For one thing, CAR gave to many a slave promise of freedom. He offered escape from orders, from routine, from boredom. He made, or seemed to make, the humble masters of their fate. By opening up the vistas of the roads, he brought back to life the pathfinder, the explorer, the romantic in us. He was really a kindly god if worshipped with common sense. But instead his cult often carried his faithful into ecstasy and hysteria.

The effects on men of CAR worship, that is of the new mechanical society, are not yet fully discernible. That society is without question one of the most remarkable in history: it is perhaps also, all its aspects considered, the most lunatic. Once again, it has not been our own creation and though Canadians are almost as ardent worshippers at these shrines as are Americans, they have not invented them. They do not resist the modern god, but he is not quite their god in the same sense as he is the Americans'. It has always been Americans who have worked up the folk-lore of this modern religion (as, for example, the stories that used to be told about the old model-T Ford such as giving a squirrel away with each one to follow it and pick up the nuts), just as it has been Americans who have supplied and taken most seriously its high priests, among them the great cardinal who did so much towards establishing it, Henry Ford himself.

37. The Middle Class

JOHN PORTER
in conversation with
DOUGLAS MARSHALL

This selection is accompanied by its own introduction. All that really needs to be added is the fact that this dialogue between Douglas Marshall and John Porter first appeared in the June 1968 issue of Maclean's *magazine.*

The interview-type essay is currently popular among newspaper and magazine writers. Essential for its success are two things: the person being interviewed must know a good deal about the subject he is being questioned on; and the interviewer must know enough to ask appropriate and searching questions.

Back in the salad days of this country, when we were even greener in judgment than we are now, a couple of extremely popular misconceptions somehow became firmly imbedded in the national consciousness. The first was that Canada, while no melting pot, was a splendid mosaic of culturally distinct ethnic groups all working harmoniously together. The second was that this New World mosaic lacked the inherently evil class distinctions of the Old, that Canada was a relatively affluent and largely middle-class democracy. This complacent picture of ourselves started to fall apart about 10 years ago, first with Quebec's Quiet Revolution and later with the publication in 1965 of John Porter's sociological bombshell, *The Vertical Mosaic*. In 600 well-documented, highly readable pages Professor Porter tabulated the enormous inequalities of income and opportunity in Canada's supposedly classless society, demonstrated that only about 10 percent of Canadian families can actually afford the middle-class life-style we think of as average, and concluded that effective power resides in a predominantly Anglo-Saxon economic elite that is only a few hundred strong. The book has since sold some 25,000 copies – phenomenal for what is basically an academic text – and remains required reading for anyone claiming to understand what Canada is all about. Prof. Porter, born in Vancouver in 1921 and a graduate of the London School of Economics, has been teaching sociology at Ottawa's Carleton University since 1949 and is now the Director of the Social Sciences Division. This interview was conducted by Staff Writer Douglas Marshall in Prof. Porter's bright corner office in one of Carleton's new high-rise towers on the bank of the Rideau River. From his seventh-floor window he can gaze across smudgy downtown Ottawa and pick out the Parliament Buildings and the Gatineau Hills beyond. His discussion, animated and fluent, ranged over the broad spectrum of Canada's social problems. But he kept returning to what he believes is the overriding priority: the need to reform our educational institutions.

MACLEAN'S: What prompted you to write *The Vertical Mosaic*?

PORTER: I decided in the early 1950s I would like to do a study of power in Canada, starting particularly with economic power as being one of the principal sources of social inequality. These problems had been studied in many other industrial societies but had not been tackled in Canada.

MACLEAN'S: Where were you then?

PORTER: I had come back to Canada after being away for some 12 years in the United Kingdom. I am Canadian-born and had lived in Canada until I was 15. I spent six years with the Canadian Army during the war, but I stayed in Britain after the war to study at the London School of Economics.

MACLEAN'S: You came back to Carleton?

PORTER: Yes, when it was a very small college. Since I had been away from Canada for some time, I spent the following summer traveling extensively and decided I would stay here and look at Canada as a society. I was back in England briefly in 1951 and there I tried to work out some sort of scheme by which I could look at power and class structure in Canada.

MACLEAN'S: You say early on in your book that the 1950s marked "the high tide of post-war affluence." Do you think we reached a peak of prosperity during that decade?

PORTER: I think that in the 1950s there was a peak in the *belief* that we were an affluent society. And indeed, compared to the underdeveloped countries, obviously we were affluent. But we weren't as affluent as we thought we were. It misled us into thinking we lived in a society where everybody enjoyed abundance. I think it's quite remarkable that the 1960s are a decade in which the whole orientation of theorizing and investigating is toward this problem of poverty and inequality.

MACLEAN'S: In your book you are generally dealing with statistics relating to the mid-1950s. Do you think there's been much change over the past 10 years?

PORTER: If you mean income distribution statistics, I don't think they've changed. Obviously, inflation has lifted the entire range higher – that is, there are more people earning more than $3,000 now than there were five or 10 years ago. But there would be very little difference in the overall income distribution in society.

MACLEAN'S: You wrote that the middle-class life-style promoted by television and consumer magazines couldn't be achieved on less than $8,000 a year. Would the cost be $10,000 now?

PORTER: I suspect it would be pretty hard to live a middle-class life-style on less than $10,000 at the present time. And by middle-class life-style I mean a separate home for the family, because you have to talk in terms of families rather than individuals. Lots of people own their own homes but they have to share them with other people. They rent out the bottom or top parts of them. So they're not necessarily leading the middle-class life.

MACLEAN'S: What else is involved in the middle-class life?

PORTER: It means holidays, sometimes abroad. It means all the necessary medical and dental facilities. It means looking forward to university training for your children. It means two cars if you live in the suburbs, and dishwashers and plenty of other kitchen and power-tool gadgetry. Middle-class people also have all kinds of status-type extras, such as sending their kids to ballet lessons or nursery schools. Central Mortgage and Housing was saying the other day that the lowest level of income eligible for an NHA mortgage was something more than $8,000. It was quite incredible, considering that the National Housing Act was supposed to benefit everybody.

MACLEAN'S: So you think that the people who can afford these things, the upper-middle class, is still a very small segment of society – about 10 percent?

PORTER: I don't see any reason to feel the basic picture has changed. The proportion of the total population represented by the top 10 percent of income families would be about the same. Because nothing has happened to change it.

MACLEAN'S: In your book you make some pretty harsh criticisms of Canada's present educational systems.

PORTER: The educational systems as they exist certainly don't educate enough Canadians for the sort of occupational structure that is now emerging. As long as our educational systems are as inadequate as they are, they cut down the opportunities for advancement to the very top.

MACLEAN'S: So you think better education is the key problem in the sort of society we are moving into?

PORTER: It's certainly the key in the sense that the more educated you are the less likely you are to become a welfare problem. The more educated the entire labor force, the more viable and the more productive this whole society becomes. But education is more than that. It is the key to the individual's opportunity to do what he wants. I would argue that the most important thing we have to do now is improve the educational systems we now have.

MACLEAN'S: What's wrong with the present systems?

PORTER: In Canada and the U.S. there are various selective factors in the schools that work against lower- and working-class kids. Any type of streaming or tracking in elementary schools tends to pattern the child's educational experience for a very long time. And if you look at the distribution by class in most of these streaming systems, it's the middle-class kid who gets an early start. The working-class child doesn't do well at the early selection procedures.

MACLEAN'S: Why not?

PORTER: Teachers don't expect him to learn quite as well as the bright, clean, middle-class child, the tidy, well-behaved, middle-class child. When middle-class children enter secondary schools they get selected and directed by guidance teachers, by principals and by a whole host of middle-class individuals who tend to operate the system with certain preconceived ideas. And so the middle class is over-represented in the academic high-school streams and the working or manual classes are over-represented in the shorter academic courses and technical courses. Canadians are quite wrong if they feel they don't have a streaming system. It's just that it operates within a public educational system. The moment you start building up school classes on the basis of performance and ability you have the social-class problem arising.

MACLEAN'S: And this is mainly because of background?

PORTER: Indeed. There's no genetic or biological reason why working-class children, on the average, aren't exactly the same as the middle-class children. But what happens is that environmental influences greatly favor the middle-class child. In my book I said that no society in the modern period can afford to ignore the ability which lies in the lower social strata. The fact remains that in absolute numbers there are more of the highly intelligent in lower classes than in the higher.

MACLEAN'S: So you are in favor of free university education?

PORTER: Absolutely. And the students should be paid a living allowance while they're at university. I think it's one of the most pressing educational reforms we need. Because even when the low-income children do get to universities they tend to take the academic programs that are the shortest and least expensive – the pass-arts degree – because it's a quick journey back into the labor market. Lower-class students seldom make it into the honors or professional courses or go on into graduate work. We've got to relate talent to training by making people's financial resources an irrelevant factor. Universally, too. I wouldn't even bother with a means test.

MACLEAN'S: Would this completely eliminate class bias in education?

PORTER: Of course not. If you look at countries that have totally free systems, you still have class-biased institutions. But removing all fees is the first stage. Only after that would it be realistic to tackle some of the other problems that make educational systems class biased. Countries like England, France and Sweden – which have free systems and liberal grants – are now in a position to work out thorough-going educational reforms.

MACLEAN'S: And you think such educational reforms take priority over any other reforms that could produce social equality?

PORTER: Yes. Mind you, I think it's important and essential to have anti-poverty programs to deal with the present adult population. It's important to have manpower retraining schemes that try to give workers skills more appropriate for the kind of economy we now have. And it's important to establish basic income levels.

MACLEAN'S: What about simply imposing a limit on incomes with pro-hibitive taxes?

PORTER: I think there are certain features of our tax system that we could certainly do a great deal with. But this idea of soaking the rich in order to redistribute it to the poor – the money doesn't go very far once you start spreading it around among the poor. All efforts to out-tax the rich every-where have tended to fail because all taxing systems have enough loopholes that ways can be found around them. So one despairs of trying to create the egalitarian society in a Robin Hood fashion. However, I think in Canada we could escalate our graduated taxes a good deal more than we have.

MACLEAN'S: So it comes back to education again.

PORTER: I suspect that if one is concerned about the egalitarian society of the future, the so-called post-industrial society, the principle of equality is best served through really implementing systems of educational opportunity. For instance, I'd pay lower-income families allowances to keep children in high school. That's absolutely essential. Because, you see, you can't really get rid of the inequalities that arise from the pressure on large low-income families to send their kids into the labor market.

MACLEAN'S: What else would you do?

PORTER: After equality on the basis of educational opportunity, I would make very substantial efforts to break up inheritance. This strikes me as one of the sources of inequality. And I would have much heavier death duties and estate duties than exist at present.

MACLEAN'S: In effect, hitting at the upper-middle class as well as the very rich?

PORTER: I certainly don't see why well-educated children who are adults should inherit large sums of money at all. That's nothing to do with incentives. I'm prepared to accept the argument that differential incomes are needed to provide incentives. But I don't think that applies to inheritance.

MACLEAN'S: One modern aim of middle-class parents is to be able to give or leave their children enough money to put a down payment on a house. Do you approve of that?

PORTER: No. That's a good example of the kind of inequality I mean. It's very nice to have middle-class parents who will put a down payment on a house. But I wouldn't consider it essential to keeping a good society going. Working-class families simply don't have such opportunities.

MACLEAN'S: Won't we reach a stage where nobody can afford a house?

PORTER: Why have houses? This again is simply a reflection of a class structure which supposes a person doesn't have status until he has a house and grounds.

MACLEAN'S: Not just status, privacy.

PORTER: I assume you can still have privacy in an apartment house. But we may have to give up such middle-class ideas as complete privacy. One is struck by the poor private housing in Europe in contrast with the very lovely public places – streets, parks and so on.

MACLEAN'S: So all in all we've got to revise our thinking about the great North American dream of affluence.

PORTER: I think we are already revising it. Politicians, for example, don't talk in those terms any more. The onward-and-upward theme that used to be the Canadian motto during the days of C. D. Howe has been dropped. Politicians now talk more of the need to create a new kind of society. All sorts of doubts have been thrown on the quality of society we have at the moment. Unfortunately, however, the federal government seems to be withdrawing as a creator of opportunities. But that's another problem.

MACLEAN'S: In other words, we're all socialists now?

PORTER: There's been a drift both toward and away from socialism. Obviously, the kinds of incentives socialists hoped they would be able to rely on haven't proved out. Increasingly, we see that high levels of consumption and high levels of output aren't necessarily related to socialistic or capitalistic forms of government. Rather, it's got something to do with industrialization.

MACLEAN'S: You said earlier we are in a post-industrial society. What do you mean by that?

PORTER: People these days are talking about the society that was spawned by the Industrial Revolution as being past. We're going through another industrial revolution, one in which the emphasis is on cybernation, science and technology with very greatly increased productive potential. This new society will radically change the character of life. It's going to be a very different kind of society.

MACLEAN'S: In that brave new world, or indeed even now, is there much point in aspiring to be very rich? What does money buy you?

PORTER: It's very foolish to downgrade the value of money for what it can provide. It can obviously provide a great range of things – all of which are, in a way, freedom. I would never want to say that poverty is blessed. I think that's one of the great misconceptions of Western Christendom. And as long as it holds as a value – the idea that money isn't very important, that not very nice people have money – it will be a great impediment to people who are re-educating themselves in order to have better jobs.

MACLEAN'S: Money must remain as a reward?

PORTER: It's very important that every society pays attention to the kind of reward system it has. The more complex the society becomes, the more arduous it is to learn and the longer people must postpone economic gratification in order to learn. There is also a greater responsibility taken on by the people who assume the higher positions. This obviously requires a system of differential rewards, differential remuneration. But we must look carefully at the kinds of differentials that are necessary to operate the system, to keep it going.

MACLEAN'S: Are some types of activities over-rewarded?

PORTER: Perhaps. Some of the highest incomes are earned not by business-men but by actors and artists and people in the cultural field. They're re-warded because they have scarce talent and scarce talent will always de-mand extra rewards. I don't think differential rewards are bad, providing they don't involve the impoverishment of others.

MACLEAN'S: What about high fees charged by lawyers and medical specialists?

PORTER: You can't ask a guy to go through the elaborate training of becom-ing a doctor without some form of reward. But some groups tend to create artificial scarcities. Doctors tend to do this in terms of the restrictions they impose on the qualifications needed to enter educational institutions. But again, these are things of the past. I think, increasingly, you'll find that the state will take over education, will take over the administration of health, and that doctors will increasingly be put on salaries. But they will have to be salaries that provide a high enough incentive for people to become doctors.

MACLEAN'S: What about the top businessmen, the corporate elite? Are they over-rewarded?

PORTER: Well, we are taxing them as much as we can. We are trying to close up tax loopholes and we are trying to narrow down the possibilities for capital gains. But unless we are prepared to establish a system of controls – which might be worse than what we have – we have to live with the mar-ket system. There is a market for a top executive and he'll be paid what the market will give him. But if you raise a man's salary say to $120,000 a year from $100,000 you are probably giving him only another $5,000 take-home pay for handling a lot more headaches.

MACLEAN'S: So the extra money probably doesn't buy him many more goods and services than he already has. But does it buy power?

PORTER: The corporate elite obviously have power in the sense that they are very important in making the major developmental decisions in this country, of what's going to be invested where. They decide what sort of demands are going to be made on governments to do certain things, to build roads instead of universities. They have a certain amount of irresponsible power when it comes to problems of pollution, for instance. Any time there is a government move against the freedom and liberty the corporate world enjoys, the economic elite usually tries to move in. The present case involv-ing drug companies and brand-name drugs is one example. So is the lobby-ing by insurance companies in relation to government-sponsored types of insurance.

MACLEAN'S: And this elite runs Canada?

PORTER: There's no doubt about that. Modern industrial societies are run by a small handful of people. And it is possible for this small handful to be very cohesive as a group, very much oriented to the same values, reflecting very much the same background and having common outlooks on many things.

MACLEAN'S: And the elite in Canada perpetuates itself by recruiting its members from among the very rich or the upper-middle class? You discovered that there was very little movement from the lower-middle to the upper-middle class.

PORTER: That's absolutely right. It's largely an exclusive elite in the sense that it is almost totally British – in some sectors the French are even excluded. It is a relatively small group of native-born Anglo-Saxons. But in some other societies the political system is much more independent, much more active in mobilizing the resources of the society in terms of overall goals. It's not so much that Canadian elites are unified, but that the political elite at the national level is so totally ineffective.

MACLEAN'S: Why is that?

PORTER: Well, in my book I showed that the majority of the political leaders in Canada have been drawn from the middle class. The upper class doesn't seem attracted to the turbulence of politics, and in any case the privileges they enjoy are not threatened by the holders of political power. Nor is there any tradition of working-class participation in politics. Canada has never produced political leaders through the trade-union or working-class movement. There has been no Lloyd George, no Ernest Bevin, no Ben Chifley.

MACLEAN'S: And there haven't been many academics in government either.

PORTER: That's right. And this, of course, is why everyone is so interested in Trudeau. I think the real problem with Canada is that its political system is being dismantled in a way and is ineffective to cope with national problems. Education is a very good example. The very treatment of education is scandalous when viewed as a problem of national resources. Politicians talk of mineral resources and forest resources, but neither of these are anything compared to the importance of human resources. The political system leaves the definition of major goals – and therefore the power – to the corporate elite. I think this is one of my major criticisms of contemporary Canada.

MACLEAN'S: What do you think of Pierre Berton's *The Smug Minority*? Could he have written it without your original research?

PORTER: A lot of people have said that he couldn't. I've only read the last part and thought it was a very brilliant piece of writing. A journalist has a role to present ideas in a somewhat more simplified, more straightforward, more popular form than academics.

MACLEAN'S: Talking about elites, do you yourself happen to belong to Ottawa's Rideau Club?

PORTER: Good God, no.

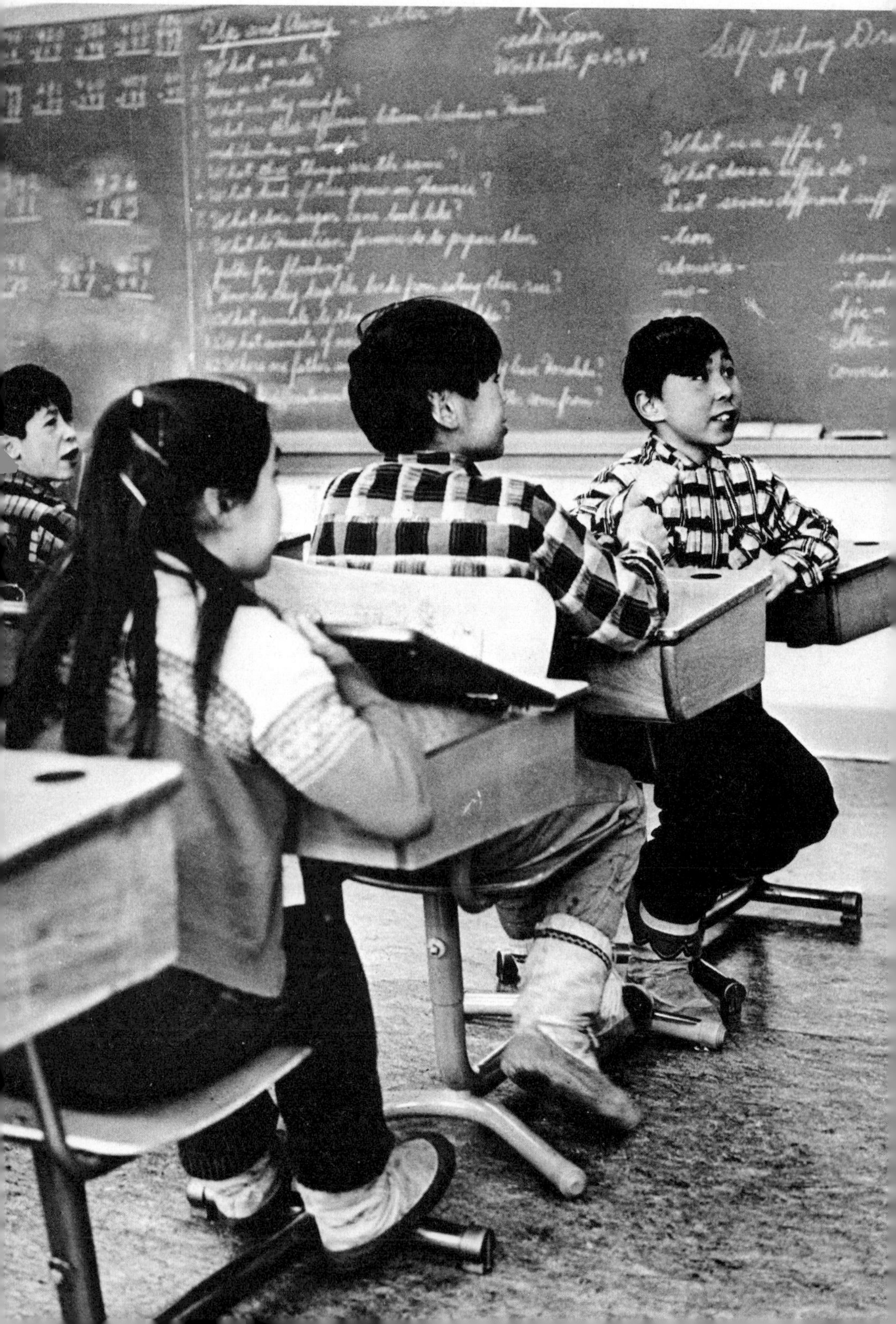
#9
What is a suffix?
What does a suffix do?

V. Canadian Issues

Despite its relatively envied position in the contemporary world, Canada
is not without its serious social and political problems. Most historians agree
that the issues at present of major concern to Canadians have come about
as the result of three unresolved tensions: the conflict between French
and English Canadians, the power struggle between provincial and federal
authorities, and the continuing threat of economic domination by the
United States. Such tensions, it is obvious, have causes that lie in the past,
causes that must be understood if the solutions looked for in the future
are to be realized. Most of the authors of these comments on basic Canadian
issues do make some reference to the past, although none of them has been
so bold as to come forth with tomorrow's easy solution. Rather, their
intention has been to define the issues clearly. The first of the eight
selections, a poem by Earle Birney, provides a kind of check-list of Canada's
problems. Four of the main issues are then developed at greater length in
the quartet of expository essays by Messrs. Julien, Cook, Craig, and Fraser.
The section closes with three lyrical comments on two further issues by
A. M. Klein, Dan George, and Alden Nowlan.

38. Canada: Case History

EARLE BIRNEY

Although it was written nearly twenty-five years ago, "Canada: Case History" still serves as a useful introduction to the problems that face contemporary Canadians. (For a brief biographical note on Earle Birney, see No. 4.)

As in the essay by A. R. M. Lower (No. 36) the unifying device in the poem is an analogy. But where Lower uses his extended comparison for satirical inflation *(the car is compared to a god), Birney uses his for satirical* diminution *(the country is compared to an adolescent boy).*

This is the case of a highschool land
deadset in adolescence
loud treble laughs and sudden fists
bright cheeks   the gangling presence
This boy is oriented well to sports
and the doctors say he's healthy
he's taken to church on Sunday still
and keeps his prurience stealthy
Doesn't like books (except about bears)
collects new coins   old slogans   jets
and never refuses a dare
His Uncle spoils him with candy of course
but shouts him down when he talks at table
You'll note he has some of his French mother's looks
though he's not so witty and no more stable
He's really much more like his Father and yet
if you say so he'll pull a great face
He wants to be different from everyone else
and daydreams of winning the global race
Parents unmarried and living apart
relatives keen to bag the estate
schizophrenia not excluded –
will he learn to grow up before it's too late?

39. A Mosaic of Provinces

CLAUDE JULIEN

This excerpt from Canada: Europe's Last Chance *(published in French in 1965, and in English translation in 1968) examines several aspects of the federal-provincial tension. In his book Claude Julien, who is foreign affairs editor of the Paris newspaper* Le Monde, *develops as his major thesis the notion that a strong and independent Canada is necessary if a balance of power between Europe and the United States is to be maintained. Hence the title of his book.*

Mr. Julien's essay is structurally complex. The central theme is each province's "obsession with local concerns", and, although the author is primarily interested in Quebec, all of the provinces are discussed in some detail, beginning with British Columbia and moving east. Throughout the essay this central theme is introduced, stated, restated, and supported with a considerable amount of statistical evidence. In dealing with prose of this complexity, the reader must make a conscious effort to see how each of the writer's separate statements contributes to the total plan of the essay.

If language tends to separate Quebec from the other provinces, does it follow that language tends to bind the nine English-speaking provinces together? Quebec's claims do not diminish a more general uneasiness which weighs heavily on the country as a whole. The federal government is aware of this and does not hesitate to discuss it. "In times of economic crisis or war," they say in Ottawa, "the provinces turn to the federal authorities for help and safety; in times of internal prosperity and peace, the provinces demand autonomy and national ties stretch dangerously thin."

In the provincial capitals, it is a rare person who thinks of the country as a whole. Public opinion is concerned with more immediate questions: schools, hospitals, roads, construction, etc., which come under provincial jurisdiction. Provincial politicians echo these local concerns rather than worrying about national problems. . . . Some federal ministers talk about a "new nationalism" which is to unite the country, but there is no evidence that it really exists. When Canadians talk about "the government" they mean the provincial government.

This attitude is partly explained by the demographic evolution of the country. During the last ten years, the population of Montreal has risen by nearly 50 per cent (from 1,471,000 to nearly 2,110,000 inhabitants). In the same period, a city such as Calgary, which did not even exist eighty years ago, has more than doubled in size (from 145,000 to 300,000). Toronto's population has risen by 50 per cent, Vancouver's by 40 per cent, Edmonton's by 96 per cent, Ottawa's by 46 per cent, Halifax's by 37 per cent, and so on. Yet in the same ten years, the total population of the country rose by only 3.6 per cent.

This urban concentration is the product of recent and intense industrialization. It has reached such proportions that municipalities face severe financial problems in providing the necessary services for their citizens. The cities look to the provincial authorities for funds; the provincial authorities are faced with increased demands for schools, industry, and general provincial development, and they turn to Ottawa for a greater share of the fiscal resources. The federal government satisfies their demands. Outside Ottawa scarcely anyone worries about whether or not the central government is holding back enough resources for its own internal and international responsibilities. Yet provincial spending amounts to more than half that of the federal government. Can a country survive when the state shrinks while provincial autonomies flourish from Atlantic to Pacific?

This obsession with local concerns and interests is a greater obstacle to the growth of Canadian identity than either the size of the land (twenty times that of France) or the lack of population.

British Columbia, cut off from the rest of the country by the Rocky Mountains, calls itself the most dynamic of the provinces. Industrial production has more than doubled in thirteen years; it supplies 60 per cent of the cut wood in Canada; its production of crude oil has risen from $2.7 million (1961) to $25.4 million (1963). *Per capita* income is 113 per cent that of the national average. With one-quarter the population of Ontario, it supplies one-fifth of Canada's exports. In minerals alone, its exports to Japan ($58 million) almost equal Canada's total exports to France. When the hydro-electric dams now under construction on the Columbia and Peace rivers are finished, its production of electricity will be higher than Ontario's and second only to that of Quebec. Giddy with its own dynamism, British Columbia looks west, where Japan is its best client, and south, where California provides capital funds and markets, but rarely to the east to the other Canadian provinces. It is a matter of geography and provincial interests. Thus, in September 1964, British Columbia signed an agreement with the United States that brought in a $254 million cheque for joint development of the Columbia River on which three large dams will be built. An additional sum of $64 million will be received when the hydro-electric systems go into operation. With its neighbour to the south British Columbia is undertaking a far larger project than would have been possible with the

228

other Canadian provinces. In the same way, its $250-million-a-year mineral production – zinc, asbestos, silver, lead, iron, copper, nickel, molybdenum – is largely exported to the United States and to Asia. While Quebec has Arvida, British Columbia has Kitimat, one of the world's greatest centres of aluminum, almost the entire production of which is exported. Foreign markets receive some 40 per cent of its wood production, 65 per cent of its paper, 80 per cent of its mining. And after local needs are satisfied, little is left for interprovincial trade. According to the provincial government, 50 per cent of the 591,000 salaries depend on foreign exports, while the rest are derived from local sources. British Columbia could, if necessary, carry out its economic development without any contact with the other provinces. It could even get industrial products as cheaply from the United States as it does from Ontario and Quebec.

From Vancouver it takes a day to cross the Rockies by train. Beyond Banff spreads the huge plain, all the way to Lake Winnipeg. It is the bread-basket of Canada. Is it one unit? Rectilinear frontiers mark out Alberta, with a Social Credit government, Saskatchewan, with a Liberal government after twenty years of "socialism", and Manitoba, governed by the Progressive Conservative Party. Moreover, the economy of each of these three provinces is markedly different. Alberta, rich in natural gas and oil, is the leader in mining and industry. Agricultural production is only slightly lower here than in Saskatchewan where, from 1944 to 1964, a very mild "socialism" frightened off the foreign capital that could have permitted similar mining and industrial development. Alberta, with oil, with ranching, and with wheat, is the Texas of Canada. Authorities in neighbouring Saskatchewan told me: "We have less oil than Alberta, but more wheat, and, above all, we have the richest potash deposit in the world. We have returned to free enterprise, and the future is ours!" In Manitoba, the Conservatives told me: "We have less wheat, less oil, less potash, but our economy is more diversified, more stable, and can develop under better conditions."

The three Prairie Provinces come together on only one point: when they talk about "*the East*", lumping together English Ontario and French Quebec, they are talking about the greedy provinces that between them have locked up four-fifths of Canadian industrial production. This industry could not have developed without the sheltering tariff barriers that protected it from American competition. The equipment that the Prairie farmers order from Montreal or Toronto could be obtained from across the border for less money and with lower transportation charges.

Except for this common complaint against "the East", the three Prairie Provinces have scarcely any feeling of belonging to one geographical and economic region. Yet they do not have British Columbia's excuse of being hemmed in by the Rockies and the Pacific. Only two thin lines traced on the map separate the three and they have many similar problems. They could unite their efforts to solve them, but such action would be interpreted as an attack on their sovereignty. They provide almost half the agricultural production of the country, yet they have not worked out any co-ordination of their efforts. Though they account for only 8 per cent of the country's industrial production, each works out its own plan for industrial development. Faced with similar problems, they have not made it any easier to find a common solution by giving themselves three governments from three rival parties.

The traveller leaves the Prairies, where a sprinkling of people live mainly on agriculture, for the richest and most heavily populated of the provinces, Ontario. One-third of Canada's population lives between the Great Lakes and Hudson Bay and is responsible for half the industry of the country, 30 per cent of its mining, and 30 per cent of its agriculture. Ontario knows that it is the richest province and that without it the country's economy would founder. Annual *per capita* income is $2,011, compared with the national average of $1,734. Each year Ontario attracts over half (51 per cent) of the immigrants coming to Canada and 34 per cent of the capital investment. This assures it of a smoother and faster development, both of its population and of its economy, than any other province. Its mining production doubled from 1949 to 1963; its industrial production rose by 20 per cent between 1956 and 1963. The unemployment rate is lower (3.8 per cent in 1963) than the national average (5.5 per cent) or the American average (5.7 per cent). Two-thirds of Canada's mechanical industry is in Ontario. The province is responsible for 90 per cent of Canada's production of electrical equipment.

Ontario's leaders, more than those of the other provinces, have a truly national outlook. Toronto knows that a good part of its industrial production is sold to the agricultural provinces and that their purchasing power depends on the harvest, on large wheat sales to the U.S.S.R. and to China, on federal protection to farmers, on credit regulations from Ottawa, etc. The provincialism of British Columbia or Saskatchewan is rarely found in Ontario, either among businessmen or among politicians. "Our economic development depends not only on the federal government and Ontario, but on co-operation with the other provinces," says Stanley Randall, Minister of Economics and Development. "Some provinces have set up programs to encourage their own industrial development. These efforts could make a major contribution to the economic growth of Canada, as long as the advantages of specialization and of planning according to local resources are respected, and the waste of duplicated effort is avoided. If the development plans of the various provinces are mutually conflicting, we must work out a way of harmonizing them with an eye to the national interest."

The minister added: "The economy of Ontario is more closely tied to the Canadian market than those of the other provinces, which means that it is in Ontario's vital interest to encourage the growth of the other parts of the country. For example, the Prairie farmer is a major factor in the increased demand this year for Ontario products, for the wheat sales to the communist countries have brought him extra revenue."

None of this means that Ontario is not proud of its distinctive characteristics and does not sometimes yield to "provincialism". For example, part of Ontario's trade crusade has been to open bureaus in New York, Chicago, London, Dusseldorf, and Milan. Quebec, to mention only one other province, has "delegations" in Paris, London, and New York. There is no theoretical reason why each of the ten provinces could not open offices in three or four foreign countries, in spite of the absurd waste of effort. In fact this process has already begun, and Ontario has pushed it the farthest, even though it has a strong voice in the federal government which has representatives in all of the countries that could possibly interest that province's economy.

But Ontario is less regional than the other provinces and has a greater sense of national reality and national interests. "There are nine separatist provinces in this country, and one federalist, Ontario," I was told by an English-speaking businessman from Manitoba. He was exaggerating slightly, for he was not taking into account New Brunswick, Nova Scotia, Prince Edward Island, and Newfoundland, the four poorest and least populated. They account for only 10 per cent of the nation's population, and their *per capita* income is much lower than the average.[1] These four Cinderella provinces hold out their hands to Ottawa, and Ottawa plays with subsidies and sliding scales to keep them alive in the federation. Separatism for them would be suicidal, and they intend to remain within Confederation. Yet, from the economic point of view these provinces are a liability and not an asset. Aware of their need to attract industry, they could well work for a better co-ordination of provincial efforts, but each puts out its own plans, on such a small scale that their viability is in question.

From the Atlantic to the Pacific, each province dreams of its own steel mill, its own chemical industry, its own expansion plans. How could it be otherwise when the federal constitution leaves to each province the full responsibility for its natural resources? The Fathers of Confederation apparently did not foresee the modern forms of development and economic planning, or they would have left those rights to Ottawa. While the federal system in the United States, especially after the New Deal and the Second

[1] New Brunswick: 66 per cent; Nova Scotia: 74 per cent; P.E.I.: 62 per cent; Newfoundland: 59 per cent.

World War, has seen federal intervention in the business of the country multiply, Canadian federalism has led naturally to a certain provincial dispersion.

The tendency is strong, and has a long history behind it. In the 1920s British Columbia wanted to meet some of its needs by imposing a tax on exports; this was thwarted by a judicial decision in 1930 pointing out that customs duties are the exclusive preserve of the federal government. Several years later Alberta wanted to regulate the banking system, and the courts prevented it from doing so since such powers belong to the federal authority. Today, British Columbia wants to establish its own bank. The Supreme Court of Canada had to nullify an Alberta law relating to news dissemination, a federal responsibility. When the courts decided in 1932 that broadcasting was a federal responsibility (apropos of the CBC), they did so in the face of opposition from Ontario and Quebec. In the same year Quebec, supported by Ontario, vainly contested the right of the federal government to regulate air traffic.

All the provinces are looking for technicians and highly specialized personnel, and all are becoming interested in organizing their own immigration campaigns in order to attract the people they need. British Columbia rather than Quebec is outstanding in this regard, for on at least six different occasions the federal authorities have annulled B.C. initiatives in this field because of federal priority. Yet it is Quebec that has several good reasons for not wanting to leave it all to Ottawa: first, prospective French-speaking immigrants are much less numerous than those who speak English, or even German or Dutch; second, the authorities arbitrarily reject twice as many French-speaking applicants as English-speaking. As a result, out of a total of 2,076,919 immigrants (1946–61), 611,983 have been British (29 per cent), 285,729 Italian, 275,065 German and Austrian (13 per cent), 155,550 Dutch (7.5 per cent), 42,480 French (2 per cent). It is possible that some day Quebec will react to the arbitrary decisions of immigration officials and to its own needs, and demand "special status" in the field of immigration. This would probably be the only method by which the province could hope to match the rising demographic charts of the English provinces and obtain the skilled personnel needed for the economic plans of the province. Though the separatists have a good argument when they talk about immigration, the Lesage government has not yet made any demand of this kind. But it is significant that British Columbia, with no linguistic factor to protect, has long been trying to modify the constitutional rules about immigration.

These few examples illustrate the provincialism that prevails in Canada. "Throughout our history, the provinces have constantly tried to encroach on federal authority," writes an editorialist in the *Winnipeg Free Press* after long study of the matter. The unconscious priority given to provincial problems is the major danger to Canadian unity today. As grave as it is, this tendency is rarely criticized by the very people who have set themselves up as guardians of federalism. They prefer to label Quebec the one and only reason for today's unrest. But Quebec's provincialism is founded on the same economic considerations as that of all the other provinces; the provincial economy must be brought up to date. And of course, this provincialism is coupled with a nationalism that becomes virulent when the French language and culture are in danger. Quebec nationalism has traditionally stressed linguistic and cultural arguments that do not exist in British Columbia or Alberta. English Canadians claim to be annoyed by it all. They forget that their nationalism nourished French Canada's; they close their eyes to the way they have violated certain principles of federalism; they wrap themselves up in their own provincial preoccupations, and accelerate the centrifugal forces that threaten to shatter the country.

The Ottawa government knows very well that Quebec is not the only province that holds to its own ways. The Lesage government knows it too, and makes skilful use of it – Lesage won certain concessions in the fiscal negotiations because of support from the other provinces that also need the supplementary resources. But French Canadians, as ignorant as English Canadians of the rest of the country, do not know this. They are annoyed, blustering, and angry, convinced that only French Canadians want changes made in the country's structures. They do not realize that Newfoundland, poor, sparsely settled, and physically separated from the continent, is no more isolated than the Western provinces caught up in feverish development. Too much attention and effort are centred on provincial problems to allow the sense of being a Canadian to triumph. The trees are hiding the forest.

Quebeckers complain that their income is only 87 per cent of the national average, unaware that the Manitoban is equally frustrated because he has not yet reached 96 per cent. Alberta is above the national average but unsatisfied, for it is still behind Ontario. The growth of a spirit of nationalism is also hindered by the great disparity in standards of living from coast to coast. Obviously, even further tinkering with subsidies and equalization payments could not bring about a uniform standard of living. Instead, it is partly a question of preventing wasteful duplication of effort across the country and partly one of common financing of productive investments, always with the national interest and the needs of the have-not provinces in mind. It would be an illusion to think individual income could be equalized rapidly. But the country cannot survive indefinitely if these serious regional inequalities are not corrected. Harmonious efforts at the development of the different provinces could help the country to a new awareness of its

233

unity. Unity cannot adapt itself to the present contrast between rich-cousin and poor-cousin provinces.

Quebec is "different" mainly on the cultural level. This upsets the other provinces much more than the poverty of Newfoundland, where the inhabitants have to get along on half the average income of Ontarians. But the cultural flowering of Quebec is closely tied to its economic development. The "French fact" would quickly have degenerated to the folklore level if Quebec had not undertaken its economic revolution in order to leave the agricultural age for the industrial, since education is largely paid for by corporation taxes. And in return, the modernization of teaching means a supply of the trained workers needed for economic expansion. For different reasons, and with less justification, economic provincialism is as strong in British Columbia as in Quebec. The frustrations of the poor provinces and the excitement of the booming provinces combine to make Canada a mosaic of provincial strongholds that a sense of national membership cannot transcend.

---

40. The Canadian Dilemma

RAMSAY COOK

The following selection is part of a book-length discussion of the French-English issue in Canada. The book from which it has been taken is entitled Canada and the French-Canadian Question, *published in 1966. Its author, who was born in 1931, has already established himself as one of Canada's most brilliant historians.*

Professor Cook's essay provides a valuable exercise in reading prose that develops in a careful and objective way a step-by-step argument. In order to follow the progression of this argument, the reader must pay close attention to the several cause-and-effect relationships that lead the writer to his conclusions.

"There are two miracles in Canadian history," Professor F. R. Scott of McGill University once maintained. "The first is the survival of French Canada, and the second is the survival of Canada." Almost always in the past English Canadians and more particularly French Canadians have believed instinctively that these two miracles were linked indissolubly together. Most French Canadians were convinced that *la survivance de la nation canadienne-française* depended on an alliance with English Canada, and even on the protection of the British Empire. The theme that the "last cannon-shot which booms on this continent in defence of Great Britain" will be "fired by the hands of a French Canadian" is an important one in the history of French Canada.

Then, too, one of the most frequently repeated arguments in favour of the acceptance of Confederation in 1865 was that it was the only alternative to annexation. That argument has often been adapted for modern usage. Pointing out the weakness of the French-Canadian separatist case a few years ago, M. André Laurendeau wrote: "Above all, one of the principal motives which led to the creation of Canada: the proximity of a large country to the south and the necessity of gathering together the British colonies in order to allow them to exist beside the United States, this motive has become more imperious. A segmented Canada would have scarcely more influence than one of the little republics of central America: would it even be able to exist?" From the French-Canadian viewpoint it has always been obvious that although they were a minority in Canada, they would be an even smaller and more precarious group, and therefore less capable of resisting absorption into the United States, if they attempted to exist apart from English Canada.

The irony of today's situation is that while a growing number of English Canadians have concluded that the survival of Canada can best be guaranteed by continuing the French-English association, there are now a growing number of French Canadians who are no longer convinced that the miracle of *la survivance* depends on this alliance. This latter is not yet a predominant view, but it is threatening enough to cause James Eayrs to remark recently: "This crisis of nationhood presents to a Prime Minister of Canada an issue transcending all others in urgency and importance. For many years it was his main concern so to conduct his countrymen's affairs that there would continue to be two sovereign governments in North America, not one. Today his main concern is that there continue to be two sovereign governments not three."

Canada's present "crisis of nationhood" is at least partly explained by the old symbol of "two solitudes". For reasons attributable largely, though certainly not exclusively, to the majority, French and English Canadians have rarely understood one another's purposes. That is the central failure of the Canadian experiment and one for which we are bound to continue paying heavily until it is rectified. In Canada we have only rarely conformed to

Durham's famous description of "two nations warring in the bosom of a single state". But, what may be worse, we have been two nations each talking to itself within the bosom of a single state.

Perhaps the most extraordinary thing about Canada is that while French and English Canadians have interacted upon each other to an immeasurable extent, the two people hardly know one another. What is today fashionably called a "national style" is, in Canada, almost wholly a reflection of the delicately balanced relationship between French- and English-speaking Canadians. Few if any other countries exemplify the obsession with that holy grail of all Canadian politicians, "national unity". That is only one example of what has been called the "bifocal" character of Canada. Nor should it be necessary to insist that the character of French-Canadian nationalism can only be understood when it is placed in the matrix of French-English relations in Canada. But despite the obvious impact of each group on the other, there is only a very limited interchange between the two groups. English Canadians read American and British newspapers, magazines, and novels, and of course watch American movies and television programs. Most of them could not, even if they wanted to, read a French-Canadian novel or understand a French-language television commentator. It is almost certainly true that an undergraduate in an English-Canadian university spends more time reading about the history of Great Britain and the United States than he does reading about the history of French Canada. Whatever else a young French-Canadian undergraduate in history may learn, he spends very little time on the history of English Canada except where it relates to *la survivance*. Mr. George Ferguson, a shrewd observer of the Canadian scene, once observed that "because of differences of race and language, culture and tradition, and, to some extent, religion, Quebec remains a *terra incognita* to almost all English Canadians." And English Canada is almost as much of a mystery to French Canadians.

While language is obviously an important wall between French and English Canadians, history, perhaps, divides us even more. The central event in the history of Canada is the British Conquest in 1760. Whatever this event may have meant in the lives of eighteenth-century French Canadians (and there is a good deal of scholarly dispute on that subject) it is nevertheless true that since the beginning of the nineteenth century French-Canadian nationalists have been attempting to overcome it. And the French-Canadian nationalist quite naturally identifies the Conqueror of 1760 with his rather indirect heir, the contemporary English Canadian. Actually, though one occasionally hears crude remarks about the Plains of Abraham, English Canadians are largely unconscious of their Conqueror's role. But consciously or not the Conquest dominates English-Canadian nationalism, just as it does French-Canadian nationalism, giving the former a sense of belonging to the winning side, the latter a yearning for lost glories. The Conquest, then, is the burden of Canadian history.

It is at least partly the Conquest that explains the different public philosophies of French and English Canada. Because they are a conquered people and a minority, French Canadians have always been chiefly concerned with group rights. Their public philosophy might be called Rousseauian: the expression of a "general will" to survive. The English Canadian, as is equally befitting his majority position, is far more concerned with individual rights and with that characteristic North American middle-class ideal, equality of opportunity. The English Canadian's public philosophy might be somewhat grandly described as Lockean. The English Canadian has therefore tended to look upon privileges asked for or granted to groups as inherently undesirable, indeed undemocratic. This means, then, especially since the dominant English-Canadian tradition is Protestant, that rights granted to groups *as* French Canadians or *as* Roman Catholics are at best an unfortunate deviation from the democratic norm, at worst a devilish plot to undermine Canadian, that is English-Canadian Protestant, civilization. The English Canadian instinctively makes the natural but nevertheless arrogant majoritarian assumption that the only fair and just way to run a society is according to the well-known Australian principle of "one bloody man, one bloody vote". The French Canadian just as instinctively makes the no less natural, and not always less arrogant, minoritarian assumption that a truly fair and just society would be based on something closer to the principle of representation by groups. And most French Canadians insist that there are only two groups in Canada.

It is this basic difference in public philosophy that divides Canadians. To an extent, I think to a quite successful extent, our political and constitutional machinery was designed to overcome or at least blur this difference. The federal system has meant, or at least was intended to mean, that those things most fundamental to the survival of the minority culture are placed safely beyond the reach of the majority. By defending provincial autonomy French Canadians could, in the past, defend at least a large part of the French-Canadian nation. At the same time our federal parties have usually worked in such a way as to ensure that if vigorous leaders were sent to Ottawa by Quebec something very near to a French-Canadian veto could be exercised within the federal cabinet, at least in matters that touched on French-Canadian affairs. It is true that the veto has not always been effective, though history unfortunately records more clearly those cases where it failed – Riel, conscription, and so on. History says less about the cases where the veto succeeded. When the complete story of Canadian foreign policy in the inter-war years is revealed, the influence of a man like Ernest Lapointe will almost certainly appear enormous. But the main point is, and it has often been made, that the Baldwin–Lafontaine, Macdonald–Cartier, Laurier–Sifton, King–Lapointe, St. Laurent–Howe tradition has given French Canadians a role in federal politics somewhat greater than a strict adherence to the principle of representation by population would have provided. Within the federal cabinet, the leading French Canadian is not a minister like the others.

But while our federal constitution allows Quebec a large measure of autonomy and our federal parties are especially susceptible to French-Canadian influence, one part of the French-Canadian community is left unprotected in practice if not in theory. These are the French Canadians living beyond the frontiers of the mother province. And it is here that English Canada's Lockean approach takes its toll. While Quebec is a constitutionally bilingual province, the other provinces, except for a brief two decades in Manitoba, have been unilingual. English-speaking Protestant majorities in every province, as far as the constitution permitted, have reduced the privileges of Roman Catholic and French-speaking minorities to a minimum. Whether the reason has been religious or national is difficult to decide with certainty, though it was probably religious in Manitoba in 1890 and national in Ontario in 1912. While the constitution in some cases (Ontario for example) has protected religious separate schools in a limited way, it gives no protection to French-language rights. The Fathers of Confederation had not seen fit to provide such guarantees; so where French-language schools existed by custom they have been eliminated by measures that are, according to the courts, within the letter of the constitution. Whether these measures are also within the spirit of the constitution is a matter that neither courts nor historians can decide with certainty. The effect of these actions has been to make French Canadians outside Quebec a minority like any other, subject, in matters of education, to the same laws as others.

Nowhere has this point been better established than in the case of Manitoba. Under the Laurier–Greenway settlement of 1897, which was designed to restore some of the privileges that the Roman Catholic and French-speaking minorities had been deprived of by the Manitoba School Act of 1890, bilingual schools meant English and *any* other language demanded by a minority group. And in 1916, when these bilingual schools were abolished, the public-school system's *Kulturkampf* was directed not only against German, Ukrainian, and Icelandic immigrants, but also against Franco-Manitobans. The survival of the French-speaking minorities outside Quebec, and they have survived in varying degrees, is a minor miracle attributable only to the will of these people to live according to the dictates of their culture. It is only recently, and very belatedly, that a growing number of English Canadians have recognized that the survival of the French-speaking minority groups is one important guarantee of Quebec's continued interest in Confederation.

Not unnaturally, French Canadians have developed a profound sense of grievance about the manner in which their compatriots were treated in the other provinces. This sense of grievance has been deepened enormously, of course, by the presence in Quebec of an English-speaking minority enjoying complete equality of rights in the educational system and bilingualism in public affairs, and to a large extent dominating the economy of the province. Despite repeated rebuffs in their attempts to extend French-language rights outside Quebec, most French-Canadian nationalists before 1913 refused to abandon the hope that one day the minorities in the other provinces would receive more equitable treatment. In 1913 Henri Bourassa stated the basic argument for this view when he said: "The Canadian Confederation . . . is the result of a contract between the two races, French and English, treating on an equal footing and recognizing equal rights and reciprocal obligations. The Canadian Confederation will last only to the extent that the equality of rights will be recognized as the basis of public law in Canada, from Halifax to Vancouver." As long as the French-Canadian nationalist believed that a bicultural Canada was possible, then he refused to identify the nation with the province.

Since 1945, and especially during the last decade, there has been a growing tendency for French-Canadian nationalists to write off the minorities, maintaining that the unending ransom being paid for these hostages to Confederation is a poor investment. As René Lévesque commented, referring to the Royal Commission on Bilingualism and Biculturalism: "It is infinitely more important to make Quebec progressive, free, and strong than to devote the best of our energies to propagating the doubtful advantages of biculturalism." The assumption underlying this view is, of course, that the province is identified with the nation. This explains the significance of the recent but now common usage, *l'Etat du Québec*.

41. Northern Miracle?

GERALD M. CRAIG

The United States and Canada, the book from which the following selection has been taken, was published in 1968. The passage reprinted below is the book's opening chapter. It provides a synoptic view of the relationship that exists between Canada and the United States, the country that is, as Gerald Craig points out, Canada's "only neighbour". The author of this lucid essay is a professor of history at the University of Toronto. He is the author of two earlier historical studies: Early Travellers in the Canadas *(1955), and* Upper Canada: the Formative Years *(1966).*

The type of development employed in this essay involves making a series of comparisons *and* contrasts *in relation to the attitudes of Canadians and Americans. In the comparisons, similarities are stressed; but in the contrasts, it is the differences that the writer is most concerned with.*

Canadians sometimes say that their country is a miracle of survival. Occasionally they also wonder whether the miracle will last. From the beginning of their history they have lived next door to one of the most vigorous, expansive, and powerful societies that the world has ever known, one that has pushed out its authority across a continent and one that has exerted a magnetic pull upon the minds of millions of people, even in distant places. These southern neighbors have always been at least ten times as numerous as Canadians, with corresponding economic and military weight. Nor have Canadians had a unified and positive sense of national identity with which to confront the attractions of the American Way of Life. Canadians keep worrying whether they really are different from Americans, while they go on being separate.

Moreover, the Canadian miracle is dual: a miracle within a miracle. Not only has Canada endured and grown, but within the larger entity French Canadians have survived as a distinctive group (some would say nation). This small people, numbering not many more than five million and unaided for over two hundred years by any significant recruitment through immigration, now faces three times as many English-speaking Canadians and forty times as many English-speaking North Americans. Yet they have retained their language as well as customs and institutions that clearly distinguish them from all other residents of the continent. Today they worry about whether they can resist the pressures that they feel all around them, and they are more determined than ever not only to go on surviving but to make "the French fact" in North America a positive and flourishing reality.

It is immediately clear, then, that Canadians and Americans look out upon the world with very different perspectives, despite close friendship and similar ways of life. The differences begin with contrasting historical outlooks; Americans can view their history with only the most infrequent references to Canada, but the United States is constantly to the fore in the telling of Canadian history. No two countries are so intimately bound together, but still they look at each other from opposite ends of the telescope.

This contrast sometimes leads to irritation on the Canadian end. That few Americans have any accurate knowledge of Canadian geography, government, or society is almost an article of faith north of the border. It is generally agreed that there is usually a vague sentiment of benevolent good will toward Canada, but this feeling often seems to be close enough to condescension to produce more resentment than satisfaction. Canadians find it difficult to realize that as long as they are stable, cooperative, and rather unobtrusive neighbors, they will seldom come to the notice of Americans, who will continue to think more about trouble spots and areas of crisis. And perhaps Canadians fail to realize that there may be some real advantages in being unnoticed by so close and so powerful a neighbor.

For their part, Americans have often been genuinely upset or mystified to come suddenly upon evidences of resentment or even hostility in a people who for the most part seem to be so much like themselves. When this happens, as it often does, Americans may be tempted to think that Canadians are being perverse, or that something has suddenly gone wrong, or that troublemakers are at work. With so many problems around the world, Americans should at least be able to count on the good will and understanding of the people on the other side of the four thousand miles of undefended boundary!

Nor is it altogether easy for an American to bring Canada into focus. One can readily grasp differences that arise out of language or political tradition or religion or economic conflict or military ambition. But to his north the American finds another American country of roughly the same geographical extent but much smaller in population, wealth, and power. It stands for no distinctive social system, its people are not easily identified when they travel abroad, and only in fairly recent years have they attained full political independence. For the most part they speak English with the same kind of accent that the majority of Americans have. To be sure, a third of them have French as a mother tongue, but Americans are used to a heterogeneous ethnic scene. This northern country is a federal state, with shapeless, non-ideological political parties and with legal institutions that have developed from the same origins as those in the United States. Economic practices and orthodoxies are shared, as are a whole range of religious and social institutions.

Awareness of this northern neighbor, when there is any, may prompt an American to no more than mild interest. Perhaps Canada is a rather pale reflection of the American republic, a little more sedate, a little less enterprising, which for some curious but not very important reason did not share fully in the great adventure of pursuing the American dream. Perhaps the Canadian blood was a bit too thin for so bold a task. Perhaps the northern people, oddly assorted rejects of history, were merely passed by, left on the shelf. Perhaps, finally, they will yet want to claim fuller membership in the American community. However hard he has focused, the American's view of Canada, apart from some clearly visible details, has tended to be rather opaque. What is there to see?

First, given the vast role of the United States in world affairs, an American will want to see where Canada stands in relation to his own country's defense and foreign policies. He finds that the two countries have been united in the defense of the continent by the Permanent Joint Board on Defense of 1940 and the North American Air Defense Command of 1957 as well as by many other agreements and enterprises. He learns that they became formal allies during the Second World War and that they renewed their alliance through the North Atlantic Treaty Organization of 1949. The record shows that Canada fought with the United States in the Korean War of the early 1950's and that her leaders have often gone out of their way to defend American foreign policy at the United Nations and in foreign countries. Yet an inquiring American will also discover that the tone of Canadian newspapers and of public discussion generally is more often critical than friendly with respect to the conduct of the United States on the world scene. In many areas where the United States is heavily committed, Canada offers no military assistance and often only the most tepid diplomatic support. The northern neighbor may seem to be a less reliable and less faithful ally than several more distant countries.

In trade and economic relations, however, we see a clearer and surer pattern. Here it is easiest for the American to grasp the importance of Canada to his own country, for it can be done by absorbing a few simple yet gigantic facts. In this field the interaction between the two nations has reached an unprecedented magnitude. They exchange the world's greatest volume of bilateral trade. Canadian natural resources and sources of energy have also begun to figure prominently in American economic calculations. Americans have more capital invested in Canada than in any other foreign country, with the result that strategic sectors of the northern economy are controlled or heavily influenced from the United States. (Conversely, per capita Canadian investment in the American economy is even larger.)

Canadian railroads, highways, air lines, and pipelines are intimately linked with their American counterparts: in the realm of transportation and communications the border is crossed by a traffic of enormous size and complexity. The majority of Canada's unionized workers belong to organizations that have their international headquarters in the United States. There is literally no equivalent anywhere in the world, no economic and financial interrelationship between two national states that is so vast and so intricate. But the United States itself is so large and its interests now so ramified that it can carry on this continental activity with little awareness that a border is being crossed. By contrast, to Canadians it is the most important fact of economic life, but in it perils and prosperity are inextricably mixed.

Finally, an American may try to see his northern neighbor as a political and social entity, apart from considerations of foreign policy and economics. It is in this sphere that his vision is likely to be most clouded. Canada is obviously in the hemisphere, stretching across more than four thousand miles of it, yet unlike all other American states it never made an open break with its imperial mother country. Today it remains a member of the Commonwealth and does not belong to the Organization of American States. It is a monarchy in a hemisphere of republics, and many of the old ceremonial forms are carefully preserved.

In addition, the American finds that there are two kinds of Canadians. One group speaks an English which for the most part is indistinguishable (except perhaps to a speech expert) from that heard in the northern states along the border. Of British and western European origins (like Americans), English-speaking Canadians have attitudes and customs which do little to distinguish them from residents of Buffalo, Bismarck, or Bellingham. Yet it is in this group that there is the strongest opposition to the elimination of "colonial" symbols. On the other hand there are the French Canadians, who have attitudes and institutions not found elsewhere in North America and who often express their opposition to "Americanization." Yet it is this group which most strongly supports the adoption of constitutional practices and symbols that grow out of life on this continent. Clearly, Canada is an American country with a number of differences.

Again, then, we come up against the problem of perspective. The peoples of the two countries are so close to each other, their affairs are so intermingled, that it is hard for them to stand back for a clear look. Every year millions of people cross the border in each direction, with a minimum of formality and for a multitude of purposes: recreation, business, education, to search for jobs, to go to conventions, or to settle permanently. It is a vastly larger human movement than between any other two countries elsewhere on the globe. Whether their stays are short or long, Canadians and Americans usually find themselves easily at home in the other country and are

243

rarely visible as strangers or outsiders. It is commonplace of Canadian-American occasions and intercourse that the two peoples are not "foreigners" to each other, but instead neighbors and friends who enjoy the same games, TV programs, and tastes in foods.

It is perhaps the beginning of wisdom in Canadian-American affairs to realize that "hands across the border" talk falls very differently upon Canadian ears from American lips than does the same discourse in the reverse direction. Very often, Americans, from presidents down, have been moved to say that they did not think of Canadians as foreigners, or that the problems of the two countries were like those of a large family or one's hometown. Such well-intentioned remarks, even when coming from the most popular and respected of American spokesmen, make Canadians feel uneasy. And when a speaker's good will becomes so expansive that he wonders why there needs to be a border at all between peoples so much alike, a Canadian listener becomes downright apprehensive. He begins to wonder whether the speaker is confusing his country with another state or group of states in the Union.

In turn, such a reaction suggests an unnecessary testiness on the part of Canadians or at least an excessive concentration upon the possible consequences arising out of their proximity to the United States. Admittedly, it is hard for Canadians to escape from this preoccupation. They are but a narrow band of people strung out irregularly for some four thousand miles, most of them living very close to the American border. They might well echo the old Mexican saying: "So far from God, so near to the United States"; indeed, they are even nearer than the Mexicans, because they adjoin many heavily populated states and, for the most part, lack the defense of a different language. This immensely vigorous society is their only neighbor; they must travel thousands of miles to make contact with any other country. Small wonder, perhaps, that Canadians spend so much time worrying about the protection of their "national identity" from American influence.

Yet many Canadians are coming to see that such a preoccupation is unhealthy and unnecessary, even perhaps rather mean-spirited. It leaves out of account the exhilarating and productive gains, touching all phases of Canadian life, that have always come and still come from contact with a free, lively, and wealthy society. Unnecessary because it sees American influence where it should see the more general trends of modern life. And unhealthy because it takes attention away from the need to make an attack on Canadian problems and leads all too easily to the view that these problems cannot be solved because they originate south of the border.

There are signs of a better balance. American interest in Canada will always be sporadic and fragmented; indeed, Americans, caught up in their own vibrant life, are not noted for their readiness to devote sustained attention to any other society for its own sake. To many Americans Canada will continue to be an "unknown country," where the fishing is said to be good and the Mounties wear red coats. But Canadian studies now have a secure place in several American universities, and there are a growing number of people in government, business, and other fields who have a detailed, even expert, knowledge of Canada. And among the general public, always on the move, there are probably many hundreds of thousands who have traveled more extensively in Canada than have most Canadians. On the other side, as a valuable dividend, the recent stresses and strains upon the fabric of Canadian unity have made Canadians more interested in their own country than they have been for a long time. It has become strikingly, even brutally, clear that there are Canadian problems that only Canadians can solve. Canadians will never cease from keeping a close watch on American events and personalities, but it has come as a revelation to many of them that absorbing matters closer to home demand careful attention and imaginative treatment if the Canadian "miracle" is to endure. And if Canadians find constructive solutions to their problems, they will find that there is interest enough in what they are doing, in the United States as well as elsewhere.

42. The Luxury of Dissent

BLAIR FRASER

When Blair Fraser was drowned in a canoeing accident on the Petawawa River in May of 1968, Canada lost one of its leading political journalists. Mr. Fraser, who was born in Nova Scotia in 1909, was for many years Ottawa editor of Maclean's Magazine. *The following discussion of four of Canada's minor political parties is a chapter from Blair Fraser's last book,* The Search for Identity, *a journalist's history of the years 1945 to 1967.*

The over-all structure of this essay is based on a logical division of the material that is to be dealt with. In the introductory section, the author makes the point that there is little ideological difference between Canada's two main political parties. He then proceeds to discuss separately each of the four parties that do enjoy the luxury of dissent.

Canada's political system is founded, perhaps appropriately, on a contradiction in terms.

The British North America Act proclaims, in writing, that the Canadian Constitution shall be "similar in principle" to the British. But the British Constitution is not written. It is a millennium's accumulation of precedent and tradition, at once flexible and durable, molded to and by the British national character. The Canadian Constitution is written, dogmatic, rigid but vulnerable to legalistic casuistry, originally (and to some extent still) a product of bargaining among scattered colonies whose national character did not exist. Small wonder that a century's use has transformed the Canadian system from one "similar in principle" to the British into one that is peculiar if not unique.

True, the basic machinery is much the same. The Cabinet is responsible to a Parliament that must be elected not less often than every five years, but can be dissolved at any time on request of the Prime Minister. (In practice, in both countries, the usual length of a Parliament is about four years.) Defeat in the House of Commons, on a major issue, compels the Government to hold a general election and submit to the judgment of the people; this happens seldom in either country, but in Canada it happened in 1925 and again in 1963. Parliamentary rituals, though not identical, are similar. But traditions and practices are sharply different. In Britain, a unitary country, the Prime Minister may choose the men he thinks most able to form his Cabinet. In Canada the Prime Minister must choose at least one minister from each province (unless, as often happens, his party has no elected members in one or more provinces). He must keep a traditional balance between English and French, Protestant and Catholic, east and west. By a tradition still new but already stern, one minister should be a woman. An obvious result is that a federal Cabinet always includes some members less able than other MPs who, because they come from the wrong city or the wrong religion, must remain backbenchers.

Another difference is the structure of political parties. The two strongest in Canada, Liberals and Progressive Conservatives, inherit their names from Britain but not their natures. Canadian parties, unlike British, do not represent social classes.

What they do represent is hard to say. The major parties, the only ones ever to hold office nationally, do not represent anything in particular. They differ in historic origins – the Liberals are descended from Reformers of the nineteenth century, Conservatives from the Tories who then supported

246

the Establishment – but this distinction has vanished from all but the vocabulary of political invective. Some Conservatives still call Liberals "crypto-republicans," some Liberals call Conservatives "puppets of Big Business" or "colonialists," but nobody takes this kind of talk seriously any more. Today no difference between the major parties can be defined in general terms that both would accept. Each tries to appeal simultaneously to all five regions, all religions, all ethnic groups, all income brackets. Both rely mainly on the same contributors for funds.

But Canada also has four minor parties, often miscalled "splinter" parties, and among them the differences are considerable. None has yet developed nation-wide strength, but each is formidable in certain regions.

Social Credit is in some ways the most formidable of the four. Never powerful in federal politics, it nevertheless holds office in two provinces, Alberta and British Columbia. In Alberta it has been in power since 1935 and still seems unbeatable. In British Columbia it has not been seriously threatened with defeat since it was first elected in 1952.

As a philosophy or socio-economic theory, Social Credit was developed in the 1920s and early 1930s by an Englishman, Major C. H. Douglas. Its principal tenet is currency reform – a currency based on the productive capacity of the nation rather than gold, a "social dividend" to all citizens which would maintain purchasing power while inflation would be averted by a "just price." Douglas' theories sound less heretical now, in these days of Keynesian economics and anti-cyclical budgeting, than they did in the 1930s, but they have never convinced any economist of national repute. Also, Douglas had a paranoid streak. He tended to believe the world's ills were the work of a vast conspiracy of international bankers allied, for some unexplained reason, with international Communists and "international Zionists," a euphemism to disguise his anti-Semitism.

Douglas' followers might now be forgotten along with the Technocrats, the Townsendites, the Single-Taxers, and the many others who were about to save the world in the 1930s, if Douglas' monetary theories had not caught the eye and imagination of a radio preacher in Alberta, William Aberhart. As founder and dean of the Calgary Prophetic Bible Institute he had built up a tremendous following on the farms and ranches of Alberta, and his adoption of the Douglas doctrine gave it instant appeal.

This was in 1932. Depression and drought were bringing widespread misery to the prairies. When in 1934 a scandal broke out involving Premier J. E. Brownlee, the United Farmers Government which had ruled Alberta since 1921 fell to pieces. Aberhart and his new Social Credit Party swept into office in the general election of 1935, and have been invincible ever since. On Aberhart's death in 1943 the leadership devolved upon his ex-pupil and protégé Ernest C. Manning, who had become Aberhart's pro-

247

vincial secretary at the age of twenty-seven and who at fifty-nine gives no sign of any loss of political potency.

Social Credit in practice under Aberhart and Manning has shown no resemblance to the Social Credit of Douglas' theory. Aberhart tried to put the theory into effect in his first few years of power, but found it went beyond provincial jurisdiction under the British North America Act. Thirty-seven of his statutes were either ruled unconstitutional by the Supreme Court of Canada and the Privy Council in London, then the Commonwealth's final court of appeal, or else they were disallowed by the federal Government in Ottawa. Thus frustrated in their attempt to make Social Credit an actuality, Aberhart and Manning settled down to give Alberta "sound," honest, and rather conservative administration, to the apparent satisfaction of practically everybody. The wartime boom brought prosperity, which was maintained after the war by the discovery of oil. Manning's more devout followers believe that Alberta's present affluence is literally the work of God – that the oil wealth, which had been there since Paleozoic time, was not revealed to sinful men until a godly government was there to exploit it.

In British Columbia the history of Social Credit is shorter and less theological. Premier W. A. C. Bennett was a Conservative, ex-candidate for the provincial Conservative leadership, until a few months before the election that brought the Social Credit Party to office. Its victory was caused by the collapse of a Liberal-Conservative coalition, originally formed to head off the threat of Canada's socialist party, the Cooperative Commonwealth Federation.

Cooperative Commonwealth Federation was the unwieldy name (normally shortened to CCF) of a left-wing group formed in 1932 by an alliance of various labor, farmer, and cooperative organizations plus a rather academic society of intellectuals called the League for Social Reconstruction. The founding conference was held in Calgary in August 1932, but the meeting more often described as the birthplace of the CCF was its first party convention in Regina, Saskatchewan, the following year. This was the rally that produced the CCF program better known as the Regina Manifesto, a fourteen-point platform that ended with this ringing paragraph:

"No CCF Government will rest content until it has eradicated capitalism and put into operation the full program of socialized planning which will lead to the establishment in Canada of the Cooperative Commonwealth."

The responsibilities of twenty years of office in one province, Saskatchewan, plus observation of socialism in other countries and also, no doubt, the normal effects of advancing age have somewhat tempered these high ideals. But they were certainly the mood of the moment at the Regina convention of 1933, and they still express the political aspirations of the

248

CCF. Perhaps the phrase "to eradicate capitalism" has now become too strong, but "the Cooperative Commonwealth" is still the ideal.

Chief founder and first president of the CCF was James S. Woodsworth, a former Methodist minister who had been an MP on the Labor ticket since 1921, and whose memory still commands a respect amounting to reverence. As a lifelong pacifist he could not accept his party's support of the war in 1939, and he abdicated the leadership at that time, but the parting came without rancor or any loss of mutual regard. His successor was his former chief lieutenant, M. J. Coldwell, who remained CCF leader until after his personal defeat in the election of 1958.

As its name suggests, the CCF was intended to be a federation of farmer and labor groups, but in its first years it elected few Labor members. Woodsworth himself was succeeded, after his death in 1942, by another labor MP, Stanley Knowles, in his riding, Winnipeg North Centre, and a few union men were elected from the east and west coasts. But the backbone of the party from 1935 to 1958 was its farm bloc from Saskatchewan.

The Diefenbaker sweep of 1958 wiped out this rural strength; the remnant of the CCF was mainly labor. In 1961 a formal attempt was made to unite, once again, the farm and labor movements, and the old CCF became the New Democratic Party (NDP), which drew its financial support mostly from labor but hoped to draw electoral support from both. At least in the early years, the hope proved vain. The NDP won twenty-one seats in the election of 1965, a total it had only once exceeded in the past, but its members did not include a single farmer.

The other two minor parties are French Canadian and operate only in Quebec, yet they have nevertheless their own significance in federal politics.

Ralliement des Créditistes was the title adopted by the Quebec wing of the Social Credit Party after it split from the group led by Robert Thompson of Alberta, after the election of 1963. Like the western Social Crediters (or Socreds as they are called), the Créditistes do not lean heavily on monetary theory. A favorite slogan of their leader, Réal Caouette, in the 1962 election was "You don't have to understand Social Credit in order to vote for it." Another slogan, even more effective among the disgruntled poor of Quebec, was "What have you got to lose?"

Caouette came back from the 1962 election with twenty-six Quebec seats. Thompson, the party's "national leader," had only four. The English-speaking tail continued to wag the French-speaking dog for the short Parliament of 1962-63, but this could not be expected to last. When the break came, only a handful of French-speaking MPs stayed with Robert Thompson, and all were defeated in 1965. Only nine of Caouette's party survived the 1965 election, and in 1966 it dropped to eight when Gilles Grégoire, his chief lieutenant, also broke away and became an independent.

His differences with his former colleagues were apparently more personal than ideological, for all are French-Canadian nationalists whose ideas vary mainly in intensity.

Union Nationale is the name of a Quebec party founded in 1935 by a rebel group of Quebec Liberals, dissatisfied with the aged and corrupt regime then in power, and the Quebec Conservatives led by Maurice Duplessis. It routed the provincial Liberals in 1936, lost power again for the duration of World War II, but came back in 1944 and remained unbeaten until after the death of Duplessis in 1959. In Quebec provincial politics it replaces the Progressive Conservatives, who have no provincial organization in Quebec.

The Union Nationale has no federal arm and no federal ambitions; it is a Quebec party pure and simple. But from time to time, and in various ways, it has more impact on federal politics than many a party, living or dead, which has nourished ambitions to rule all Canada.

---

43. Indian Reservation: Caughnawaga

A. M. KLEIN

The Caughnawaga Indian Reservation on the south bank of the St. Lawrence River opposite Lachine, Quebec, has a history that goes back to the seventeenth century. In this poem, first published in 1948, Mr. Klein presents an ironic series of contrasts between what the Indian people once were, and what they have been allowed to become in their "grassy ghetto". (For a brief biographical note on Mr. Klein, see No. 2.)

In this selection we find illustrated the fact that a poetic image can express in a few words an idea that would take many words in prose. The reader who has not understood everything that is implied by such compressed phrases as "the feathered bestiaries", "fur on their names", and "a grassy ghetto" cannot really claim to have "read" the poem.

Where are the braves, the faces like autumn fruit,
who stared at the child from the coloured frontispiece?
And the monosyllabic chief who spoke with his throat?
Where are the tribes, the feathered bestiaries? –
Rank Aesop's animals erect and red,
with fur on their names to make all live things kin –
Chief Running Deer, Black Bear, Old Buffalo Head?

Childhood, that wished me Indian, hoped that
one afterschool I'd leave the classroom chalk,
the varnish smell, the watered dust of the street,
to join the clean outdoors and the Iroquois track.
Childhood; but always, – as on a calendar, –
there stood that chief, with arms akimbo, waiting
the runaway mascot paddling to his shore.

With what strange moccasin stealth that scene is changed!
With French names, without paint, in overalls,
their bronze, like their nobility expunged, –
the men. Beneath their alimentary shawls
sit like black tents their squaws; while for the tourist's
brown pennies scattered at the old church door,
the ragged papooses jump, and bite the dust.

Their past is sold in a shop: the beaded shoes,
the sweetgrass basket, the curio Indian,
burnt wood and gaudy cloth and inch-canoes –
trophies and scalpings for a traveller's den.
Sometimes, it's true, they dance, but for a bribe;
after a deal don the bedraggled feather
and welcome a white mayor to the tribe.

This is a grassy ghetto, and no home.
And these are fauna in a museum kept.
The better hunters have prevailed. The game,
losing its blood, now makes these grounds its crypt.
The animals pale, the shine of the fur is lost,
bleached are their living bones. About them watch
as through a mist, the pious prosperous ghosts.

44. Lament for Confederation

CHIEF DAN GEORGE

The following speech by Chief Dan George of the Burrard Indian Reserve in North Vancouver, British Columbia, was first read at a public ceremony in Vancouver's Empire Stadium on July 1, 1967. In reporting the event, the Vancouver Sun *noted that "the jubilant crowd of 32,000 was silenced by the moving – and bitter – soliloquy".*

The point of view and some of the thoughts expressed by Chief Dan George have already been stated many times. What makes his particular development of this theme an effective one?

How long have I known you, Oh Canada? A hundred years? Yes, a hundred years. And many many *seelanum*[1] more. And today, when you celebrate your hundred years, oh Canada, I am sad for all the Indian people throughout the land.

For I have known you when your forests were mine; when they gave me my meat and my clothing. I have known you in your streams and rivers where your fish flashed and danced in the sun, where the waters said come, come and eat of my abundance. I have known you in the freedom of your winds. And my spirit, like the winds, once roamed your good lands.

But in the long hundred years since the white man came, I have seen my freedom disappear like the salmon going mysteriously out to sea. The white man's strange customs which I could not understand, pressed down upon me until I could no longer breathe.

When I fought to protect my land and my home, I was called a savage. When I neither understood nor welcomed this way of life, I was called lazy. When I tried to rule my people, I was stripped of my authority.

My nation was ignored in your history textbooks – they were little more important in the history of Canada than the buffalo that ranged the plains. I was ridiculed in your plays and motion pictures, and when I drank your fire-water, I got drunk – very, very drunk. And I forgot.

Oh Canada, how can I celebrate with you this Centenary, this hundred years? Shall I thank you for the reserves that are left me of my beautiful forests? For the canned fish of my rivers? For the loss of my pride and

[1]A Squamish Indian word meaning "lunar months".

authority, even among my own people? For the lack of my will to fight back? No! I must forget what's past and gone.

Oh, God in Heaven! Give me back the courage of the olden Chiefs. Let me wrestle with my surroundings. Let me again, as in the days of old, dominate my environment. Let me humbly accept this new culture and through it rise up and go on.

Oh God! Like the Thunderbird of old I shall rise again out of the sea; I shall grab the instruments of the white man's success – his education, his skills, and with these new tools I shall build my race into the proudest segment of your society. Before I follow the great Chiefs who have gone before us, oh Canada, I shall see these things come to pass.

I shall see our young braves and our chiefs sitting in the houses of law and government, ruling and being ruled by the knowledge and freedoms of *our* great land. So shall we shatter the barriers of our isolation. So shall the *next* hundred years be the greatest in the proud history of our tribes and nations.

---

45. The Execution

ALDEN NOWLAN

In 1968, Canada began a five-year period of testing the practicability of abolishing capital punishment. Although the following poem does not comment directly on the capital punishment issue, it does imply many things. Mr. Nowlan, who was born in 1933, lives in New Brunswick. His occupation is that of newspaper editor, but he is also the author of seven books of poems. "The Execution" appeared in The Things Which Are, *published in 1962. For his work,* Bread, Wine and Salt, *Alden Nowlan was awarded the 1967 Governor General's Award for poetry.*

The perceptive reader can discover a number of implied questions in this dramatic poem. Is the poet asking, for example, whether it is society itself – as represented by the Press – that is the real victim when a man is executed? But, in order to understand fully the questions raised in the poem, the reader must be clear about what is meant by the references to "Press", "Reverend Press", "Padre", and "Mr. Ellis".

On the night of the execution
a man at the door
mistook me for the coroner.
"Press," I said.

But he didn't understand. He led me
into the wrong room
where the sheriff greeted me:
"You're late, Padre."

"You're wrong," I told him. "I'm Press."
"Yes, of course, Reverend Press."
We went down a stairway.

"Ah, Mr. Ellis," said the Deputy.
"Press!" I shouted. But he shoved me
through a black curtain.
The lights were so bright
I couldn't see the faces
of the men sitting
opposite. But, thank God, I thought
they can see me!

"Look!" I cried. "Look at my face!
Doesn't anybody know me?"

Then a hood covered my head.
"Don't make it harder for us," the hangman whispered.

VI. Contemporary Issues

In this final section, the scope of the readings is extended beyond Canada to issues that have potential relevance for all inhabitants of the twentieth-century world. As in the previous section, the main achievement of the writers has been to raise the questions provocatively, not to provide magical answers. The subjects discussed are, for the most part, of the type where conflicting points of view are to be expected, and although only one side of these two-sided issues has been presented here, it is hoped that under the stimulus of these strongly voiced opinions the reader will be inspired to define the other side of the argument for himself. Of the nine topics discussed, four have been approached in a comic vein. This flippant approach to serious matters by Art Buchwald, Norman Ward, Noel Perrin, and M. J. Arlen, is defensible on the grounds that laughter has long been considered a human and even a healthy response to certain types of frustration. The five serious discussions that complete this section do not, unfortunately, complete the possible list of problems that face mankind in these tense middle years of the twentieth century. And these problems, raised by such writers of international reputation as Aldous Huxley, Rachel Carson, Ralph E. Lapp, Bertrand Russell, and Martin Luther King, may not even be the most pressing contemporary ones. But they are all matters of considerable importance, and each has been discussed by a writer with a strong and individual voice.

46. Fold, Bend, Mutilate

ART BUCHWALD

Art Buchwald is a widely syndicated Washington columnist whose work appears regularly in a number of Canadian newspapers. There have been several collections of his columns: I Chose Capital Punishment *(1963),* Son of the Great Society *(1966), and* Have I Ever Lied to You? *(1968).*

The comic technique employed by Mr. Buchwald involves taking some everyday situation (such as the fact that "most bills are now sent out on perforated business machine cards") and extending it for satirical purposes to its humanly illogical conclusion. The value of such a satirical comment will depend, of course, on whether the writer has put his finger on some actual threat inherent in the situation he satirizes.

Most bills are now sent out on perforated business machine cards that say in large letters DO NOT FOLD, BEND OR MUTILATE. I have a friend who doesn't like to be told what to do with a bill, and one day, to my horror, I saw him fold, bend and mutilate a card right in front of my eyes.

"You did not have to do that," I said, quivering. "There is a curse on anyone in the United States who folds, bends, or mutilates a bill."

He laughed at me. "That's an old wives' tale. This is a free country, isn't it?"

"Only if you don't fold, bend, or mutilate."

"You're chicken," he said. "No computer is going to tell me what to do."

I didn't see my friend for several months. Then I finally ran across him in a bar. He was unshaven, dirty and obviously had been on a bender.

"What happened?" I asked.

"The curse," he croaked. "The curse got me."

Then he told me his story. He had sent back the folded, bent and mutilated card to the company and received another card in a week, saying, "We told you not to F. B. or M. THIS IS YOUR LAST CHANCE."

"I crumpled up the card and sent it back," he said. "Still thinking I had the upper hand. Then it started.

"First my telephone went out on me. I could not send or receive any messages. I went to the phone company and they were very nice until they looked up my name. Then the woman said, 'It says here that you mutilated your bill.'

" 'I didn't mutilate my phone bill.'

" 'It doesn't make any difference what bill you mutilated. Our computer is aware of what you did to another computer and it refuses to handle your account.'

" 'How would your computer know that?'

" 'There is a master computer that informs all other computers of anyone who folds or bends or mutilates a card. I'm afraid there is nothing we can do about it.' "

My friend took another drink. "The same thing happened when my electricity was cut off and my gas. Everyone was sorry but they all claimed they were unable to do anything for me.

"Finally pay day came but there was no cheque for me. I complained to my boss and he just shrugged his shoulders and said, 'It's not up to me. We pay by machine.'

"I was broke, so I wrote out a check on my bank. It came back marked 'Insufficient respect for IBM cards.' "

"You poor guy," I said.

"But that isn't the worst of it. One of the computers got very angry and instead of canceling my subscription to the 'Reader's Digest' it multiplied it. I've been getting 10,000 Reader's Digests a month."

"That's a lot of Digests," I said.

"My wife left me because she couldn't stand the scandal, and besides she was afraid of being thrown out of the Book of the Month Club."

He started crying.

"You're in bad shape," I said. "You better go to the hospital."

"I can't," he cried. "They canceled my Blue Cross, too."

---

47. Grave New World

NORMAN WARD

Norman Ward is a Canadian writer with two strings to his literary bow. One is his ability to produce scholarly essays on political science (Mr. Ward is a professor at the University of Saskatchewan); the other is his talent for writing short comic pieces on a wide range of subjects. The essay by which he is represented here was published in 1960 in Mice in the Beer, *the first of two collections of Mr. Ward's comic writing.*

Like Art Buchwald, Norman Ward in this essay makes use of satirical extension. *He also makes effective use of a rhetorical device called* paranomasia, *or, more simply, the pun. The reader can decide for himself whether Mr. Ward is punning when he gives the name "Welter" to the little man caught in the bureaucratic tangles of tomorrow's grave new world.*

For several months I've been deriving satisfaction from the occasional perusal of two newspaper clippings sent me by friends about whose motives I am not at the moment prepared to speculate. One clipping concerns a chimpanzee who broke out of his cage while being flown across the Atlantic as the ward of a lady who had some difficulty subduing him. The other is about a handicapped lad named Bill who kept losing his glass eye on the way home from school, playing marbles.

The case of the lady and the chimpanzee is obviously a logical outcome of the woman-suffrage movement that wracked the civilized world thirty-five years ago. In its own way, the clipping that sets forth the relevant facts is a work of art, requiring neither comment nor exposition. Consider the picture. Across the Atlantic, miles high, drones a sleek aluminum machine that represents one of the great triumphs of man's inventive genius. At the controls sits a keen-eyed man in whose training has culminated the progress of countless centuries of Western culture. And in the cargo space is Emancipated Woman, wrestling with a chimpanzee. The only point I don't know, and would like to know, is whether the editors who published the story ran it as a straight news item, or consigned it to the Women's Page.

The tale of Bill the marble player strikes a different note. The woman-suffrage movement, as the above attests, has clearly attained most of its original aims. But Bill's predicament is not an echo of the past but a foretaste of the future. Bill's glass eye was not purchased for him by his family, or presented to him by an admirer. It was supplied to him free under a government health scheme, and the Government took a dim view of equipping him with eye after eye as his losses mounted in the schoolyard. Oddly enough, so far as I can discover, nobody in the Government thought of sending Bill to some institution where he could be trained at government expense to shoot a better game of marbles.

The important thing to note is that the Government presumed to have an interest in Bill's glass eye even after the eye had left the Civil Service and been installed in Bill. This opens up for speculation a vast new field of politics, for governments are becoming increasingly prone to supply citizens not only with services like education which can be taken or left alone, but also with concrete objects that citizens can put to many uses beyond the reach of even the longest arm of the law. Glass eyes, eye-glasses, false teeth, wigs, and artificial limbs have been thrust upon grateful recipients by their governments within living memory, and the end is not in sight.

And what legal liability is accepted by a government if, for instance, a gentleman finds after being fully outfitted at the local health warehouse that he is so effectively disguised that he can with impunity commit bigamy right in his own neighbourhood? Suppose, while reclining comfortably on some sunny bank, a lens of the gentleman's free glasses acts as a magnifying glass and starts a brush fire which ultimately destroys the embassy of a previously friendly power? Who is responsible if the Leader of the Opposition gets kicked by an artificial leg supplied by the Government? These are deep waters, and little comfort can be found in the stern official attitude taken towards marbling Bill. Bill seems to have been instructed to treat the Government's gift with greater respect, and to keep a civil eye in his head.

The Government was of course in a position to argue that all government property was the taxpayers', so that Bill, in being careful, was only caring for his own. Bill was thus enjoying an eye in which he shared the property rights with several million other fellows, although only he, presumably, had the right to use the eye on any given day. It's too bad that Plato, who thought well of communal property under some circumstances, didn't live long enough to help us work out some of the philosophical implications of that one.

None of the mishaps that Bill might have had with his eye are nearly so interesting as the possibilities that come to mind in connection with false teeth. How does a government go about keeping an eye on the teeth after they are being gnashed by taxpayers? I like to think of the case of Mr. J. C. Welter, a minor civil servant whom I invented a while ago for the purpose of being thought about. Welter is employed in a small way as a tax collector, and not long ago qualified for a government issue of false teeth under a compulsory fitness plan. When he went around to the teeth office to pick up his share of the welfare state, he was asked to sign a receipt for the teeth after trying them on. He was understood to say that in order to get the teeth he had already filled out more forms than ought to exist in any single country, and now that he had them had no intention of signing any more forms, ever. Welter remained so impenetrable to reason that the teeth people felt obliged to perform a summary salvaging job, and in the ensuing struggle an Administrative Assistant, Grade II, was bitten. Welter was then had up for assault.

Since Welter had signed no receipt for the teeth, the administrator started off with a weak case, for the teeth were technically government property at the time of the alleged assault. As Welter was a civil servant himself, his lawyer was naturally able to make much of the constitutional argument that the Crown in one capacity cannot be held liable for putting the bite on the Crown in another capacity. The judge, however, seized on the fact that Welter was a tax collector, and pointed out that the powers of tax collectors had not yet been extended to include the actual biting of citizens, no matter whose teeth are used.

Welter thus lost his case. He also lost the teeth, for he was obliged to submit them as Exhibits A and B at the trial, and an alert bureaucrat beat both Welter and the sheriff to them after it was all over. The teeth are now back in Her Majesty's Stores, where they will stay until some other approved citizen of the right size comes along.

48. The Wooden Bucket Principle

NOEL PERRIN

The issue raised by this letter to the editor of The New Yorker *may not in itself be a crucial one, unless the tendency its author writes of (imagining "almost anything in the country as simpler and more primitive and kind of nicer than it really is") is symptomatic of a widespread doubt about the complete adequacy of life in the modern megalopolis. Noel Perrin is a teacher of English who frequently contributes humorous articles to American magazines. This essay in the form of a letter appeared in the June 6, 1963, issue of* The New Yorker.

Mr. Perrin's essay provides a further illustration of the basic type of essay structure that has already been discussed at several points in this anthology. Two of Mr. Perrin's variations on this basic structure are worth noting. First is his trick of using a somewhat oblique introduction. He ends his first paragraph by noting, "But that's not what I'm writing you about." Second is the device of skilfully repeating in new contexts several of the main details of the essay.

Under the heading "Incidental Intelligence (Is Nothing Sacred? Division)," you lately reported that some Vermont farmers are using plastic bags rather than wooden buckets to catch the sap from maple trees. This is true, though plastic tubes that eliminate the need to catch the sap at all (they run it directly from inside the tree down to the sugarhouse) are more popular still. But that's not what I'm writing you about.

I am unable to decide whether you really believe that maple-sugar producers, in Vermont or out of it, were using wooden buckets until the plastic apparatus came along. Since wooden sap buckets started to go out not long after the Civil War ("I like tin," said the Secretary of the Vermont Board of Agriculture in 1886), and since they had pretty well disappeared, even on hill farms such as mine, by about 1920, it seems improbable. On the other hand, city people plainly haven't been following the development of sugaring at all closely. For example, every spring your magazine publishes one or two cartoons that show some farmer gathering sap from buckets of the wrong shape, without covers, hung too high on what look to be beech trees, or possibly box elders. Most farmers do still hang buckets (they're made of galvanized steel, with peaked lids to keep the snow out), and we mostly still boil down over wood fires, rather than over oil fires, but we never tap box elders. If you can swallow those cartoons, I don't suppose you have much trouble believing in the wooden buckets.

Actually, I don't blame either you or your cartoonists at all. I think there's something I shall henceforth call the Wooden Bucket Principle at work here. By this I mean a tendency to imagine almost anything in the country as simpler and more primitive and kind of nicer than it really is. Picture calendars are the most familiar example. Every time I see a calendar decorated with a color photograph of a New England village, I look, and I'm never disappointed. There's the little village, nestled among the hills. There's the white church. What about the filling station? It's been cropped. There are never gas stations in pictures of New England villages. Those big orange school buses don't generally get into such pictures, either, nor does the town shed, with a couple of modern road scrapers lying around out front.

I also find the Wooden Bucket Principle operating in the books that we have begun to buy for my daughter, who is now two. Some of these are books written and published in the United States in the last four or five years – animal ABCs, I-Can-Do-This-or-That books, and so forth. Supposedly, they are both about and for contemporary American children. Yet I was reading from one just tonight that shows a little girl saying, "Pick. Pick. Pick. I'm a little chick." Behind her are five chicks, about a dozen hens, and two roosters, all wandering freely about in front of a quite charming henhouse, picking for corn. Real American chickens, of course, do no such thing. They neither wander nor pick. Instead, they spend their time in lots of ten thousand or a hundred thousand, locked in battery houses, never walking an inch. The cages are too small. I think their feed has aureomycin in it.

There's a similar discrepancy in a slightly more advanced book my daughter has. This one shows a girl a little older helping to drive in some cows. Not yet in Vermont, maybe, but on modern dairy farms there's no place to drive cows in from. The modern cow spends her days in a concrete enclosure, receiving her feed – alfalfa, mostly – from an overhead conveyor. In this setup, a little girl would just get in the way. Besides, she'd fall and skin her knees on the concrete. I understand that in California the same method is being used for beef cattle. (One of its advantages is that permanent indoor life gives steers paler flesh. The meat thus has more room to darken once it's cut up and put on display in a supermarket.) Yet for all my daughter will learn from her books, the cows in California all hang around in the sunlight, just like Californians.

As a matter of fact, the Wooden Bucket Principle isn't simply a country thing. I come to New York fairly often, and I've seen it in use by the Port of New York Authority. A couple of summers ago, while the second level of the George Washington Bridge was being built, the Authority started handing out explanatory leaflets at the toll booths. I have several. I well remember getting the first. It made the customary apology for the delay, and the customary explanation that it was for my future safety and convenience. It also showed an artist's rendering of the work in hand. The bridge was in the background, looking very handsome but somehow only three lanes wide. The foreground was taken up with sketches of two genial-looking workmen busy widening the New Jersey approaches. They were using for this purpose a shovel and a pickaxe, respectively. I had only to look out the car window to see the scene in actuality: the eight lanes of traffic, streaming across, the earth movers and giant power shovels roaring about on the Jersey approaches. There wasn't a workman in sight except dimly, inside some fifty-ton piece of equipment. (I suppose bridgebuilders' flesh is paler these days, too.)

I have no idea where all this is going to end. I may still be writing letters to the editors of *The New Yorker* when the whole magazine is put together by plastic tubes. On the other hand, I may by then have got into a wooden sap bucket and pulled down the lid.

Yours,
NOEL PERRIN

49. After Progress, What?

M. J. ARLEN

Like the previous selection, this essay first appeared in The New Yorker.
*When it was published in October 1959, Mr. Arlen noted in a sub-title that
his essay was "A few notes on Rockets, Missiles, Satellites, Space and so
forth, jotted down after reading one too many articles on the subjects".*

*This selection is an illustration of that special type of comic writing
termed parody, that is, the conscious imitation of a particular writing style,
either as a means of satirizing the style itself, or making fun of some situation that the writer finds ludicrous. Here Mr. Arlen is parodying what can
best be described as popular science reporting. What are some of the characteristics of this type of writing that the author treats lightly? What aspects
of contemporary science does he make fun of?*

The largest rocket made so far in the United States is the new five-stage
Wozzek. The Wozzek is 95 feet tall, weighs 94,500 lbs., and is constructed
entirely out of a heat-resistant planum. Built at a cost of fifteen million
dollars, the Wozzek is designed to be fired from a standing position. After
firing, thrust from the first three stages will accelerate the rocket to a speed
of roughly 15,000 feet per second. When the rocket reaches an altitude of
450 miles, the first three stages will fall off and drop into downtown Ta-
coma, Washington. Power for the Wozzek is supplied by 23 lbs. of Gebirium,
a sticky gelatinous fuel that delivers upward of 35,000 eisenstaedts per cubic
foot – enough power to drive three cruisers of the Comstock class from New-
port to the Bay of Fundy, via the Cape Cod Canal.

When completed, the Wozzek will contain 230,000 movable parts and is
expected to attain a range of 23,000 miles (equivalent to five times the
distance between South Bend and Moscow, nine times the distance between
Montreal and Dakar, or twice the total trackage of the New York Central
system, not counting the West Shore Branch). In flight, the Wozzek will be
guided by the new Zeitz Directional Computer. Based on an invention by
Hector Zeitz and manufactured under patent by General Transistor (a division of the National Luncheon Meat Company), the ZDC combines basic
principles of light-wave refraction, astrodynamic parallax, and long division
to keep the rocket on a straight line between the star Sirius and the Hayden
Planetarium. The Wozzek also contains two short-wave radio transmitters,

encased in pink vinyl plastic, and if the rocket should start travelling upside down, this information would be relayed instantly to the ground.

Air Force authorities consider that a rocket of the Wozzek configuration could conceivably be used for launching man into space. To date, fifteen rockets of the Wozzek configuration have been built and fired. Unfortunately, owing to failures in the Gebirium release indicator, the linear mono-wave transmission, the steering mechanism, and the rudder and clutch, and the apparent total breakdown of the Zeitz Directional Computer, each of these rockets either failed to leave the pad or was destroyed in midair. Air Force spokesmen have pointed out that the IJ-4G triggering device, which makes it possible to destroy a rocket immediately after launching, is the only device of its kind in the non-Communist world.

Scientists, doctors, and dietitians have declared, however, that before an actual attempt is made to launch man into space, they would "like to know more about" several problems that have not yet been answered to their satisfaction. Foremost among these problems is that of weightlessness, so called from the tendency of travellers in space to lose weight, look peaked, catch colds, and suffer from nosebleeds and stuffed-up ears, all in direct proportion to the duration of the space flight. Almost as challenging are difficulties posed by re-entry (the Passport Division of the State Department is preparing a definitive statement on this matter) and by food intake.

Stated briefly, the central problem of food intake (or "eating") has been to find a way for the space traveller to intake (or "eat") food during a seven-month space journey without removing his pressurized helmet. To solve this obstacle, two beefed-up special programs are now under way – a 300 million dollar crash project at Oswego Field, where the Air Force has been investigating the possibilities of shrinking ordinary ham sandwiches down to tablet size, and the Navy's 1.5 billion dollar crash program, Project Astrolunch, in which 32 recent honors graduates of the Naval Academy have been subsisting since February, 1958, entirely on brewer's yeast and frozen pineapple-grapefruit juice squirted into their ears.

At present, plans for putting man into space call for the following sequence of events: (1) Launching of the giant experimental piloted missile "Herbert Hoover." The fastest missile of its kind ever built, the Herbert Hoover contains 250 lbs. of special electronic equipment, and will be fired, at 22,000 miles per hour, 3,000 miles out into the South Atlantic. It is expected to be caught before striking the water, somewhere between 55 and 520 miles northwest of Saint Helena, in a huge fish net towed by fifteen planes of the Air Force's 17th Missile Retrieval Squadron. (2) Launching of the Wozzek rocket containing two dogs. (3) Launching of the Wozzek Major rocket containing two dogs and one large rabbit. (4) Launching of the Zeus, the

266

United States' first manned satellite, containing two dogs, one large rabbit, and one veterinarian.

United States space advisers consider that when all pertinent information has been received from the Zeus and other sources, manned flight to the moon and to other planets will be feasible. At the moment, some of this country's most daring pilots are undergoing rigorous tests to determine which one of them will be chosen to ride the first United States rocket ship to the moon. These tests, which are being conducted jointly by the Department of Defense and Time-Life, Inc., include celestial navigation, syntax, gym, and elements of narrative prose.

Last week, in a signed article in *Life*, Milton Berlinger, 39, one of the potential U.S. spacemen, described his own deep, personal feelings toward the forthcoming moon flight: "Like most Americans my age, I have a normal desire to be shot off into space. I have given this whole thing a good deal of thought, and the way I see it, getting to the moon is the biggest challenge left to man now that things have gotten so dull down here. People often tell me that it can't be done. Well, if I remember aright, they said that nobody would ever climb to the top of Mount Everest, or beat the Yankees, or go over Niagara Falls in a barrel and live. Taking into account the physiological-stress factor, possible guidance malfunction, discomfort, and the personal-fear characteristic, we expect that the pilot should have a 76.524 percentile chance for a successful mission. Columbus didn't have odds like that, and, besides, he wasn't in shape."

Military planners have pointed out the patriotic and moral advantages of an early moon landing by the United States. In a recent address to the graduating class at Densher Junior College, Major General Melvin Belfrage acclaimed the approaching moon expedition as an event "of the greatest magnitude in the history of man's achievement," and added that a United States lunar outpost might provide priceless strategic benefits in our ability to drop "small objects" back onto the earth, and would allow us to maintain a "friendly round-the-clock vigil" on any space ventures that might be conducted in the future by other major powers, including France.

Scientists, for their part, admit that to date little is known about exact conditions on the moon, but are quick to agree with Dr. Heinz Bamberg, the so-called Father of Space Flight (formerly Professor of Explosives, Heidelberg), that it is of "the utmost importance to humanity" that we get a man up there, preferably a U.S. citizen, as soon as possible. Experts have already privately named June, 1965; May, 1972; or September, 1980, as final target date for the first flight.

50. Overpopulation

ALDOUS HUXLEY

In his novel Brave New World, *written in 1931, Aldous Huxley made a number of predictions (not all of them cheerful) about what he thought the world of the future would be like. Twenty-seven years later, he published* Brave New World Revisited *in which he noted (again not too optimistically) that many of his earlier predictions seemed to be coming true much earlier than he had expected. The following discussion of the perils of overpopulation is from the first chapter of* Brave New World Revisited. *Aldous Huxley (1894–1963) is one of the twentieth century's major writers. Among his many successful books are the novels* Point Counter Point *and* Antic Hay, *and a collection of essays entitled* Music at Night.*

This selection offers an example of the type of essay structure where the main idea comes towards the end, having been arrived at through a progression of logical arguments. In understanding and evaluating prose of this type, the reader must be prepared to distinguish between statements that present a verified fact and those that offer an opinion.

On the first Christmas Day the population of our planet was about two hundred and fifty millions – less than half the population of modern China. Sixteen centuries later, when the Pilgrim Fathers landed at Plymouth Rock, human numbers had climbed to a little more than five hundred millions. By the time of the signing of the Declaration of Independence, world population had passed the seven hundred million mark. In 1931, when I was writing *Brave New World*, it stood at just under two billions. Today, only twenty-seven years later, there are two thousand eight hundred million of us. And tomorrow – what? Penicillin, DDT and clean water are cheap commodities, whose effects on public health are out of all proportion to their cost. Even the poorest government is rich enough to provide its subjects with a substantial measure of death control. Birth control is a very different matter. Death control is something which can be provided for a whole people by a few technicians working in the pay of a benevolent government. Birth control depends on the co-operation of an entire people. It must be practised by countless individuals, from whom it demands more intelligence and will power than most of the world's teeming illiterates possess, and (where chemical or mechanical methods of contraception are used) an expenditure of more money than most of these millions can now afford. Moreover, there are nowhere any religious traditions in favour of unrestricted death, whereas religious and social traditions in favour of unrestricted reproduction are widespread. For all these reasons, death control is achieved very easily, birth control is achieved with great difficulty. Death rates have therefore fallen in recent years with startling suddenness. But birth rates have either remained at their old high level or, if they have fallen, have fallen very little and at a very slow rate. In consequence, human numbers are now increasing more rapidly than at any time in the history of the species.

Moreover, the yearly increases are themselves increasing. They increase regularly, according to the rules of compound interest; and they also increase irregularly with every application, by a technologically backward society, of the principles of Public Health. At the present time the annual increase in world population runs to about forty-three millions. This means that every four years mankind adds to its numbers the equivalent of the present population of the United States, every eight and a half years the equivalent of the present population of India. At the rate of increase prevailing between the birth of Christ and the death of Queen Elizabeth I it took sixteen centuries for the population of the earth to double. At the present rate it will double in less than half a century. And this fantastically rapid doubling of our numbers will be taking place on a planet whose most desirable and productive areas are already densely populated, whose soils are being eroded by the frantic efforts of bad farmers to raise more food, and whose easily available mineral capital is being squandered with the reckless extravagance of a drunken sailor getting rid of his accumulated pay.

In the Brave New World of my fable, the problem of human numbers in their relation to natural resources had been effectively solved. An optimum figure for world population had been calculated and numbers were maintained at this figure (a little under two billions, if I remember rightly) generation after generation. In the real contemporary world, the population problem has not been solved. On the contrary it is becoming graver and more formidable with every passing year. It is against this grim biological background that all the political, economic, cultural and psychological dramas of our time are being played out. As the twentieth century wears on, as the new billions are added to the existing billions (there will be more than five and a half billion of us by the time my granddaughter is fifty), this biological background will advance, ever more insistently, ever more menacingly, towards the front and centre of the historical stage. The problem of rapidly increasing numbers in relation to natural resources, to social stability and to the well being of individuals – this is now the central problem of mankind; and it will remain the central problem certainly for another century, and perhaps for several centuries thereafter. A new age is supposed to have begun on October 4th, 1957. But actually, in the present context, all our exuberant post-Sputnik talk is irrelevant and even nonsensical. So far as the masses of mankind are concerned, the coming time will not be the Space Age; it will be the Age of Overpopulation. We can parody the words of the old song and ask,

> Will the space that you're so rich in
> Light a fire in the kitchen,
> Or the little god of space turn the spit, spit, spit?

The answer, it is obvious, is in the negative. A settlement on the moon may be of some military advantage to the nation that does the settling. But it will do nothing whatever to make life more tolerable, during the fifty years that it will take our present population to double, for the earth's under-nourished and proliferating billions. And even if, at some future date, emigration to Mars should become feasible, even if any considerable number of men and women were desperate enough to choose a new life under conditions comparable to those prevailing on a mountain twice as high as Mount Everest, what difference would that make? In the course of the last four centuries quite a number of people sailed from the Old World to the New. But neither their departure nor the returning flow of food and raw materials could solve the problems of the Old World. Similarly the shipping of a few surplus humans to Mars (at a cost, for transportation and develop-ment, of several million dollars a head) will do nothing to solve the problem of mounting population pressures on our own planet. Unsolved, that prob-lem will render insoluble all our other problems. Worse still, it will create conditions in which individual freedom and the social decencies of the democratic way of life will become impossible, almost unthinkable.

Not all dictatorships arise in the same way. There are many roads to Brave New World; but perhaps the straightest and the broadest of them is the road we are travelling today, the road that leads through gigantic numbers and accelerating increases. Let us briefly review the reasons for this close correlation between too many people, too rapidly multiplying, and the formulation of authoritarian philosophies, the rise of totalitarian systems of government.

As large and increasing numbers press more heavily upon available re-sources, the economic position of the society undergoing this ordeal becomes ever more precarious. This is especially true of those underdeveloped regions, where a sudden lowering of the death rate by means of DDT, penicillin and clean water has not been accompanied by a corresponding fall in the birth rate. In parts of Asia and in most of Central and South

America populations are increasing so fast that they will double themselves in little more than twenty years. If the production of food and manufactured articles, of houses, schools and teachers, could be increased at a greater rate than human numbers, it would be possible to improve the wretched lot of those who live in these underdeveloped and overpopulated countries. But unfortunately these countries lack not merely agricultural machinery and an industrial plant capable of turning out this machinery, but also the capital required to create such a plant. Capital is what is left over after the primary needs of a population have been satisfied. But the primary needs of most of the people in underdeveloped countries are never fully satisfied. At the end of each year almost nothing is left over, and there is therefore almost no capital available for creating the industrial and agricultural plant, by means of which the people's needs might be satisfied. Moreover, there is, in all these underdeveloped countries, a serious shortage of the trained manpower without which a modern industrial and agricultural plant cannot be operated. The present educational facilities are inadequate; so are the resources, financial and cultural, for improving the existing facilities as fast as the situation demands. Meanwhile the population of some of these underdeveloped countries is increasing at the rate of three per cent per annum.

Their tragic situation is discussed in an important book, published in 1957 – *The Next Hundred Years*, by Professors Harrison Brown, James Bonner and John Weir of the California Institute of Technology. How is mankind coping with the problem of rapidly increasing numbers? Not very successfully. "The evidence suggests rather strongly that in most underdeveloped countries the lot of the average individual has worsened appreciably in the last half-century. People have become more poorly fed. There are fewer available goods per person. And practically every attempt to improve the situation has been nullified by the relentless pressure of continued population growth."

Whenever the economic life of a nation becomes precarious, the central government is forced to assume additional responsibilities for the general welfare. It must work out elaborate plans for dealing with a critical situation; it must impose ever greater restrictions upon the activities of its subjects; and if, as is very likely, worsening economic conditions result in political unrest, or open rebellion, the central government must intervene to preserve public order and its own authority. More and more power is thus concentrated in the hands of the executives and their bureaucratic managers. But the nature of power is such that even those who have not sought it, but have had it forced upon them, tend to acquire a taste for more. "Lead us not into temptation," we pray – and with good reason; for when human beings are tempted too enticingly or too long, they generally

271

yield. A democratic constitution is a device for preventing the local rulers from yielding to those particularly dangerous temptations that arise when too much power is concentrated in too few hands. Such a constitution works pretty well where, as in Britain or the United States, there is a traditional respect for constitutional procedures. Where the republican or limited monarchical tradition is weak, the best of constitutions will not prevent ambitious politicians from succumbing with glee and gusto to the temptations of power. And in any country where numbers have begun to press heavily upon available resources, these temptations cannot fail to arise. Overpopulation leads to economic insecurity and social unrest. Unrest and insecurity lead to more control by central governments and an increase of their power. In the absence of a constitutional tradition, this increased power will probably be exercised in a dictatorial fashion. Even if Communism had never been invented, this would be likely to happen. But Communism has been invented. Given this fact, the probability of overpopulation leading through unrest to dictatorship becomes a virtual certainty. It is a pretty safe bet that, twenty years from now, all the world's overpopulated and underdeveloped countries will be under some form of totalitarian rule – probably by the Communist Party.

How will this development affect the overpopulated, but highly industrialized and still democratic countries of Europe? If the newly formed dictatorships were hostile to them, and if the normal flow of raw materials from the underdeveloped countries were deliberately interrupted, the nations of the West would find themselves in a very bad way indeed. Their industrial system would break down, and the highly developed technology, which up till now has permitted them to sustain a population much greater than that which could be supported by locally available resources, would no longer protect them against the consequences of having too many people in too small a territory. If this should happen, the enormous powers forced by unfavourable conditions upon central governments may come to be used in the spirit of totalitarian dictatorship.

The United States is not at present an overpopulated country. If, however, the population continues to increase at the present rate (which is higher than that of India's increase, though happily a good deal lower than the rate now current in Mexico or Guatemala), the problem of numbers in relation to available resources might well become troublesome by the beginning of the twenty-first century. For the moment overpopulation is not a direct threat to the personal freedom of Americans. It remains, however, an indirect threat, a menace at one remove. If overpopulation should drive the underdeveloped countries into totalitarianism, and if these new dictatorships should ally themselves with Russia, then the military position of the United States would become less secure and the preparations for defence and retaliation would have to be intensified. But liberty, as we all know, cannot flourish in a country that is permanently on a war footing, or even a near-war footing. Permanent crisis justifies permanent control of everybody and everything by the agencies of the central government. And permanent crisis is what we have to expect in a world in which overpopulation is producing a state of things in which dictatorship under Communist auspices becomes almost inevitable.

---

51. The Human Price

RACHEL CARSON

When Rachel Carson's Silent Spring, *the book from which the following selection has been taken, first appeared in 1962, it caused a storm of controversy that has not yet subsided, partly because the threats she warned of will be corroborated or disproved only by time. Rachel Carson, who died in 1964, was a biologist with a gift for writing lucidly about her subject.* Silent Spring *and* The Sea Around Us *(1951) are her best-known books.*

This discussion of the possible dangers of chemical contamination provides an example of a writer making effective use of direct and indirect quotation in developing an idea. Notice how skilfully Rachel Carson has introduced the quoted passages into the flow of her own prose by using a variety of introductory phrases.

As the tide of chemicals born of the Industrial Age has arisen to engulf our environment, a drastic change has come about in the nature of the most serious public health problems. Only yesterday mankind lived in fear of the scourges of smallpox, cholera, and plague that once swept nations before them. Now our major concern is no longer with the disease organisms that once were omnipresent; sanitation, better living conditions, and new drugs have given us a high degree of control over infectious disease. Today we are concerned with a different kind of hazard that lurks in our environment – a hazard we ourselves have introduced into our world as our modern way of life has evolved.

The new environmental health problems are multiple – created by radiation in all its forms, born of the never-ending stream of chemicals of which pesticides are a part, chemicals now pervading the world in which we live, acting upon us directly and indirectly, separately and collectively. Their presence casts a shadow that is no less ominous because it is formless and obscure, no less frightening because it is simply impossible to predict the effects of lifetime exposure to chemical and physical agents that are not part of the biological experience of man.

"We all live under the haunting fear that something may corrupt the environment to the point where man joins the dinosaurs as an obsolete form of life," says Dr. David Price of the United States Public Health Service. "And what makes these thoughts all the more disturbing is the knowledge that our fate could perhaps be sealed twenty or more years before the development of symptoms."

Where do pesticides fit into the picture of environmental disease? We have seen that they now contaminate soil, water, and food, that they have the power to make our streams fishless and our gardens and woodlands silent and birdless. Man, however much he may like to pretend the contrary, is part of nature. Can he escape a pollution that is now so thoroughly distributed throughout our world?

We know that even single exposures to these chemicals, if the amount is large enough, can precipitate acute poisoning. But this is not the major problem. The sudden illness or death of farmers, spraymen, pilots, and others exposed to appreciable quantities of pesticides are tragic and should not occur. For the population as a whole, we must be more concerned with the delayed effects of absorbing small amounts of the pesticides that invisibly contaminate our world.

Responsible public health officials have pointed out that the biological effects of chemicals are cumulative over long periods of time, and that the hazard to the individual may depend on the sum of the exposures received throughout his lifetime. For these very reasons the danger is easily ignored. It is human nature to shrug off what may seem to us a vague threat of future disaster. "Men are naturally most impressed by diseases which have obvious manifestations," says a wise physician, Dr. René Dubos, "yet some of their worst enemies creep on them unobtrusively."

For each of us, as for the robin in Michigan or the salmon in the Miramichi, this is a problem of ecology, of interrelationships, of interdependence. We poison the caddis flies in a stream and the salmon runs dwindle and die. We poison the gnats in a lake and the poison travels from link to link of the food chain and soon the birds of the lake margins become its victims. We spray our elms and the following springs are silent of robin song, not because we sprayed the robins directly but because the poison traveled, step by step, through the now familiar elm leaf-earthworm-robin cycle. These are matters of record, observable, part of the visible world around us. They reflect the web of life – or death – that scientists know as ecology.

But there is also an ecology of the world within our bodies. In this unseen world minute causes produce mighty effects; the effect, moreover, is often seemingly unrelated to the cause, appearing in a part of the body remote from the area where the original injury was sustained. "A change at one point, in one molecule even, may reverberate throughout the entire system to initiate changes in seemingly unrelated organs and tissues," says a recent summary of the present status of medical research. When one is concerned with the mysterious and wonderful functioning of the human body, cause and effect are seldom simple and easily demonstrated relationships. They may be widely separated both in space and time. To discover the agent of disease and death depends on a patient piecing together of many seemingly distinct and unrelated facts developed through a vast amount of research in widely separated fields.

We are accustomed to look for the gross and immediate effect and to ignore all else. Unless this appears promptly and in such obvious form that it cannot be ignored, we deny the existence of hazard. Even research men suffer from the handicap of inadequate methods of detecting the beginnings of injury. The lack of sufficiently delicate methods to detect injury before symptoms appear is one of the great unsolved problems in medicine.

"But," someone will object, "I have used dieldrin sprays on the lawn many times but I have never had convulsions like the World Health Organization spraymen – so it hasn't harmed me." It is not that simple. Despite the absence of sudden and dramatic symptoms, one who handles such materials is unquestionably storing up toxic materials in his body. Storage of the chlorinated hydrocarbons, as we have seen, is cumulative, beginning with the smallest intake. The toxic materials become lodged in all the fatty tissues of the body. When these reserves of fat are drawn upon the poison may then strike quickly. A New Zealand medical journal recently provided an example. A man under treatment for obesity suddenly developed symptoms of poisoning. On examination his fat was found to contain stored dieldrin, which had been metabolized as he lost weight. The same thing could happen with loss of weight in illness.

The results of storage, on the other hand, could be even less obvious. Several years ago the *Journal* of the American Medical Association warned strongly of the hazards of insecticide storage in adipose tissue, pointing out that drugs or chemicals that are cumulative require greater caution than those having no tendency to be stored in the tissues. The adipose tissue, we are warned, is not merely a place for the deposition of fat (which makes up about 18 per cent of the body weight), but has many important functions with which the stored poisons may interfere. Furthermore, fats are very widely distributed in the organs and tissues of the whole body, even being constituents of cell membranes. It is important to remember, therefore, that the fat-soluble insecticides become stored in individual cells, where they are in position to interfere with the most vital and necessary functions of oxidation and energy production.

52. Tickling the Dragon's Tail

RALPH E. LAPP

In the preceding selection, Rachel Carson called radiation and chemical contamination the two major "environmental health problems" facing the world. The following selection from Ralph E. Lapp's Atoms and People *does not directly discuss radiation as a public health problem, but it does describe vividly the effects that an overdose of radiation can have upon the human body. The author of this selection is himself a successful atomic physicist who has written several books on his subject. Among these are* Must We Hide? *(1949) and* Kill and Overkill *(1962).* Atoms and People *was published in 1956; the events described in "Tickling the Dragon's Tail" took place in 1946.*

This selection illustrates a basic convention of writing: the subject should be dealt with in a way that is appropriate to the audience for whom it was written. Here Mr. Lapp has dealt with a highly technical subject in a way that can be understood by the non-technical reader. What are some of the means he has employed in making his description of Louis Slotin's experiment clear to the non-scientist?

Ordinary or natural uranium is quite harmless for it will not, by itself, sustain chain reaction. Only when it is embodied in an enormous matrix of some light element like graphite or heavy water does it sustain a slow chain reaction. Were this to be allowed to run out of control, it would not in general produce anything like an explosion. Heat would be produced and some inner parts of the reactor might melt, but it would not qualify as a bomb.

Enriched uranium or plutonium is quite different from ordinary uranium. Assemble too much of it in one place, and the chain reaction will automatically run away. Thus, it was rather important for the people at Oak Ridge and at Hanford to know how much was "enough" so that safety precautions could be taken. At Los Alamos the experts refined their calculations as to the size of the critical mass, but it was essential to have experimental measurements.

The man who headed up the "critical assembly" group was a good friend of mine. I knew Louis Slotin while an undergraduate at the University of Chicago and liked him very much for his pleasant manner and friendly advice. He was never too busy to help out a Ph.D. aspirant, and I remember that he gave me valuable pointers on making Geiger counters. On my visits to Los Alamos I used to stop by to see Slotin and give him the news of Chicago. He was a short, wiry youth with dark hair and soft sad eyes. Somehow or other, he always ended up doing jobs nobody else wanted. He never complained, and I respected the cheerful way that Slotin did dirty work.

Slotin had nerves of iron and he needed them for his critical experiments with the "nukes." Here is essentially what he did in making a critical assembly, or in "tickling the dragon's tail," as we called it. He would set up a table with a neutron counter and a rack. On the rack he would place two pieces of bomb stuff, each one being somewhat less than a critical amount. Then he would push the two pieces, often in the form of hemispheres the size of a split baseball, toward each other. As the gap narrowed between the pieces, he would measure the buildup of the chain reaction inside the assembly. He used a small source of neutrons to amplify the effect, rather than waiting for stray neutrons to come from cosmic rays or from the material itself. He determined the tempo of the buildup by listening to the clicks in an amplifier connected to the neutron counter and in watching a recorder trace out a jagged red line on a moving roll of graph paper.

As the hemispheres came closer and closer, more and more of the neutrons would tend to be caught within the bomb stuff and fewer would be lost through the narrowing air gap. The chain reaction would build up, and, just before it was ready to rip, Slotin would calmly stop the experiment, measure the separation and deduce just how big the critical mass was. He grew quite adept at the experiment for he repeated it fifty times or more. His nonchalance amazed Fermi who once warned him, "Keep doing that experiment that way and you'll be dead within a year." Some of Slotin's colleagues tried to get him to build in automatic safety devices, like powerful springs, which could be triggered to hurl the two hemispheres apart when the neutrons built up too fast. He turned aside this suggestion with this retort:

"If I have to depend upon safety devices I am sure to have an accident."

Slotin was asked to repeat the experiment "just one more time" to demonstrate the technique to others in the laboratory. So he gathered the group of six people behind him in the sunlit room where he did his work. One man, Dr. Alvin Graves, had his hand almost on his shoulder as Slotin proceeded to demonstrate his technique. He used two hemispheres that he had worked with before and holding a screwdriver he moved the two pieces of bomb material together to form a "nuke" or nuclear core. Slowly, at first, then more quickly the counters clicked away and the red line moved upward on the white paper chart.

Suddenly the counters screamed and the red ink indicators swung off scale. There had been an accident! The chain reaction was running away. Almost as if by reflex action Slotin hurled himself forward and tore the reacting mass apart with his bare hands. The others gasped and, turning around, Slotin, his face whitely reflecting his terror, motioned them to leave the room.

Slotin telephoned the hospital and said that there had been an accident. Then he telephoned his close friend, Phil Morrison. He was nauseated but, always the true scientist, paused in the hallway and drew a pencil sketch of the room and marked everyone's position, putting a big X for himself. Then he scribbled the time, 3 : 20 P.M., and hustled the group off to the hospital, all of them jamming into two jeeps.

The big question in the mind of everyone was: how much dose did Slotin get? The neutrons and X-rays which flashed through his body before he tore the assembly apart caused biological damage to his body. This we measure in certain units – called roentgens or r-units. A total of about 400 r over the entire body is considered the lethal amount for most people. This deadly amount does not produce immediate effect but takes time . . . weeks . . . or days . . . depending on the dose.

Phil Morrison, gifted theoretical physicist, worked feverishly to recon-struct the accident and to learn how serious was his friend's plight. Slotin's very blood had been made radioactive by the burst of neutrons which riddled his body, and a small sample of his blood gave a clue to the dose. Of course, Slotin was hospitalized and became ill rather soon, but during the first few days he was cheerful and would ask when visited by Morrison, "Well, what's the dose?" Nobody really knew and it took a long time to find out. Before they did, the tide had changed in Slotin's reaction to the radiation. His differential blood cell count told the story – a picture so hopeless that the attending Army nurse, hardened to hospital routine, broke down and sobbed when she saw the results.

Slotin had been most severely irradiated around the hands and arms. These parts of his pain-ridden body swelled grotesquely and the skin

278

sloughed off. The nation's best doctors were flown to the Army hospital at Los Alamos but they could do little for the weakening patient. Nor could we do much more today.

Technicians strung a telephone connection into the bare hospital room and Slotin talked with his mother in Winnipeg, Canada. The next day, his parents were flown to New Mexico by special Army plane, and they stayed at their son's bedside until he breathed his last. The end came early on the morning of the ninth day after the accident.

The man who stood behind Slotin, Dr. Graves, was severely injured by the accident but he recovered and went on to become associate director of Los Alamos in the postwar period. He had this to say of Slotin: "I can perhaps tell you as much about his personality and character as I could in very many words if I merely quote to you his first statement when we were alone together in the hospital room. He said, 'I'm sorry I got you into this. I am afraid that I have less than a fifty-fifty chance of living. I hope you do better than that.'"

Slotin was not destined to be a great or a famous man. He was one of the many scientists who worked devotedly and unselfishly throughout the war. The young scientist gave his life, just as did many of his comrades in arms.

Slotin's experiment was outlawed at Los Alamos. With the development of television and remote-control gadgetry, it became possible to do the critical assembly operations with no one within a quarter of a mile. White-coated technicians, principally women, control the assembly and make all their observations without the slightest danger to themselves.

---

53. Let's Stay Off the Moon

BERTRAND RUSSELL

Even though Bertrand Russell was born as long ago as 1872, he is still actively concerned in human affairs, especially as a critic of anything he considers "human folly". Lord Russell's major achievements have been in the disciplines of mathematics and philosophy, but he is also the author of a number of books on a wide variety of subjects. His most recent works are the first two instalments of his autobiography published in 1966 and 1968. The essay that appears below was first published in the August 30, 1958, issue of Maclean's *Magazine.*

Lord Russell points out in his opening paragraph that he is aware that the subject he is writing about has "arguments on both sides", and he will "try to set them forth impartially". However, he makes it quite clear where his sympathies lie. A careful examination of the vocabulary employed by this master stylist will reveal how skilfully he has made this particular attack on "folly".

My generation was familiarized in boyhood with the idea of traveling to the moon by Jules Verne, who wrote admirable science fiction and stimulated the imagination of adventurous youth. I still remember vividly the thrill with which I read his story called From the Earth to the Moon. But I hardly thought, and I suppose that other young readers hardly thought, that an actual journey to the moon might become possible during the lifetime of those who were enjoying Jules Verne's fantasies. Yet this is what has been happening. Already the technical capacity exists to send a projectile to the moon. As yet such a projectile cannot be made large enough to carry human beings on the journey. But there is reason to expect that, before many years have passed, it will become possible for men to land on the surface of our satellite. The thought of such an adventure is exciting, especially to those who are still young. But those who are no longer young are troubled by doubts and hesitations as to whether the conquest of the moon will really do anything to ameliorate our human lot. I see arguments on both sides, and I shall try to set them forth impartially, without any attempt to reach a dogmatic conclusion.

Let us first attempt to see the question in a context of past technical achievements. When I was a boy, electric light had just been invented and telephones were still regarded as a rare curiosity. The fastest thing on the road was the push bicycle, which was regarded with apprehension as a danger to pedestrians and a cause of terror to horses. I was grown up when I first saw a motor car, and nearly forty when I first saw an aeroplane. In World War I everybody marveled when the Germans constructed a gun which would carry a shell some seventy miles. Those who are still young do not easily apprehend how much that is now commonplace in daily life is of quite recent invention.

It is not only in the sphere of new inventions, but also in that of adventure, that our age is making unprecedented advances. When I was young, large parts of Africa were still unexplored and both poles had so far remained unreachable. Everest remained, for a time, the last terrestrial challenge for the explorer, but it yielded at last to the ardent spirit of adventure. Love of adventure has been a distinctive human characteristic ever since men began to be civilized, and I think it is a characteristic deserving of all the admiration which is usually given to it. I should not wish to see it decay or be stifled under a blanket of fear. Such general considerations lead one to applaud those extraterrestrial voyages which are beginning to be within scientific possibility. The conquest of the poles and of Everest was generally considered worthy of applause, and, without doubt, rightly so. We also justly admire the exploration of the depths of the sea and of the upper air which has been inaugurated in recent years, but of which the greater part still remains to be done. The same sort of applause, in even greater degree, will be deserved by those who first venture on the journey to the moon.

But whether anything more than the admiration of courage and skill will be gained when men reach the moon is, I think, very doubtful.

The first question that as yet remains in doubt, is whether people will be able to live on the surface of the moon, or whether they will have to return to earth after a few hours or days. The moon has no atmosphere, or, at most, a very tenuous one. It has no water and no vegetation. At first, therefore, people landing on the moon will have to manufacture the air they breathe, and will have to be encased in an armor which will prevent the too rapid escape of the air that their apparatus is manufacturing. They will have to bring with them enough food and water to keep them alive during their stay. For these reasons, the moon will be even less habitable than the summit of Everest. At any rate this will be the situation at first and for many long years.

There are those, however, who think that physical conditions on the moon can gradually be changed by scientific manipulation. I have read a curious recent Russian work containing the kind of very serious science fiction which the Soviet government considers good for its more youthful subjects. In this book it was suggested that, in time, chemical means would be found of turning lunar rocks into gases and gradually creating something that would do as an atmosphere. If once an atmosphere had been created, hydrogen and oxygen extracted from minerals could be made to produce water. Low forms of life might then become capable of living in the newly created pools, and gradually the biologists might coax these forms of life up the ladder of evolution.

Let us not say that it is impossible: much has been achieved that, even a hundred years ago, seemed utterly beyond human power, and it would be very rash to place unalterable limits upon what science may do in later centuries.

But, however that may be, there is certainly no *near* prospect of life on the moon except as a brief incursion with very elaborate and expensive apparatus. It will be a very long time, if ever, before the moon offers an outlet for problems of over-population or a refuge for groups of unpopular deportees.

A number of scientists wish for delay in any attempt to fire a projectile at the moon. Their grounds for delay are two: they say that the moon's surface is covered with cosmic dust which might be disturbed by the arrival of a missile, but, if left undisturbed, will give valuable data for the past history of the universe. They say, also, that if the moon has a little atmosphere, as it may have, the explosion of a rocket would contaminate this atmosphere. I cannot but be amused by this concern for a hypothetical lunar atmosphere and cosmic dust in view of the fact that at the present moment the governments of Britain and the United States are deliberately engaged in poisoning the earth's atmosphere and its soil and the water that we drink and the food that we eat, although they know that they are thereby causing cancer and idiocy.

To my mind there is a lack of proportion in this meticulous care for the moon combined with wanton damage to our own planet as the bearer of life. But I suppose this shows that I am unpatriotic. A true patriot does not mind how many of his compatriots become idiots, provided a greater number of his country's enemies will suffer a like affliction.

Unfortunately, this spirit of ruthless competition is infecting projects for reaching the moon. These projects are not being considered in a spirit of scientific detachment, or as redounding to the credit of the human race. They are regarded, instead, as an opportunity for a race between rival Great Powers. It is felt that the important thing is not that the moon should be reached, but that it should be reached by our side (whichever that may be) sooner than by the other. This is paltry, and makes the whole enterprise one in which it is difficult for sane men to see much of value.

Man has his merits and also his demerits. If the latter are to be spread over the cosmos, if our follies are to be transplanted, first to the moon, then to Mars and Venus, and perhaps, at a later date, to more distant regions, by savage pilgrims of hate who have grown old during the long journey, if all this is to be the outcome of our silly cleverness, I cannot see that we have any reason to rejoice in the prospect. And yet, unless the nations repent and reform, this is exactly what we have to expect if man continues to exist. Men will not be content to land upon the moon and try to make it habitable. They will land simultaneously from Russia and the United States, each party complete with H-bomb and each intent upon exterminating the other. It would be cheaper to shoot each other at home, and more humane to supply each with a poison capsule and sentence the rivals to a painless death.

There are some who seem to imagine that space travel will, of itself, lead to some cure for our terrestrial troubles. I cannot see any reason to think this. Europe had troubles before the Western hemisphere was discovered. After it was discovered, the wars to which the Old World was accustomed were transplanted to the "New World." Unless we amend our ways, the same thing will happen if we extend our silly empires into outer space.

There is no reason whatever to suppose that the new possibilities of travel will do anything to promote wisdom. On the contrary they will, as air travel has already done, cause people to spend more time in locomotion and, therefore, less in thought. Already, the foreign ministers of the Great Powers spend so much time in visiting each other's countries, and also those smaller countries which they hope to influence, that they have become unable to acquire even those elements of knowledge which are of most importance if their policies are to have even a modicum of good sense. Bustling activity will more and more take the place of reasonable consideration. A foreign minister who is traveling to the moon will be filled with a sense of public duty nobly performed and will retain, without shame, all the foolish beliefs with which he started on his journey. It is not by bustle that men become enlightened. Spinoza was content with The Hague; Kant, who is generally regarded as the wisest of Germans, never traveled more than ten miles from Königsberg.

For my part, I should wish to see a little more wisdom in the conduct of affairs on earth before we extend our strident and deadly disputes to other parts. Mars and Venus shine very effectively and are a joy to behold in the night sky. I should not derive more pleasure from their brightness if debates were being conducted in Congress as to which of the two should be admitted to statehood, it being understood that one of them favors the Republicans and the other the Democrats. It is for us to grow to the stature of the cosmos, not to degrade the cosmos to the level of our futile squabbles.

Conquerors have almost always been ruthless. There have been some exceptions, of which the most notable were the Romans in Greece. But, in general, the men who take to a life of conquest tend to be men who are indifferent to the higher values of civilization. The conquistadors, when they went into Mexico and Peru, sought only to acquire great masses of gold. They carelessly destroyed two remarkable civilizations which subsequent historians and archæologists have patiently labored to rediscover. I do not suppose that there is anything similar on the moon. But, although I spoke somewhat slightingly of the scientists who are concerned about cosmic dust, I have nevertheless more respect for their point of view than for that of the men who wish to embroil the moon in the struggles of what, with cosmic impertinence, we magniloquently call "The Great Powers."

There is something that may perhaps be called respect for those things in the world that have not been created with modern technique. There is something which might almost be called impiety in the ruthless disregard of everything already existing, which characterizes those in whom a mechanistic outlook is unchecked by imagination and contemplation. It is not the whole of what should make up human life to cause changes, however vast and however clever. Contemplation, also, must play its part. If we allow it to do so, some element of wisdom in human affairs may be reflected into our lives from the contemplation of the heavens. But, if we think of the heavens only as something which we can change, until the universe is degraded to the level of the most trivial of human concerns, we shall only widen the sphere of folly and shall deserve the disasters which it will bring upon us. We need less ruthlessness and more respect. If we have them, our cosmic conquests may be a matter for rejoicing; but, if not, we shall bring upon ourselves the punishment we shall deserve for our impiety.

---

54. Impasse in Race Relations

MARTIN LUTHER KING

Prior to his assassination in April of 1968, Martin Luther King was the most articulate advocate of non-violence in the American civil rights movement. His eloquence survives in the several books and hundreds of speeches in which he described the Negro's plight. "Impasse in Race Relations" is a talk Dr. King delivered over the CBC radio network in November 1967. This talk, along with four others that followed it, was later reprinted in a book entitled Conscience for Change.

One aspect of Martin Luther King's style that is immediately apparent is the powerful rhythm of his prose, a prose that was written to be read aloud. What are some of the devices of rhetoric and sentence structure that the author has made use of in creating this powerful style?

It is a deep personal privilege to address a nation-wide Canadian audience. Over and above any kinship of U.S. citizens and Canadians as North Americans there is a singular historical relationship between American Negroes and Canadians.

Canada is not merely a neighbor to Negroes. Deep in our history of struggle for freedom Canada was the north star. The Negro slave, denied education, de-humanized, imprisoned on cruel plantations, knew that far to the north a land existed where a fugitive slave if he survived the horrors of the journey could find freedom. The legendary underground railroad started in the south and ended in Canada. The freedom road links us together. Our spirituals, now so widely admired around the world, were often codes. We sang of "heaven" that awaited us and the slave masters listened in innocence, not realizing that we were not speaking of the hereafter. Heaven was the word for Canada and the Negro sang of the hope that his escape on the underground railroad would carry him there. One of our spirituals, "Follow the Drinking Gourd", in its disguised lyrics contained directions for escape. The gourd was the big dipper, and the north star to which its handle pointed gave the celestial map that directed the flight to the Canadian border.

So standing today in Canada I am linked with the history of my people and its unity with your past.

The underground railroad could not bring freedom to many Negroes. Heroic though it was, even the most careful research cannot reveal how many thousands it liberated. Yet it did something far greater. It symbolized hope when freedom was almost an impossible dream. Our spirit never died even though the weight of centuries was a crushing burden.

Today when progress has abruptly stalled and hope withers under bitter backlashing, Negroes can remember days that were incomparably worse. By ones and twos more than a century ago Negroes groped to freedom, and its attainment by a pitiful few sustained hundreds of thousands as the word spread through the plantations that someone had been reborn far to the north.

Our freedom was not won a century ago – it is not won today but some small part of it is in our hands and we are marching no longer by ones and twos but in legions of thousands convinced now it cannot be denied by any human force.

Today the question is not whether we shall be free but by what course we will win. In the recent past our struggle has had two phases. The first phase began in the early 'fifties when Negroes slammed the door shut on submission and subservience. Adapting non-violent resistance to conditions in the United States we swept into southern streets to demand our citizenship and manhood. For the south with its complex system of brutal segregation we were inaugurating a rebellion. Merely to march in public streets was to rock the *status quo* to its roots. Boycotting busses in Montgomery, demonstrating in Birmingham, the citadel of segregation, and defying guns, dogs, and clubs in Selma, while maintaining disciplined non-violence, totally confused the rulers of the south. If they let us march they admitted their lie that the black man was content. If they shot us down they told the world they were inhuman brutes. They tried to stop us by threats and fear, the tactic that had long worked so effectively. But non-violence had muzzled their guns and Negro defiance had shaken their confidence. When they finally reached for clubs, dogs, and guns they found the world was watching, and then the power of non-violent protest became manifest. It dramatized the essential meaning of the conflict and in magnified strokes made clear who was the evil-doer and who was the undeserving victim. The nation and the world were sickened and through national legislation wiped out a thousand southern laws, ripping gaping holes in the edifice of segregation.

These were days of luminous victories. Negroes and whites collaborated for human dignity. But there was a limitation to our achievements.

Negroes were outraged by inequality; their ultimate goal was freedom. Most of the white majority were outraged by brutality; their goal was improvement, not freedom nor equality. When Negroes could use public facilities, register and vote in some areas of the south, find token educational advancement, again in token form find new areas of employment, it brought to the Negro a sense of achievement but it brought to the whites a sense of completion. When Negroes assertively moved on to ascend the second rung of the ladder a firm resistance from the white community developed. This resistance characterized the second phase which we are now experiencing. In some quarters it was a courteous rejection, in others it was a stinging white backlash. In all quarters unmistakably it was outright resistance.

The arresting of the limited forward progress by white resistance revealed the latent racism which was deeply rooted in U.S. society. The short era of widespread good will evaporated rapidly. As elation and expectations died, Negroes became more sharply aware that the goal of freedom was still distant and our immediate plight was substantially still an agony of deprivation. In the past decade little had been done for northern ghettos. All the legislation was designed to remedy southern conditions – and even these were only partially improved. A sense of futility and frustration spread and choked against the hardened white attitudes.

Non-violence as a protest form came under attack as a tactical theory and northern Negroes expressed their dismay and hostility in a succession of riots.

The decade of 1955 to 1965 with its constructive elements misled us. Everyone underestimated the amount of violence and rage Negroes were suppressing and the amount of bigotry the white majority was disguising.

The riots are now in the center of the stage, and are being offered as basis for contradictory positions by whites and Negroes. Some Negroes argue they are the incipient forms for rebellion and guerrilla tactics that will be the feature of the Negro revolt. They are represented as the new stage of Negro struggle replacing the old and allegedly outworn tactic of non-violent resistance. At the same time some white forces are using riots as evidence that Negroes have no capacity for constructive change and in their lawless behavior forfeit all rights and justify any form of repressive measures. A corollary of this theory is the position that the outbursts are unforgivable, ungrateful, and menace the social order.

I would like to examine both questions: Is the guilt for riots exclusively that of Negroes and are they a natural development to a new stage of struggle?

A million words will be written and spoken to dissect the ghetto outbreaks, but for a perceptive and vivid expression of culpability I would submit two sentences written a century ago by Victor Hugo: "If the soul is left in darkness, sins will be committed. The guilty one is not he who commits the sin, but he who causes the darkness."

The policy makers of the white society have caused the darkness; they created discrimination; they created slums; they perpetuate unemployment, ignorance, and poverty. It is incontestable and deplorable that Negroes have committed crimes; but they are derivative crimes. They are born of the greater crimes of the white society. When we ask Negroes to abide by the law, let us also declare that the white man does not abide by law in the ghettos. Day in and day out he violates welfare laws to deprive the poor of their meager allotments; he flagrantly violates building codes and regulations; his police make a mockery of law; he violates laws on equal employment and education and the provisions for civic services. The slums are the handiwork of a vicious system of the white society; Negroes live in them but they do not make them, any more than a prisoner makes a prison.

Let us say it boldly that if the total slum violations of law by the white man over the years were calculated and were compared with the lawbreaking of a few days of riots, the hardened criminal would be the white man.

In using the term white man I am seeking to describe in general terms the Negro's adversary. It is not meant to encompass all white people. There are millions who have morally risen above prevailing prejudices. They are willing to share power and to accept structural alterations of society even at the cost of traditional privilege. To deny their existence as some ultra-nationalists do is to deny an evident truth. More than that it drives away allies who can strengthen our struggle. Their support serves not only to enhance our power but in breaking from the attitudes of the larger society it splits and weakens our opposition. To develop a sense of black consciousness and peoplehood does not require that we scorn the white race as a whole. It is not the race *per se* that we fight but the policies and ideology that leaders of that race have formulated to perpetuate oppression.

To sum up the general causes of riots we would have to say that the white-power structure is still seeking to keep the walls of segregation and inequality substantially intact while Negro determination to break through them has intensified. The white society unprepared and unwilling to accept radical structural change is resisting firmly and thus producing chaos because the force for change is vital and aggressive. The irony is that the white society ruefully complains that if there were no chaos great changes would come, yet it creates the circumstances breeding the chaos.

I am not sanguine but I am not ready to accept defeat. I believe there are several programs that can reverse the tide of social disintegration and beyond that I believe that destructive as the riots may be they have been analyzed substantially in a one-sided fashion.

There is a striking aspect to the violence of riots that has stimulated little comment and even less analysis. In all of the riots, taken together, the property damage reached colossal proportions (exceeding a billion dollars). Yet the physical injury inflicted by Negroes upon white people was inconsequential by comparison. The bruising edge of the weapon of violence in Negro hands was employed almost exclusively against property – not persons.

It is noteworthy that many distinguished periodicals and leaders of the white community, even while the conflict raged, in clear terms accepted the responsibility for neglect, evasion, and centuries of injustice. They did not quibble nor did they seek to fasten exclusive culpability on the Negro. They asked for action and a facing-up to the need for drastic social reformation. It is true that not all were motivated by morality. The crisis of Negro aspirations intersects with the urban crisis. Some white leaders may not be moved by humanity to save Negroes but they are moved by self interest to save their cities. But even their moral and selfish motives which merge toward a constructive end have not yet made government act. It is preoccupied with war and is determined to husband every resource for military adventures rather than for social reconstruction.

Negroes must therefore not only formulate a program but they must fashion new tactics which do not count on government good will but instead serve to compel unwilling authorities to yield to the mandates of justice.

We are demanding an emergency program to provide employment for everyone in need of a job or, if a work program is impracticable, a guaranteed annual income at levels that sustain life in decent circumstances. It is now incontestable that the wealth and resources of the United States make the elimination of poverty perfectly practicable.

A second feature of our program is the demolition of slums and rebuilding by the population that live in them.

There is scarcely any division among Negroes for these measures. Divisions arise only around methods for their achievement.

288

I am still convinced that a solution of non-violence remains possible. However, non-violence must be adapted to urban conditions and urban moods. The effectiveness of street marches in cities is limited because the normal turbulence of city life absorbs them as mere transitory drama quite common in the ordinary movement of masses. In the south, a march was a social earthquake; in the north, it is a faint, brief exclamation of protest.

Non-violent protest must now mature to a new level to correspond to heightened black impatience and stiffened white resistance. This higher level is mass civil disobedience. There must be more than a statement to the larger society; there must be a force that interrupts its functioning at some key point. That interruption must however not be clandestine or surreptitious. It is not necessary to invest it with guerrilla romanticism. It must be open and, above all, conducted by large masses without violence. If the jails are filled to thwart it the meaning will become even clearer.

The Negro will be saying: I am not avoiding penalties for breaking the law – I am willing to endure all your punishment because your society will not be able to endure the stigma of violently and publicly oppressing its minority to preserve injustice.

Mass civil disobedience as a new stage of struggle can transmute the deep rage of the ghetto into a constructive and creative force. To dislocate the functioning of a city without destroying it can be more effective than a riot because it can be longer lasting, costly to the larger society but not wantonly destructive. Finally it is a device of social action that is more difficult for the government to quell by superior force.

The limitation of riots, moral questions aside, is that they cannot win and their participants know it. Hence, rioting is not revolutionary but reactionary because it invites defeat. It involves an emotional catharsis but it must be followed by a sense of futility.

Where does the future point? The character of the next period is being determined by the response of white decision-makers to this crisis. It is a harsh indictment, but it is an inescapable conclusion, that Congress is not horrified with the conditions of Negro life but with the product of these conditions – the Negro himself. It could, by a single massive act of concern expressed in a multi-billion-dollar program to modernize and humanize Negro communities, do more to obviate violence than could be done by all the armies at its command. Whether it will summon the wisdom to do it is the question of the hour.

It is a shattering historical irony that the American Revolution of 1776 was the consequence of many of the same conditions that prevail today. King George adamantly refused to share power even in modest degree with the colonies. He provoked violence by scorning and spurning the appeals embodied in non-violent protests such as boycotts, peaceful demonstrations, and petitions. In their resort to violence the colonists were pressed ideologically beyond their original demands and put into question the system of absolute monarchical rule. When they took up arms and searched for the rationale for independence they broke with all traditions of imperial domination and established a unique and unprecedented form of government – the democratic republic.

The Negro revolt is evolving into more than a quest for desegregation and equality. It is a challenge to a system that has created miracles of production and technology to create justice. If humanism is locked outside of the system, Negroes will have revealed its inner core of despotism and a far greater struggle for liberation will unfold. The United States is substantially challenged to demonstrate that it can abolish not only the evils of racism but the scourge of poverty of whites as well as of Negroes and the horrors of war that transcend national borders and involve all of mankind.

The first man to die in the American Revolution was a Negro seaman, Crispus Attucks. Before that fateful struggle ended the institution of absolute monarchy was put on its death bed.

We may now only be in the initial period of an era of change as far-reaching in its consequences as the American Revolution. The developed industrial nations of the world, which include Canada, as much as the United States, cannot remain secure islands of prosperity in a seething sea of poverty. The storm is rising against the privileged minority of the earth, from which there is no shelter in isolation and armament. The storm will not abate until a just distribution of the fruits of the earth enables man everywhere to live in dignity and human decency. The American Negro of 1967, like Crispus Attucks, may be the vanguard in a prolonged struggle that may change the shape of the world, as billions of deprived shake and transform the earth in their quest for life, freedom, and justice.

Index of
Rhetorical Terms